New Explorations in Italian American Studies

Proceedings
of the
25th Annual Conference
of the
American Italian
Historical Association

Washington, D.C.
November 12-14, 1992

Richard N. Juliani
Sandra P. Juliani
Editors

31012597

Volume XXV in the series of Annual Proceedings of the American Italian Historical Association.

Copyright (1994) by the American Italian Historical Association, Inc.

American Italian Historical Association. Conference (25th: 1992: Washington, D.C.)
New explorations in Italian American studies: proceedings of the 25th Annual Conference of the American Italian Historical Association, Washington, D.C., November 12-14, 1992/Richard N. Juliani, Sandra P. Juliani, editors.

      p. cm.

Includes bibliographical references (p.) and index.
ISBN 0-934675-31-7 (hardcover). -- ISBN 0-934675-32-5 (softcover)
1. Italian-Americans--History--Congresses. I. Juliani, Richard N. II. Juliani, Sandra P. III. Title.
E184.I8A524 1992
973'.0451--dc20   94-32166
                              CIP

Published in the United States of America by
The American Italian Historical Association
209 Flagg Place
Staten Island, New York 10304-1148

Printed by Harbinger Publications, 18 Bluff Road, Columbia SC, 29201

Printed on Recycled Paper

CONTENTS

ACKNOWLEDGMENTS

The 25th Annual Conference of the American Italian Historical Association was held in Washington, D.C. on November 12-14, 1992. The planning for the event had actually begun two years earlier at the New Orleans conference in 1990. Due to some unfortunate and unanticipated events, however, almost all of that planning had to be abandoned. In late May, 1992, although numerous proposals had been received from members who intended to make presentations, we had to make new arrangements if the annual meeting, now only less than six months away, was to take place. The situation represented a rather critical challenge to the AIHA.

We were fortunate, however, to overcome these difficulties in a manner and to a degree that amply demonstrated that the AIHA possessed considerable internal resources and strengths. In particular, the outcome revealed that the Association did not need to look beyond itself to other organizations for the successful implementation of its programs and the preservation of its integrity. Indeed, during the days of the annual meeting, several participants expressed their view that it was, in fact, the best conference of the Association that they had yet attended. In short, what had perhaps once been an incipient crisis actually developed into an opportunity from which the AIHA emerged as a stronger and more autonomous organization. It was also an experience from which many of us learned a great deal about ourselves as well as about the relationship of the AIHA to other organizations. And as a scholarly society, we recognize the importance of opportunities for learning in whatever forms they come.

The solution to the problems of the successful planning and execution of the 1992 conference rested to a very large extent upon the dedication and labor of several individuals. Most conferences come and go without the participants being well aware of those persons who really performed the critical tasks, often rather invisibly, without which such programs could not take place. Their contributions deserve our recognition and gratitude. William V. D'Antonio, an old and constant friend to our efforts, took valuable time away from a very busy schedule in order to play an essential part in securing and negotiating our local arrangements. His recommendations and activities in obtaining meeting space and accommodations provided for an essential component of the conference.

Diane Francesconi Lyon, similarly, devoted extensive time and energy in a number of tasks before and during the conference, particularly in regard to her diligent, but always affable, work in staffing the registration desk. The Association especially ought to commend individuals, such as she represents, who register for the conference, but who then spend much of their hours in selflessly serving other members.

If the 1992 conference had a distinctive element that is likely to be remembered by the members who attended, it was unquestionably the special entertainment provided at the annual banquet. After suffering through so many grim, patronizing, eminently forgettable, and certainly regrettable after-dinner speakers at other affairs, the planning for this conference consciously committed itself to the providing of an entertaining and enjoyable banquet program. Fortunately, we were able to secure the services of Marco Pezzano and Anthony Rauche, both also members of the Association, who have previously participated in regular sessions. In this case, Pezzano and Rauche provided an after-dinner program of popular traditional Italian *canzoni*. Before their program ended, however, Pezzano and Rauche had converted their audience into a unique chorus in a memorably moving singalong. Certainly, this aspect of the program engendered more fraternity and cohesion among the members than any other previous event in the history of the Association. It was our intention that this event would become a regular feature of the annual banquet in the future.

In the preparation of these *Proceedings*, a special note must be made of the extraordinary and indispensable services provided by Rachel Levy of the Sociology Department of Villanova University for her technical assistance. She has contributed immeasurably by her keen and diligent efforts in the preparation of these materials for publication in this volume.

In addition, as usual, all the participants of the conference deserve to be recognized for their energetic labors in the field of Italian American studies as well as their continued support of the Association. Despite the difficulties and frustrations of organizing a conference, the rank-and-file members of the Association ultimately make it a worthwhile enterprise. This organization, unlike any other scholarly body, rests upon a membership of individuals who transcend their professional roles and become friends and almost kinfolk. The study of the Italian American experience has frequently emphasized the concept of *paesani* as a central tool in understanding immigration and resettlement. With the passage of time, we ordinarily understand the transformation and dissolution of the reality which that concept describes. In the distinctive character of the Association and the activities through which it brings all of us together, whether of Italian ancestry or not, we still find relationships that are, indeed, like those of the immigrants we seek to describe and understand. Consequently, the success the 1992 program and every other conference also depended upon this special quality of its collective membership, and no less than the contribution of any individual member deserves to be acknowledged.

Finally, we wish to note that while previous volumes of the *Proceedings* have been prepared by co-editors, the present number represents the first occasion that the co-editors have been married to each other. In fact, this collaboration was instrumental both in bringing about the conference and in compiling the papers for this volume. In addition, despite what tribulations those tasks entailed, the marriage has survived as well. In this instance, the volume is actually the result of our long term shared interest and commitment to the field of Italian American studies. It is also a reflection of a deep concern for all things related to Italy from its ancient past to its present situation. Similarly, it includes a continuing dialogue on the current condition of Italian Americans and the future of their ethnic identity and culture. It includes questions that are solved in the kitchen as well as in the library. For both of us, it is a continuing and joyful celebration of our own personal origins as Americans of Italian descent and the families from which we have proceeded. In this effort, we have also been able jointly to pay homage in a very special way to those who have preceded us and whom we fondly, but privately, choose to remember.

Richard N. Juliani
Sandra P. Juliani
Wynnewood, Pennsylvania

FOREWORD

During the course of the 25th Annual Conference of the American Italian Historical Association, nearly 75 participants made some type of presentation in 24 scheduled sessions over a two day period. In the weeks after the conference, many of the participants submitted their work in consideration for the *Proceedings* of the conference. Each submitted item was read by members of an editorial committee, whose labor can be acknowledged here, even if their names are not revealed. The determination of the papers that were selected for the *Proceedings* was neither entirely a pleasant, nor an unpleasant task. On one hand, it involved the reading of a number of important essays and poems that we are pleased to be able now to make available to the public. On the other hand, it also required the elimination of other works, many of which were also interesting and valuable.

The general theme of the 25th Annual Conference was *New Explorations in Italian American Studies*. The choice of this theme was the result of a careful and deliberate process of consideration of what the year 1992 would represent for anyone in the field of Italian American studies. Obviously, it was the year of the 500th anniversary of the first voyage of exploration and discovery by Christopher Columbus. From the earliest moment, when the first plans for the 1992 conference were being made, we were aware of the significance that the year would have for all Americans, for all the world, for scholars and for the general public. It was our intention to remain very much conscious of that aspect. At the same time, however, we were equally committed to the proposition that the Italian experience in the Americas certainly reached far beyond Columbus. Consequently, while we wanted to retain an appropriate reference to the great explorer, we also intended to capture, as the AIHA has always done from its inception, the fuller range of Italian American experience that embraces the continued assimilation of third and fourth generations of descendants from the great immigration masses as well as the conditions of life facing the most recent immigrants from Italy today.

The theme of *New Explorations in Italian American Studies* was chosen, therefore, as a device that would allow some participants to present papers in which they could re-examine aspects of the Columbus saga and its implications for America as a society. The first three papers of this volume are representatives of this opportunity. In "Columbus and the Rise of American Literature", Frank J. Cavaioli traces the earliest efforts by creative writers to present as a subject of their essays and poetry as well as to elevate the Genoese explorer as a folk hero to other Americans. At the same time, Cavaioli shows us these writers used Columbus as an instrument to serve their own ends in the development of a new literature for a young society. In "Columbus's Religiosity and the Millennium", Luciano J. Rusich considers the religious beliefs, motivations and objectives of the explorer. In particular, Rusich draws our attention to the religiosity, and in fact the mysticism, that can be found within the personal character of Columbus. This series of papers is completed with "Christopher Columbus, What Have We Done to You? The Renaissance Paradigm", in which Harral E. Landry responds to present day criticisms of Columbus and his impact on indigenous peoples by placing him in the cultural context of his own times. Landry argues that we can only truly understand and assess Columbus alongside of the personalities and conditions of the period in which he lived, rather than judge him by modern standards of belief and conduct.

The theme of the conference, however, aimed to reach beyond the explorations of Columbus and to include new thinking on later aspects of the relationship between Italy and the United States. In the next set of papers, the authors consider some political issues of the 20th century that involve either the two countries or the experiences of Italians in the political domain of urban America. In "The Italian Democratic Left and Woodrow Wilson: A Venture in Political Collaboration", Charles Killinger examines the interaction between the various political factions of Italy in the period of the First World War and the diplomatic strategies of the American President afterward in seeking the restoration of order in Europe. Killinger documents the unfortunate failure of democratic politics that paved the way for the emergence of Fascism in Italy. In "The Fascist/Anti-Fascist Struggle in San Francisco", Rose Scherini describes the tensions between different elements within the Italian American community as well as the relationship of these elements to the American government. The eventual results included not only the dissolution of what had previously been a rather cohesive ethnic community, but a disturbingly unrestrained assault on the civil rights of individual Italians by officials of the American government. Finally, in his essay, "Italian Democratic Chieftains and the Making of a Democratic Majority among Italian Americans in Pittsburgh", Stefano Luconi traces the emergence of Italian Americans as a component of city and state politics during several decades at the middle of the present century. Luconi shows quite effectively how the patronage system managed by their political leaders served to maintain the affiliation and support of Italian Americans for the Democratic Party at the very moment that the rest of the state was slipping under the control of the Republican Party.

Another important dimension of "new explorations" of the experience of Italians as immigrants involved their participation in the economic life of their destinations. In his discussion of "Dun and Bradstreet's Assessments of Merchants: A Neglected Source for Italian American Studies", Luciano Iorizzo presents a rich, but relatively unknown, source of information on the entrepreneurial careers of the foreign born. Iorizzo also provides some brief capsules of substantive description that illustrate some aspects of the cases of immigrant businessmen that he has begun to explore. In his paper, "Vengo per Fare l'America: The Sojourner Businessman", Michael LaSorte implements the study of the economic dimension of immigrant adjustment by examining the careers of two Italians who came to the United States in search of prosperity as grocery shopkeepers. By his focus upon the factors that enable us to understand why one man achieved relative success, while the efforts of the other ended in failure, LaSorte depicts variation on the micro-level by the contrasts provided by two individuals. In her article, "Ligurian Merchants: Between Italy and the Americas", Adele Maiello also presents a comparative study of immigrant experience, but at the macro-level by her analysis of the differences between settlers in Argentina and in California. In her research, Maiello has attempted to use these cases to distinguish how much of their success can be explained by what Ligurians brought with them in their cultural heritage from what was more the result of conditions found in their new societies.

From its beginnings 25 years ago, however, the Association has recognized that the immigrant experience was more than simply political and economic dimensions. An adequate and comprehensive perspective could not be restricted to the measurement of the objective, material aspects of immigrant life. The work presented by participants in the annual programs has frequently explored the more subjective dimensions of images and stereotypes by which Italian immigrants and their descendants have been viewed by other members of American society. In "That's Italian...Or Is It?: (Un)Popular Images of Italians in Mass Media", John R. Mitrano and James G. Mitrano survey and describe a very broad range of how Italians and Italian Americans have been depicted by advertising, packaging and marketing as well as by motion pictures and television programs. The Mitranos show the continuation of a broad spectrum of negative portrayals of Italian Americans and call for some response to amend this situation. The 1992 conference program also included several papers which examined the depiction and reception of Gay and Lesbian Italian Americans by others. While several participants discussed how such sexual orientations presented problems within their family or community life, one paper in particular provided a rather different set of issues. In "Where is Nella Sorellanza When You Need Her?", Rose Romano described the difficulties of other Lesbians in understanding what it meant to be an Italian American Lesbian. Taken together, these two papers clearly show that whether in the mainstream of commercial market and popular culture or at the interstices of sexual orientation, the Italian American experience is still marked by misperception and distortion.

Despite its origins as an organization of historians and social scientists, the Association has also long held that the continuing exploration of immigrant experience is not restricted to those particular disciplines and fields, but includes modes of more creative interpretation. Increasingly, in the programs of recent years, the Association has included literary and film criticism and of creative writers and artists. In a similar vein, the conference programs have recognized the relevance of Italy and its people as a part of the cultural experiences of populations of Italian origins who happened to have migrated elsewhere. This broader view was well represented in the agenda of the 1992 conference. For example, in his paper on "Salvatore Giuliano: The Facts, the Myth and Cinema", Mario Aste investigates the discrepancies found in the actual life and career and in the film portrayal of the modern Sicilian bandit and folk-hero. Aste contends that the uncertainties about the actual character and events in the life of Giuliano provide the condition for the film industry to create its own myths which serve in turn as useful symbols in the Sicilian imagination. In another instance, in his paper, "On the Poetics of Joseph Tusiani's *Gente Mia*", Franco Mulas has examined the meaning of the work of perhaps the foremost Italian immigrant poet of the 20th century. In much of this work, Tusiani expresses the painful marginality of immigrant life. Completing this section of the *Proceedings,* we have included "Il Caffè" and "Figs", two pieces of the evocative and poignant poetry of Mary Russo Demetrick. In her lyric sensitivity, Demetrick reveals a later generation of Italian Americans who continue to suffer a lingering marginality.

The papers of the concluding section of the *Proceedings* of the 1992 conference return to familiar concerns of Italian American studies. Each paper, however, contains some innovative aspect. In her paper, "Adjustment and Integration: The Italian Experience in Colorado", Janet E. Worrall presents a community study, but focused upon the case of Denver, Colorado, a setting for the immigrant and ethnic experience that has been largely neglected by previous researchers. Her description and analysis mainly present the difficult material conditions of individuals and families that coincided with the evolution of the local immigrant community. Worrall's work marks hopefully not only another contribution to the continuing identification and exploration of Italian experience in places other than the more customary urban industrial centers of the northeastern states, but the initial phase of further study of Denver and its surrounding region. In "Moral Familism: Italian Americans and *Società*", Frank J. Salamone renews the discussion of a lingering question in the field of Italian American studies, namely the capacity of Italian Americans to form their own self-help organizations. In his research on the Italians in Rochester, New York, Salamone has focused upon the critical role that such organizations played in the development of ethnic identity and cohesion within the immigrant community. Finally, in his brief analytical review of previous studies, Louis J. Gesualdi also returns to some issues that remain at the center of research on the Italian experience in the United States. Gesualdi reviews the controversy over whether the adjustment and achievements of several generations of Italian Americans were helped or hindered by the values and customs that derive from the cultural heritage of their homeland. This final paper reminds us, to paraphrase the poet, T.S. Eliot, that we often must return to the point from which we have started in order to understand where we have been and how far we have come, and perhaps it is only then that we finally attain the understanding that we have sought.

The end result represented by this volume, however, is only a selective sample of the papers delivered at the conference. But these papers provide some indication not merely of the work that was presented on that occasion, but the kind of research, critical analysis, and creative writing that represents the field of Italian American studies. Although the Italian experience in the Americas has now extended over a period of 500 years, it has only been the past several decades that the serious investigation of that subject has been pursued. The reader will readily discover and appreciate the manifold themes, directions, and emphases that can be found in this now flourishing field. We can only hope that this area of scholarly and intellectual endeavor remains, however, in an early phase of its trajectory of growth and development. In the years ahead, we would want to look back upon the present period, as we do upon the meaning of Columbus's early voyages, as only the beginning of a significant time of new exploration and significant discovery. We are confident that the present volume will take its place among previous numbers of the *Proceedings of the American Italian Historical Association* as a modest contribution to that objective of serious reflection and expression.

Richard N. Juliani
Sandra P. Juliani
Wynnewood, Pennsylvania

PART I
COLUMBUS: RECONSIDERATION AND REVISION

1

COLUMBUS AND THE RISE
OF AMERICAN LITERATURE

Frank J. Cavaioli

In searching for national self-definition, Americans, through the vehicle of literature, created the image of Christopher Columbus to use as an important metaphor to overcome a divided society. Poets included the lyrical term "Columbia" in their verses to personify America. The name Columbia, as it developed earlier, signified a central unifying reference point, as articulated by poets, to promote a new democratic nation. This paper will focus upon the use and significance of the name Columbia, as derived from the name Columbus, and its relationship to the rise of an American national literature.

While no political unity existed before 1776, colonial provincialism delayed the development of a distinct American literature. The population was multi-ethnic, agrarian, and looked to Europe for cultural leadership. Minimal transportation and communication facilities further restricted intercolonial contact. It could not be expected that this frontier society produce a national literature of much note. "A literature must have behind it an independent nation, a people with hope and vision and enthusiasm."[1] However, a seminal development of an American literature appeared at the time of the American Revolution when the foundation of nationhood was first established.

At the close of the American Revolution, nationhood as we know it today did not exist. Divisions predominated as the people of the thirteen states addressed the United States in plural rather than singular terms. Essentially, Americans possessed no distinct national culture and religion; even their language was not exclusively their own. Common traditions were emerging, but there was no common national attitude toward anything at this time. Despite progress made in political liberty, a Confederation of nearly sovereign states exhibiting local prejudices prevailed beyond 1789 when the national Constitution was instituted. Persons thought of themselves as New Yorkers or Virginians. It must also be remembered, as Carl Becker had astutely observed more than 60 years ago, that the American Revolution was marked by considerable internal conflict, further fracturing society.

Americans knew they possessed concepts of natural rights that greatly differed from other people of earlier civilizations. Producing a national literature to express this concept to unite a people in a common belief provided a unique challenge. Culturally Americans had fallen behind during the revolutionary generation when political survival had become paramount. Pamphleteering and the political poem had exerted a major influence in persuading colonists to support the movement for independence, but this writing could not be classified as belle-lettres. The war had diverted Joel Barlow, Timothy Dwight, David Humphreys, and Philip Freneau to engage in political propaganda and satire. Unable to pursue careers in poetry, they entered such fields as journalism, diplomacy, religion, education, editing, and business. Pursuing republican goals consumed their energies.

Add to this record the task of settling a raw land and it can be seen that achieving a notable literature proved to be difficult. Now the opportunity for writers to develop a literature to carry the ideas of progress and liberty could lead to the rise of a republican system. In the past, literature had been the servant of royalty and aristocracy in perpetuating an elitism for their own aggrandizement. The prospect for belletristic writing in 1789 did not appear promising, particularly at a critical time when a national literature could advance political and cultural unity. It mattered little a generation later when British writer Sydney Smith wrote in the *Edinburgh Review* (1820), "Who reads an American book?" What mattered was that the most important literature to emerge from the American Revolution was political. The songs, poems, odes, and ballads clearly expressed the national spirit. Christopher

Columbus and the name Columbia played an integral part in this development as self-conscious writers felt compelled to contribute literary salvos in further defining an American identity.[2]

A group of poets stepped forward to meet the national and literary needs of the young nation. One of these, Timothy Dwight (1752-1817), grandson of Jonathan Edwards, graduate and later president of Yale, distinguished himself as a chaplain in the American Revolutionary army, and as a teacher and clergyman. He produced over fourteen volumes of writings. Although he was a conservative in politics, religion and literature, in his most ambitious work, "The Conquest of Canaan" (1774), and best long poem, "Greenfield Hill" (1794), he emphasized "the rising glory of America" in prophetic verse. Dwight demonstrated a proud New England Puritan temper. In "Greenfield Hill" he argued for the superiority of America over Europe as he applied a Columbian reference in Part IV:

> Senate august! that sway'st Columbian climes,
> Forme'd of the wise, the noble, and humane,
> Cast back the glance through long-ascending times,
> And thank what nations fill'd the western plain.[3]

But Dwight's most successful Revolutionary War poem, "COLUMBIA" (1777), instilled a fighting spirit among the soldiers. He wrote it while serving as an army chaplain at West Point. This popular poem began and ended with two pertinent lyrical lines:

> Columbia, Columbia, to glory arise,
> The queen of the world, and the child of the skies!

In the other 44 lines of the poem, Dwight extolled America's "fruitful" soil and Columbia as the "last refuge of virtue," that shall "Hush the tumult of war, and give peace to the world."[4] Didactic in purpose, Dwight, though lacking in true poetic creativity, contributed an indispensable literary element on the road to American nationality.

The process of creating a national literary culture contributed to a clarification of the American ideal of a democratic society. There was no stopping this onward march of building upon the foundation established in early American colonial civilization. It seemed that utopia was near at hand. The image of Christopher Columbus devised by Americans to serve such purpose became inevitably bound in this process. Columbus, a man of two continents, can be seen as sowing the seed of the Old World on the New World, and that seed would flourish in an unfettered environment. This Italian Renaissance man as mariner-discoverer served as a vital cultural metaphor so necessary for inspiring poets to cultivate a liberal nationalism. No other figure provided a similar function. Observing the need to fulfill patriotic purpose, one scholar commented:

> The mythmaking needs of the new nation
> reached back to embrace the whole era of
> European exploration. Thus Christopher Columbus,
> an enterprising Italian, who had served the
> colonial ambitions of monarchical Spain became
> the unlikely forefather of an English-speaking
> democracy.[5]

Composing patriotic poems and ballads continued unabated in the post-Revolutionary period. The verses were less "spontaneous" and "sincere," according to one critic, than the earlier period when Americans faced a more serious challenge. Anyone who composed verse felt an obligation to express an intense patriotic sentiment in striving for national posterity. Since the Revolution had produced a leveling effect, anyone who had the time and energy celebrated the democratic spirit. Poets continued to rely on the Columbus image, Columbia, as the personification of America. The poem, "Eulogium on Major-General Joseph Warren," written by "A Columbian," symbolized such patriotic praise. A nationalistic literary sentiment gripped the nation.[6]

Benjamin Young Prime (1733-1791), a Long Island physician and poet, first eulogized George Washington during the hero's presidency in 1791 in the pindaric ode, "Columbia's Glory, or British Pride Humbled." Prime's ode contained 1441 lines that expressed some very effective patriotic verse. Having achieved political independence, it was now time to establish American literary independence from Europe, to record American events, to extol

American personalities. The poetic soul was to be cultivated through original themes to deflect Old World models. The Old World Muses were no longer relevant.[7] Poet David Humphreys, conscious of the lack of a national history, openly admitted,

> ERATO's SEAT, ALAS, CAN'T BE FOUND,
> COLUMBIA's BARREN, 'TIS UNHALLOWED GROUND.[8]

Caught up in this expansive spirit, Prime composed his best poem, "Columbia's Glory, or British Pride Humbled." It was published five weeks before his death in 1791. This poem parodied his earlier poem on the French and Indian War that had praised the great British victory at Quebec. That poem, "Britain's Glory, or Gallic Pride Humbled" (1758), was written by Prime as a loyal British subject. Now, as a citizen of the new American nation, Prime voiced his sentiments in "Columbia's Glory, or British Pride Humbled," invoking the Columbus image.

> The muse of Britain sings no more,
> The British Laurel withers on my brow,
> COLUMBIA only is my country now;
> To her alone my services belong:
>> My head, my heart, my hands,
>> My pen, my lyre, my tongue,
> COLUMBIA'S int'rest now demands,
> Engrosses all my cares and claims my ev'ry song.[9]

Continuing along this line of development was jurist and Congressman Joseph Hopkinson (1770-1842) who composed the song, "Hail Columbia," in 1798. It was first sung by Gilbert Fox to the music of *The Presidential March* in Philadelphia at the Chestnut Street Theater. The first four lines sang praises to the new nation and its heroes:

> Hail Columbia! happy land
> Hail, ye heroes! heaven born band!
> Who fought and bled in freedom's cause,
> Who fought and bled in freedom's cause.[10]

Events in Europe continued to absorb American writers. With the rise of Napoleon to power came the fear of a Napoleonic invasion of the United States in 1798. This exaggerated fear animated poet Thomas Green Fessenden to compose the poem, "Ye Sons of Columbia." Napoleon had been assembling a large fleet in Toulon, causing Americans to believe he intended to invade their country. Actually, the fleet's destination was Egypt and not America. Nevertheless, Fessenden urged Americans to defend the Republic.

> Ye sons of Columbia, unite in the cause
> Of liberty, justice, religion, and laws;
> Should foes then invade us, to battle
>   we'll hie.
> For the GOD OF FATHERS will be
>   our ally!
> Let Frenchmen advance,
>   And all Europe join France,
> Designing our conquest and thunder;
>   United and free
>   Forever we'll be,
> And our cannon shall tell them in thunder,
> That foes to our freedom we'll ever defy,
> Till the continent sinks, and the ocean is dry![11]

The person to emerge as the "Poet of the Revolution" was Philip Freneau (1752-1832). A Jeffersonian, and patriotic and idealistic in temperament, he composed political satires and directed them against the British. He distanced himself from Federalist beliefs, and his opponents marked him as a vulgar democrat. He projected a vision of the infant United States as greater than what it was and what it had been. If times had been normal, Freneau might have devoted himself entirely to poetry. V.L. Parrington said of Freneau, "It is fitting that our first outstanding poet should have been a liberal."[12]

The chronicle of Columbus's persistent striving to secure financial backing of his enterprise had enlivened poets such as Freneau to compose lyrical lines that demonstrated a dedication to the dream. The failure of Columbus to get King John II of Portugal to sponsor his westward enterprise forced him to appeal to King Ferdinand and Queen Isabella of Spain. But they referred the project to a council in Salamanca which also rejected it. Poet Freneau, in probing the American nation's historical roots, imagined an impatient Columbus turning to King Ferdinand in the poem, "Columbus to Ferdinand."

> Illustrious monarch of Iberia's soil,
> Too long I wait permission to depart;
> Sick of delays, I beg thy list'ning ear—
> Shine forth the patron and the prince of art.

In this poem Freneau paints a courageous Columbus dreaming of new lands to the west.

> Fir'd at the theme, I languish to depart,
> Supply the barque, and bid Columbus sail;
> He fears no storms upon the untravell'd deep;
> Reason shall steer and skill disarm the gale.[13]

After having discovered a new world, Columbus had proved to be a less than able administrator of that land. At the end of his third voyage he was placed in chains, the result of court intrigue, and was returned to Spain in disgrace. His patrons had the chains removed. Aware of Columbus's vision and suffering, Freneau, in the poem, "Columbus in Chains," has Columbus pleading to his patrons and voicing displeasure of the court intriguers who refused to appreciate the magnitude of his discoveries.

> Are these the honors they reserve for me,
> Chains for the man who gave new worlds to Spain!
> Rest here, my swelling heart!—O Kings,
>   O Queens,
> Patrons of monsters, and their progeny,
> Authors of wrong, and slaves to fortune merely.[14]

Freneau, the passionate poet whose versifying vilified British usurpations, predicted a glorious future for the emerging nation in an ode delivered by his classmate, Hugh Henry Brackenridge, at the Princeton commencement. The ode, "The Rising Glory of America," hailed America's future, and it began by turning to Columbus's discovery of the New World. This event marked a major advance of western civilization, as Freneau pointed out:

> Now shall the adventurous muse attempt a theme
> More new, more noble, and more flush of fame
> Than all that went before—
> Now through the veil of ancient days renew
> The period famed when Columbus touched
> These shores so long unknown, through various toils,
> Famine, and death, the hero forced his way.
> Through oceans pregnant with perpetual storms,
> And climates hostile to adventurous men.[15]

Freneau demonstrated a national self-consciousness which had been instigated by the American Revolution in this poem. He continued by tracing major events in the New World following the discovery of America, emphasizing economic progress and praising civic liberty:

> Independent power shall hold her sway,
> And public virtue warm the patriot breast!
> No traces shall remain of tyranny.[16]

Freneau pronounced a utopian vision for America, sinless and virtuous in a pastoral setting, so common a theme among colonial writers:

> A new Jerusalem, sent down from heaven
> Shall grace our happy land . . . .[17]

In another poem, "The Pictures of Columbus" (1774), Freneau contrasted the visionary mariner urging on his quest for a new world against the realization that, once discovered, pastoral innocence would be destroyed by greed and brutality. In eighteen verse-sketches, he described Columbus charting new maps, persevering in seeking support for his enterprise, addressing King Ferdinand and Queen Isabella, urging the discontented sailors to give him more time, discovering land, afterward placed in chains, and dying quietly in retirement without honors. In one graphic scene Freneau, through the eyes of Columbus, depicts

> Sylvan scenes of innocence and ease,
> How calm and joyous pass the seasons here!
> No splendid towns of spiry turrets rise,
> No lordly palaces—no tyrant kings
> Enact harsh laws to crush fair freedom here.[18]

Columbus then comes upon a body of a native murdered by one of his men for the gold trinkets he wore and wondered if the discovery of this new land was worth it.

> Is this the fruit of my discovery!
> If the first scene is murder, what shall follow
> But havock, slaughter, chains and devastation
> In every dress and form of cruelty.[19]

Freneau juxtaposed Columbus's noble motive for discovery with selfish materialistic desires. The very reasons why men escaped from Europe were now being instituted in the New World: violence, greed, tyranny, despoilment of the environment. Columbus's (Freneau's) idealistic vision of America was now tempered by a realization that human nature could also be debased in striving for that ideal. Fleeing from European corruption to an innocent American asylum appeared not easily accomplished. Here was a forecast of the contemporary debate over Columbus's impact on the world he had discovered. Freneau, the romantic poet was now disturbed by the other side of his perceived American paradise.[20]

In one of his finest patriotic poems, "On Mr. Paine's Rights of Man" (1791), Freneau condemned monarchy and war, praised reason and freedom, and employed Columbia to address the future greatness of the new nation:

> Columbia, hail! immortal be thy reign:
> Without a king, we till the smiling plain;
> Without a king, we traced the unbounded sea,
> And traffic round the globe, through each degree;

> Each foreign clime our honour'd flag reveres,
> Which asks no monarch, to support the Stars:
> Without a *king*, the laws maintain their sway,
> While honour bids each generous heart obey.
> Be ours the task the ambitious to restrain,
> And this great lesson teach—that kings are vain;
> That warring realms to certain ruin haste,
> That kings subsist by war, and wars are waste:
> So shall our nation, form'd on Virtue's plan,
> Remain the guardian of the Rights of Man,
> A vast Republic, famed through every clime,
> Without a king to see the end of time.[21]

Freneau persisted in the tradition of depicting all republican virtues as ancient Greek goddesses by personifying America as a feminine reference in the poem, "On the Dissolution of Transatlantic Jurisdiction in America" (1795). The Jay Treaty, recently enacted with Great Britain, signaled the romantic emancipation of "vulnerable femininity" from Old World control:

> From Britain's grasp forever freed,
> COLUMBIA glories in the deed:
> From her rich soil, each tyrant flown,
> She finds this fair estate her own.[22]

Columbia merges into goddess and nation so necessary for this paean of patriotism.

To Freneau, Columbus remained the model navigator as he related a ship's plight tossed about in a hurricane near Jamaica in the poem, "The Hurricane" (1774). He wondered what new admiral would save the ship:

> No charts have we to mark that land,
> No compass to direct that way—
> What Pilot shall explore that realm,
> What new COLUMBUS take the helm![23]

Later, in the poem, "Lines Addressed to Mr. Jefferson on His Re-

tirement from the Presidency of the United States.—1809," Freneau honored
this American hero:

> At length the year, which marks his course, expires,
> And JEFFERSON from public life retires;
> That year, the close of years, which own his claim,
> And give all his honors, all his fame.
> Far in the heaven of fame I see him fly,
> Safe in the realms of immortality:
> On EQUAL WORTH his honor'd mantle falls,
> Him whom Columbia her true patriot calls.[24]

Evolving American republican institutions prompted Joel Barlow
(1754-1812), who was one of the original Connecticut Wits, but later became
a Jeffersonian liberal, to attempt an epic poem. (The Connecticut Wits, some
of whom were Timothy Dwight, Joel Barlow, John Trumbull and David
Humphreys, were educated at Yale, lived in Hartford and maintained conservative Federalist political leanings.) Seeking to capture the sweep of the history of the New World and narrating the aspirations of his age, Barlow produced *The Vision of Columbus* in 1787, which was to be revised and enlarged
twenty years later into *The Columbiad*, the only epic attempt based on Columbus by an American poet. Barlow joined patriotic poets Freneau, Dwight,
Wheatley, Trumbull, and Humphreys to respond to the need for national
self-definition through the advocacy of "universal republicanism" by stressing such virtues as peace, freedom, and progress. *The Columbiad* prophesied
a utopia; future American growth was of the highest moment in the mind of
the writer who conceived of American power leading the international community. The uncertainties of the Revolution demanded that Barlow dedicate
himself to democracy with a linkage to the rising glory of America.[25]

Barlow turned away from an epic narrative of describing
Columbus's accomplishments and instead composed a philosophic-prophetic
epic poem whereby Hesper, the guardian genius of the western continent,
pacifies Columbus's fears by describing to him the future glories of his discoveries. Barlow structured *The Columbiad* by laying out the past, present,
and future history of America as seen through the eyes of Columbus. Thus

The Columbiad begins:

> I sing the Mariner who first unfurl'd
> An eastern banner o'er the western world
> And taught mankind where future empires lay.[26]

Barlow drew inspiration from Columbus, but he identified not Columbus but America, and its free institutions, as the real hero. Columbus became a passive witness to unfolding events in the New World. The vision of a utopian society crystallized in Columbus's mind as Hesper declared:

> Here springs the day, since time began,
> The brightest, broadest, happiest morn of man.

And he continued:

> Here social man a second birth shall find,
> And a new range of reason lift his mind,
> Feed his strong intellect with purer light,
> A nobler sense of duty and right,
> The sense of liberty. . . . [27]

Such optimistic faith in the future is expressive of the Age of the Enlightenment and consistent with America's glorious destiny. The success of the American Revolution and constitutionalism led Barlow to celebrate the dawn of a new era; and instead of exalting individuals as in the epic tradition, "American readers were to accept the premise that the hero is all of us. . . ."[28]

It is not the purpose to produce here an extensive literary criticism of *The Vision of Columbus* and *The Columbiad* since numerous scholars have written on the subject. It is important to note, however, that by the time of the American Revolution, Columbus was an authentic hero.[29] Having opened the New World for the persecuted of the Old, having experienced personal hardship, having challenged the mighty oceans, having faced a new frontier, having broken with the past, having unleashed unknown forces in the world, it was logical that Americans would look to him as its natural hero who could be celebrated in an emerging national literature. Columbus was cast as a unifying symbol for a nascent nation. Barlow may have written a mediocre poem, as critics have asserted, but it served a vital function at a critical time in the early years of the United States. Such a vision of progress and freedom has remained a central part of the nation's story. Perhaps that is what V. L. Parrington had in mind when he wrote, "The child of two continents, America can be explained in its significant traits by neither alone."[30]

Clearly, *The Columbiad* did not memorialize a hero in the epic tradition but "expressed the idea of democratic order and progress. . . and is meant to celebrate the establishment of democratic order, inculcate its working in those who participate in it, project its glorious possibilities into the future." Barlow attempted through the complex figure of Columbus to fill a void in a "hero-less culture." Although Columbus provided inspiration, as he had for other writers, his achievements assumed a valuable role in the progression of American culture and republican institutions. In a literary sense, Barlow had failed to create an epic hero; however, it was logical that he turn to Columbus as other writers had done.[31]

The complex figure of Columbus provided an inherent contradiction underlying why the hero, Columbus, who later died quietly with less than hero-like ceremony, could not lend himself to the essential substance necessary in an epic figure. Columbus, brilliant navigator-mariner but inept administrator, suffered the disgrace of enchainment following his third voyage. He bore the unfair charge of critics of having introduced slavery and having destroyed native populations in the New World, a mighty burden for any historical figure to bear. Indeed, those who followed him, greedy conquistadors led by Cortez and Pizarro, plundered Aztec and Inca civilizations in their drive for wealth. At his death in 1506, Columbus adamantly clung to the belief that he had really found the long-sought western route to the Indies, when in fact he had discovered a new world.

These historical ingredients posed a challenge to poets whose function was to create heroic legend for posterity in an American setting. Italian American poet Joseph Tusiani has observed that according "to the loftiest literary examples, a pure epos never ends in tragedy." Discovering a new world, then, became subordinate to an unfolding series of historical events with subsequent blame placed on Columbus. Critics remembered him in this sorrowful context, thus weakening his reputation in history and diluting his unique accomplishments. Creating a true American epic with Columbus as its subject was bound to fail. Joel Barlow, the poet, became victimized by this dilemma.[32]

With the American Revolution came the birth of a nation and its poetry. The beacon light of freedom reflected brightly in poets' minds. A new hero emerged in George Washington whose deeds were sung in glorious verses. Yet in spite of these competing forces, American poets continued to seek inspiration from Columbus for historical continuity to justify nationhood. Barlow may have failed in writing a true American epic based on Columbus; however, he nevertheless drew inspiration from the great discoverer at a critical moment in the creation of a democratic nation and its distinctive national literature.

Classical scholar Edith Hamilton astutely provided an understanding of a nation's underlying tenet when she wrote, "A people's literature is the great text-book for real knowledge of them."[33] The relationship between the use of Columbus and Columbia and the rise of American literature have contributed significantly to a national identity unknown to Americans up to the Revolutionary era and helped to establish a tradition of unity upon which American civilization could prosper.

NOTES

1. Fred Lewis Pattee, *The First Century of American Literature: 1770-1870* (New York: Cooper Square Publishers, 1966), pp. 5-12.
2. Jay B. Hubbell, *American Life in Literature* (New York: Harper and Brothers, 1949.), pp. 203-210; Emory Elliott (ed), *Columbia Literary History of the United States* (New York: Columbia Univ. Press, 1988), pp. 156-159.
3. Jane Donahue Eberwein (ed), *Early American Poetry* (Madison: Univ. of Wisconsin Press, 1978), p. 188.
4. *Survey of American Poetry*, (Great Neck, NY: Poetry Anthology Press, 1983), pp. 118-120.
5. Peter Conn, *Literature In America* (New York: Cambridge Univ. Press, 1989), p. 101.
6. William Peter Field Trent, John Erskine, Stuart P. Sherman, and Carl Van Doren, eds, *The Cambridge History of American Literature, Part I* (New York: Macmillan, 1917), pp. 167-8.
7. Benjamin T. Spencer, *The Quest for Nationality* (Syracuse: Syracuse Univ. Press, 1957), pp. 23-8.
8. B. T. Spencer, p. 69, as quoted from.
9. James McLachlan, *Princetonians, 1748-1768* (Princeton: Princeton Univ. Press, 1976), p. 43, as quoted from.

10. *Webster's Biographical Dictionary, 5th edition,* (Springfield, MA: G. & C. Merriam, 1958), p. 728; Arthur Hobson Quinn, *The Literature of the American People* (New York: Appleton-Century- Crofts, 1951), p. 189; Alphonso Gerald Newcomer, Alice E. Andrews, and Howard Judson Hall, *Three Centuries of American Poetry and Prose* (New York: Scott, Foresman, 1929), p. 170.

11. Burton Egbert Stevenson, *Poems of American History* (Boston: Houghton Mifflin, 1922), p. 278.

12. Vernon L. Parrington, *Main Currents in American Thought, Vol. I* (New York: Harcourt, Brace, 1954), p. 374.

13. B. E. Stevenson, pp. 9-10.

14. B. E. Stevenson, p. 17.

15. Harry Hayden Clark, *Poems of Freneau* (New York: Hafner, 1968), p. 3.

16. H. H. Clark, pp. 15-16.

17. H. H. Clark, p. 16; Annette Kolodny. "The Visionary Line: Poems of Philip Freneau," in Harold Bloom (ed), *American Poetry to 1914* (New York: Chelsea House, 1987), pp. 80-8.

18. H. H. Clark, p. 254.

19. H. H. Clark, p. 255.

20. William D. Andrews, "Philip Freneau and Francis Hopkinson," in Everett Emerson (ed), *American Literature in 1764-1789, The Revolutionary Years* (Madison: Univ. of Wisconsin Press, 1977), pp. 141-3.

21. *Survey of American Poetry,* Vol. II, p. 16.

22. A. Kolodny, pp. 79-80.

23. J. D. Eberwein, pp. 236-237.

24. J. D. Eberwein, p. 243. "Him" refers to Madison, the next President and Freneau's classmate at Princeton.

25. P. Conn, p. 103; E. Elliott, pp. 159-160.

26. Roy Harvey Pearce, *The Continuity of American Poetry* (Princeton: Princeton Univ. Press, 1961), p. 63, as quoted from.

27. R. H. Pearce, p. 65, as quoted from.

28. John P. McWilliams, Jr, *The American Epic* (New York: Cambridge Univ. Press, 1989), p. 42.

29. For the significance of Columbus in early America see, Frank J. Cavaioli, "Columbus and the Name Columbia," *Italian Americana* 11 (Fall/Winter, 1992): 6-17.

30. V. L. Parrington, x.

31. Roy Harvey Pearce, "Toward An American Epic," *Hudson Review* 12 (1959): 362-6.

32. Joseph Tusiani, "Christopher Columbus and Joel Barlow," *Italian Americana* 3 (Autumn, 1976):30-44; Arthur L. Ford, *Joel Barlow* (New York: Twayne, 1971).

33. Edith Hamilton, *The Roman Way* (New York: Mentor, 1963), v.

2

COLUMBUS'S RELIGIOSITY AND THE MILLENNIUM

Luciano G. Rusich
The City University of New York
The College of Staten Island

It is not news that, to his contemporaries, Christopher Columbus appeared to be a deeply religious man. One may wonder whether his religiosity was sincere or not; whether it was the expression of a healthy and well rounded personality or the manifestation of some psychological imbalance; and whether it constituted a decisive motivation to undertake his voyages. In Europe and in the United States, scholars have answered these questions with a range of divergent opinions which goes from Columbus the saint, worthy to be canonized,[1] to Columbus the deranged and senile individual whose delusions inspired him to write the *Book of Prophecies*.[2] Fortunately, more recently, after years of studies and research, scholars have reached a more accurate and objective understanding of the religiosity of the Italian Navigator. Christopher Columbus's religiosity was sincere and allowed him to withstand the many trials and tribulations that the realization of his dreams entailed. Based on medieval thought, his faith was a form of knowledge and a way of life. Paolo Emilio Taviani, however, pointedly observed that as strong as his faith was, he could not be a saint because his exercise of the virtue of charity, essential for saintliness, was weak and erratic, at best.[3] On the whole, the consensus was that in Columbus's personality, one cannot exclude a mystical and religious component.

The obvious next question then was the possibility that the religiosity of the Discoverer was a mere reflex of the spirituality of the times in which he lived, and that it had, partly or fully, motivated him to undertake his voyages of explorations. The answer to this question had already been given affirmatively by his first biographers: Bartolomé de las Casas and Columbus's son Ferdinand. But the problem had not been taken under serious consideration or exhaustively studied by subsequent biographers. According to one of them, the French Henry Vignaud, divine inspiration did not constitute a category which allowed for critical discussion.[4] Perhaps, it would have been better to say that the spirituality of Columbus and of the period in which he lived were very different from today's spirituality and sensibility. Certainly they did not lend themselves to an easy interpretation. It is only in 1956, with the publication of *The Millennial Kingdom of the Franciscans in the New World* by John Leddy Phelan, that we see this aspect of Columbus's personality analyzed. Probably John Leddy Phelan was the first contemporary scholar to take into consideration once again the spirituality of the Genovese as a possible motivation for his voyages to the New World. According to Phelan, Columbus's spirituality cannot be doubted. Its sources may be found in the apocalyptic tradition of the Calabrian monk, Joachim of Fiore, which was so influential in shaping the spirituality of the Spanish Franciscans of Columbus's time.[5] More recently, his ideas have been followed by many others. Notably by Marianne Mahn-Lot who stressed the importance of the religious aspects of Columbus's personality in her biography of the Genovese[6] and Alain Milhou who, in his *Colón y su mentalidad mesiánica en el ambiente franciscanista español*, recreated the historical milieu and the mentality of the Franciscans of the Spain of the Catholic Monarchs, with a text full of erudite and well documented references, both literary and historical. Also for Milhou, as it was for Phelan, it was from this milieu and from this mentality that Columbus mystical spirituality derived.[7] The same conclusions were reached by Delmo C. West and August Kling in their scholarly and perceptive presentation of the *Book of Prophecies.*[8]

Before even starting a discussion on any aspect of Christopher Columbus's personality, however, it would be well to remember that he lived in a world whose ideas and values were strangely remote and different from ours. If it is true that he opened new vistas to mankind and that with his discovery, the Modern Age began, it is also true that he remained a man deeply anchored to the Middle Ages. His perceptions and cognitions were different from ours and were not subject to the same rules and to the same logic. If Christopher Columbus believed in something, he did so without critical analysis, without discriminating whether that which he believed in was a mere opinion or an article of faith. His faith was not a mere religious feeling; it was a method of knowledge that he applied to all fields of intellectual endeavor. He believed in God, in the Garden of Eden, in the authority of the Ancients, in the production of gold by way of solar rays, in the mountain of water which constituted the center of the Earth, and in the marvelous tales of Marco Polo.[9] In other words, Columbus, in this aspect of his personality was still a son of the Middle Ages. Therefore, it is expedient to define the terms "mysticism" and "prophet," as they were defined in Columbus's time.

In a wide sense, mysticism means and meant the attainment of the beatific vision of God, in this life, with the help of faith and divine grace, after having purged one's soul from sin and one's body from carnal desires. In Columbus's time, however, mysticism was a type of knowledge based on faith, as opposed to Aristotelic scholasticism in which knowledge was based on reason. In other words, Columbus may be considered a mystic not only because of his religious vision of the world, but also because he firmly believed that the knowledge of God, of infinity and of absolute truth was possible immediately and intuitively, without the help of reason, through an illumination of the intellect, with the help of the will guided by faith. For that which concerns the term "prophet", in the High Middle Ages and during the Renaissance, a prophet was not necessarily a messenger of God, one who conveyed the will of the Creator to mankind, as in the Old Testament; rather, he was someone who possessed the wisdom and the skill to interpret the Holy Scriptures, revealing their hidden truths.It is therefore natural that Columbus considered himself, and Las Casas would consider him to be, a true prophet.[10] In this context, we may legitimately speak of Columbus's mysticism which, as we shall see, showed a definite apocalyptic twist. This clarification renders even more evident the impossibility of speaking of the religiosity and mysticism of the Navigator without trying to understand the spirit of the

period in which he lived, and without being blinded by the fact that his contemporaries were the cream of the Italian Renaissance: Lorenzo de' Medici,
Leonardo da Vinci, Michelangelo Buonarroti, Domenico Ghirlandaio, Pico
della Mirandola. Above all, we must never forget that Columbus was himself an immigrant to Spain who lived and acted in the milieu of the Spanish
culture which, undoubtedly, affected him. It is only the analysis of this culture that can explain his religiosity as manifested in two fundamental documents: the Deed of Entail—*El Mayorazgo*—in which he transmitted his estate and title to his eldest son and his *Book of Prophecies* [*El libro de las
profecías*].

From *El Mayorazgo*—dated Seville, February 23, 1498—three
main components of Columbus's religiosity emerge: love of the Holy Sepulchre, loyalty to the papacy, and zeal to spread the Gospel.[11] The conquest
of Jerusalem and the rescue of the Holy Sepulchre were constants in the
political and religious ideals of Christopher Columbus. Even before the Ca-
pitulations of Santa Fé (April 1492), for instance, he had promised the Catholic monarchs to provide such a quantity of gold and spices from the "Indies"
to enable them to finance the conquest of Jerusalem. Now, with the
Mayorazgo, he established a fund imposing on his heirs the obligation to put
it at the disposal of the Spanish Crown to encourage the sovereigns to start
a crusade for the liberation of the Holy Sepulcher. Should the monarchs fail
to undertake the crusade, he enjoined his own heirs to do it. The other component, loyalty to the papacy, revealed an overwhelming preoccupation for
the future of the mission of the papacy. In effect, the Admiral of the Ocean
Sea, in this document, foresees and expresses the fear that in his lifetime, or
in the future, a schism could take place in the Church and that some of the
Christians would rebel against the pope. In this case, Columbus's heir is
under obligation to report to the pope and put himself and the family's wealth
at his disposal, to help defeat the schismatics and prevent the pope and the
Church from being deprived of the honors, privileges and estates to which
they are entitled. The penalty for failing to comply with this clause is the loss
of the primogeniture, unless the pope had been declared a heretic. The third
and last component, the zeal to evangelize, manifests itself in the testamen-
tary dispositions given to his heirs to provide for and support "four good

teachers of Holy Theology, with the purpose and the task to work for and order that work be done for the conversion to our Holy Faith of these peoples of the Indies."[12] In the same year that he signed the *Mayorazgo*, he wrote a letter to his brother Bartholomew which reveals the essence of his religiosity as expressed in the *Mayorazgo* and in all his writings. "In this as in everything—writes Columbus—it is necessary to observe the mandates of conscience, because there is no other good than to serve God, in so far as all the things of this world count for nothing whereas the other world is forever."[13]

This desire to serve God, this certainty that he had always done so by undertaking and bringing to completion his travels of discovery, as a mission entrusted to him by Divine Providence never abandoned him. On the contrary, the years that witnessed his defeat and humiliation, the years that saw him in chains, stripped of all honors, purified his religiosity to the point of imparting to it a mystical dimension. The proof that this happened can be found in the *Book of Prophecies*, compiled after his disastrous fourth voyage, between 1501 and 1504. Quite different from the *Mayorazgo* document, the *Book of Prophecies* does not have a coherent structure. It consists of miscellaneous writings collected by Columbus and the Cartusian monk Gaspare Gorrizio. Essentially it comprises passages of the Bible, of writings and quotations of famous ancient and medieval authors (Seneca, Roger Bacon, Saint Thomas Aquinas, Saint Augustine, Nicholas of Lyra, Joachim of Fiore and others) with handwritten commentaries by Columbus, Father Gorrizio, and Columbus's son Ferdinand. The other difference is psychological. The *Book of Prophecies* is written, inspired and organized by a man who, because of the injustices suffered, saw the vanity of the world and the transience of its pomp and glory, and looked at his life and at his accomplishments, *sub species aeternitatis*, as the fulfillment of the will of God as prophesied in the Bible. In the words of an Italian Columbian scholar, Cesare de Lollis,

> ... all of a sudden he saw his accomplishments devoid of any human characteristic and himself as the man prophesied in the Holy Scriptures, he who would have carried the name and the glory of the God of Israel to the farthest confines of the world. Then with great care he began to look into the Holy Scriptures and theological writings for

those passages in which he would seem to find a prediction
of his work and he collected them in the *Book of Prophecies.*[14]

Even more important than the collection of prophecies and commentaries which comprise the *Book of Prophecies* is the long letter that introduces them. It is addressed to their royal majesties Isabella and Ferdinand
of Spain with the purpose of sustaining their interest in the liberation of the
Holy Sepulchre. In it, Columbus narrates with a wealth of biographical information that since he was young, thanks to the grace of God and to His
inspiration, he always looked for the company of learned people, clerics or
laymen of every religious affiliation, "Latins, Greeks, Jews, Moslems" so that
they would teach him what they knew. He himself, by himself, studied
enough geometry, astrology, and arithmetic, that would enable him to navigate in the open sea and to draw maps. But it was not the scholars he con-
sorted with, nor the books he read, to prompt the decision to navigate westward. It was the Holy Spirit that inspired him to undertake his voyages, and
the Catholic Majesties to support him, in his endeavors, in spite of the many
enemies at court who had tried to thwart his projects. Indirectly Columbus
was exhorting Ferdinand and Isabella not to give up their project to liberate
the Holy Sepulchre even though many of their advisors considered it imprac-
ticable. Just as his voyage to the Indies was the work of God, in the same way
God shall not deny his help to those who will dedicate themselves to the holy
undertaking of liberating the Holy Sepulchre.[15] Further on in the same letter,
Columbus assumes an apocalyptic tone associating the coming of the Antichrist and the end of the world with the evangelization of the Indies and the
liberation of Jerusalem. To use his own words:

> As I said before, there are many of the prophecies which
> still have to be fulfilled and I believe that these are great
> events for the world. It is my belief that there signs that
> Our Lord is hastening these things. One of these signs is
> that is now possible to preach the Gospel in so many lands
> and to all people. The Abbot Joachim, a Calabrian, stated
> that he who was to rebuild the House of Mt. Zion would

come out of Spain. Cardinal Pierre D'Ailly wrote a lot
concerning the end of the sect of Mohammed and the coming of the Antichrist in a treaty called *De concordia
astronomie veritatis, et narrationnis historice* [Accord of
Astronomical Truth and History].[16]

As if this would not be sufficient to induce Isabella and Ferdinand
of Spain to undertake the conquest of Jerusalem, Columbus quotes another
prophecy by Joachim of Fiore, taken from the letter that the Republic of
Genoa wrote to the Spanish Monarchs on the occasion of the conquest of
Granada. In the letter the prophecy of the Calabrian Abbot is specifically
applied to the king of Spain as the liberator of the Holy Sepulchre.[17]

The recurring theme that underlies the collection of writings in the
Book of Prophecies is that all of them, somehow, seem to foretell the end of
the world. The end would take place after all nations and all peoples would
have been converted to Christianity, the infidels defeated, and the holy city
of Jerusalem reconquered by a king who would later establish a universal
empire. This empire would have paved the way for the second coming of
Christ. To dispel all doubts about the veracity of the prophecies, Columbus
even calculated the date of the Millennium, circa 1655.[18]

Because of the nature of the book, the *Book of Prophecies*, until
recently, had not been subject to a detailed analysis, especially concerning its
organization. In February of 1985, however, Paoline Moffitt Watts, in an
article published in the *American Historical Review*, with well-documented
arguments, proves that the ideal outline of the book, the choice of authors,
and the prophecies selected follow the outline of the writing included in the
Imago Mundi, a summary of the cosmological and geographical knowledge
of the time. Originally written by Cardinal Pierre D'Ailly in 1410, Columbus owned a copy of the book which he read and annotated carefully.[19] Another excellent analysis of the book was written by Delno C. West and August Kling who recapitulated their commentaries as follows:

> In summary, Christopher Columbus looked upon himself
> as a man of destiny who had been given a charismatic gift
> to understand Scripture, navigation, maps, winds, tides,

astronomy, cosmography, mathematics and related sci-
ences. His understanding of his mission, or enterprise, was
drawn from the Bible or proved by the Bible, and he knew
that he was opening up new land rich with gold and other
valuables. He believed himself a chosen person working
for the good of all Christendom in opening up the rest of
the world to the gospel message. . . and he believed most
strongly that the proper utilization of those new lands
would enable the Spanish monarchs, and all Christendom,
to recapture the Holy Temple in Jerusalem. . . . All of these
goals were unintelligible to many of his contemporaries
and to nearly all of his biographers and readers in the suc-
ceeding five hundred years. But the goals were perfectly
clear in the light of his biblical sources and world events
as seen through the eyes of prophecy.[20]

It is obvious that the study of great historical figures demands a
deep, objective, and documented knowledge of the period and of the milieu
in which they lived and acted. The lack of such knowledge may cause the
historian either to create a heroic myth or to engender a monster. This is even
more important in the case of Columbus because many books dealing with
him have not been written on the basis of objective historical analysis,but on
the basis of certain hypotheses to correct and refute other hypotheses.It is,
therefore, indispensable to relate what has been said about the *Mayorazgo*
and the *Book of Prophecies* with the conditions of the historical and social
milieu in which they were written.

In 1492, in Florence, Marsilio Ficino wrote his famous letter which
proclaimed the coming of the Golden Age by discussing all the achievements
in the fields of literature, the arts, architecture, music, and astronomy, and the
invention of the printing press. All of them were to usher in this marvelous
period of progress. In spite of the optimistic tone of this letter, however, the
anguish for the future of the world was increasing. In Italy, it manifested itself in the apocalyptic sermons delivered by Savonarola and in the splendid
frescoes by Luca Signorelli in the Chapel of Saint Brizio in the Orvieto Ca-

thedral (Antichrist, End of the World, Resurrection of the Dead,etc.). In the whole of Europe, as if to counterbalance the splendor of the Renaissance, there was a feeling of impending doom, of pessimism. Spain was not exempted from it. The successful conclusion of the wars against the Moors, with the conquest of Granada, had left its treasury exhausted and its trade in the Mediterranean and in Castille seriously endangered by Genovese competition. If this were not enough, Castillian expansionism in the Atlantic had come into open conflict with Portuguese expansionism.[21] Italy was not faring better. The rivalry between Spain and France, with its religious undertones, had made Italy a battlefield and the papacy a source of scandal for all of Europe. In the feud between Ferdinand of Spain and Charles VIII of France, it was not only the Kingdom of Naples which was at stake, but the very authority of the papacy that was being challenged. Charles VIII and his ministers favored the independence of the Church of France (Gallicanism) and were staunch supporters of Conciliarism, the theory of the supremacy of a general council over the pope. Ferdinand was a steadfast supporter of the supremacy of the authority of the pope. The only two cases in which he conceded that a council of bishops could pass judgement on the person and on the actions of a pope were if the pope had become a heretic or if more than one pope had been elected, as it had already happened during the Great Schism (1378-1449).[22] Ferdinand had expressed these principles through his ambassadors to the Fifth Lateran Council of 1512. Columbus had heard and had lived them during his stay at the Spanish court,fifteen years earlier. The clauses of his *Mayorazgo* clearly reflected these preoccupations that affected the whole of Christianity.

Neither were these the sole preoccupations which caused fear and apprehensiveness at the Spanish court. Europe was being threatened by the Turkish army that, after having conquered Constantinople in 1453 and destroyed the Eastern Roman Empire, was now turning its might against the West. In 1463, the Turks conquered Bosnia; in 1467, Erzegovina fell into their hands; in 1478, Albania was annexed to the Ottoman Empire. Two years later, they landed in Italy and, on August 11, they conquered Otranto, in Apulia, killing all the defenders who had refused to convert to Islam. Sixtus IV proclaimed a crusade whose objectives were to liberate Otranto, to occupy key strategic positions, and to stop the Turkish advance. Only the first objective was reached. Otranto was liberated, but the Moslem threat remained not only for Italy, but also for the rest of Europe. In particular, for Austria, Moldavia, Hungary and all of present day Dalmatia and Croatia, which were in turn invaded or conquered. Islam was triumphing over Christianity because, in the mentality of the period, the victory of the Turks meant the triumph of Islam.[23] The conflict was seen as a war not only for territory, but also for religious supremacy.

In this conflict, Spain occupied a position of particular importance. With the conquest of Granada, Spain was the only frontier of Christianity in which Islam was in retreat. After this triumph of the *Reconquest*, perceived as a crusade, the very idea of the crusade became for the Spaniards a spiritual incentive to establish the universal kingdom of Christ. This idea did not permeate the political agenda of any of the other European sovereigns. The Spanish monarchy was the only one, spurred as it was by the spirit and the ideals of the *Reconquest*, that made the crusade an urgent and preeminent item of its political agenda. Queen Isabella died leaving to her people the imperative of an African campaign. Cardinal Cisneros, one of the best political minds of his time, tried to carry it out. He was only partially successful with a program which aimed at completing the work of the *Reconquest* with the invasion of North Africa, the defeat of Islam, the liberation of the holy city of Jerusalem, and the restoration of Christianity to the purity of its beginnings.[24]

These were the courses of action, political and religious, that opened up with the taking of Granada. Columbus knew of them, because he was there and they were evident even in the popular poetry of the time. The famous *romance*, "En memoria de Alixandre", sung at court, foretold that, after Granada, Spain would liberate Jerusalem and that the imperial crown was waiting for the Spanish monarchs in the church of the Holy Sepulchre.[25] Nobody at the Spanish court ignored that one of the purposes of the education of Don Juan, heir to the throne, was to prepare him for the conquest of Jerusalem. This conquest could open up a secure route through which Christians could safely visit the Holy City and the sepulcher of the Redeemer.[26] This aspiration was reinforced by the fact that Don Juan was the direct descendant of the Aragonese kings who considered themselves protectors of the holy places and, with the Anjou of Naples, aspired to the crown of Jerusalem as descendant of the last king of Jerusalem, Frederick II of Hohenstaufen, king of Sicily and Jerusalem.[27] Columbus lived at the Spanish court, his sons Diego and Ferdinand were page-boys to Don Juan. Nothing was more natural therefore than that he absorbed these ideals, and that helps us understand why they appear consistently in his writings. Perhaps, at the beginning, with this dream of the conquest of Jerusalem, Columbus tried to comply with the desires of the Catholic monarchs, especially Queen Isabella. With the gold of the Indies the sovereigns would have acquired the means necessary to undertake the crusade to liberate Jerusalem. If this were true, we could not speak of ideals. Rather we should speak of a scheme to convince Ferdinand and Isabella to finance his voyages of exploration. It is common knowledge, however, that the liberation of Jerusalem is one of the constants of his writings. It was a fixed idea that pursued him since his first voyage to the Indies (and even before that, according to Paolo Emilio Taviani), as it appears from his *Journal*. Later, this very idea coalesced into commands never to be disregarded by his heirs in the *Mayorazgo*, and finally reappeared suffused with mystical and apocalyptic overtones, in the *Book of Prophecies*.[28] It is these essentially medieval aspects of Columbus's personality which baffle the modern researcher.

In the Middle Ages, people were not obsessed with the duration of human life. Life was considered an obligatory and temporary stage that a person ought to endure on one's way to eternity. Man was merely in transit on this earth. *Homo viator*, man the traveller, was much more than a rhetorical or metaphysical expression. It was a philosophy of life, a *Weltanschauung*, as attested by the pilgrimages and the missionary travels of the period. Every Christian saw oneself as a pilgrim travelling through time and space, searching and working for one's own personal salvation and waiting for the second coming of Christ.[29] The second coming, according to the book of Apocalypse (20, 4-7), would see the beginning of the millennium of the kingdom of Christ on earth, the regeneration of mankind and the establishment of a new order. When and how this would happen was written in the Bible, allegorically, metaphorically, and symbolically. And the Bible was open to the interpretation of the prophets—men whose intelligence, inspired by the Grace of God, could interpret the Sacred Scriptures. Guided by these prophecies which predicted the coming of an emperor who would bring peace to the world, convert all nations to Christianity, liberate the Holy Sepulchre, and precede the coming of the Antichrist, Columbus and his contemporaries searched for their roles in this cosmic drama of the Redemption. This drama, which began in the Garden of Eden with Adam and Eve, was now being played unremittingly before their very eyes and was bound to reach its conclusion with the terrifying vision of the Last Judgment. To personally participate in the fulfillment of the prophecies was the duty of every Christian who, in collaborating with the divine will, would assure for himself, eternal salvation.[30]

In fact navigators, like Christopher Columbus, and missionaries such as the Franciscans Giovanni del Pian delle Carpine and Giovanni da Montecorvino who, with merchants, such as the Polos, in the middle of the thirteen century, travelled overland to central and eastern Asia, considered their travels of evangelization, discovery, and colonization a fulfillment of the prophecies of the Apocalypse.[31] The popes and the Christian rulers of the 13th century entertained the fallacious hope to convert the then polytheistic Tartars to Christianity and enlist their support in the fight against Islam. Inspired by the same imperative was the exploration of Africa, in the search for the mythical Prester John. The Franciscan mystic Johannis of Rupescissa, who wrote in the middle of the 14th century, deeply influenced by the apocalyptic theories of Joachim of Fiore (1145-1202), prophesied that the Tartars and the Jews would soon convert to Christianity and that, with the help of the Tartars, the Christians would defeat the Moslems in spite of the fact that, by 1345, the Tartars had already converted to Islam. The source of inspiration of Rupescissa's millenarianism is to be found in the history of the Franciscan movement and in Joachim of Fiore's concept of history. The Calabrian mystic had divided history into three great epochs, each one of them corresponding to one person of the Holy Trinity. The period from Adam to Christ corresponded to God the Father. This was the laymen's Church. The period from Christ to 1260 corresponded to God the Son. This was the priests' Church. The third period the one of the Holy Ghost, would begin in 1260. This was to be the friars' Church. It would be initiated by the appearance of a new Adam or a new Christ who would be the founder of a monastic order. The Franciscans of strict observance (Spirituals) considered themselves to be the very religious order that, according to Joachim of Fiore's prophetic vision, would inaugurate the friars' Church and the Age of the Holy Spirit, harbinger of the millennial kingdom of the Apocalypse.[32] Rupescissa was one of the first to integrate in an eschatological scheme the possibility of converting the peoples of Asia, that is to say the rest of the world then known. For this reason, according to John Leddy Phelan, this Catalan friar may be considered the precursor of Columbus. Just like Rupescissa, the Genovese was also one of the few to see the necessity to convert all nations to Christianity, in the context of a messianic vision - one fold, one Shepherd—with an apocalyptic finality.[33] This, of course, does not surprise us, because Columbus's attachment to the Franciscans is well known. Of all the religious orders, they helped him and comforted him in the most critical moments of his life. It is not by chance that he appeared in the streets of Seville, after the second voyage, dressed in the penitential garb of a Franciscan and that he took the Franciscan habit on his deathbed.

It is extremely difficult to establish, documentally, the intensity of these religious and mystic ideals. And it is even more difficult to ascertain the effect they had on Columbus's motivation to undertake the first and second voyage of exploration. We know for certain, however, that the mystic trait in the personality of the Admiral of the Ocean Sea began to surface unequivocally during the third voyage (1498-1500), when he identified the estuary of the Orenoco river with one of the four rivers of the Garden of Eden. This trait assumed a definite apocalyptic characteristic in the compilation and the writing of the commentaries of the *Book of Prophecies* and in his account of the fourth voyage (1502-1504).[34] In part his mysticism may be understood as a sort of sublimation, as

> . . . the response of a man of ardent temperament and failing health who found his ambitions being thwarted and his contractual prerogatives ignored. But it would be an error to stress only this explanation. Columbus's unique historical perspective must not be forgotten. He was looking back

through fifteen hundred years of Christianity. It seemed to
him that his discoveries represented the grandiose climax
of Christian history. His opening of the "door of the Western Sea" promised the speedy fulfillment, after a delay of
fifteen hundred years, of the words of Mark 16:15, " Go
out all over the world and preach the gospel to all creation."[35]

One fact is certain, as it is well documented: many of his famous
contemporaries interpreted the discovery of the New World the way Columbus had done, namely as an eschatological event that would herald the end
of the world, just as much as the conversion of all peoples to Christianity, and
the rescue of the Holy Sepulchre. As it happens the encounter of the Old with
the New World did not spell the Millennium. But it certainly was an apocalyptic event. It revealed to each other two different worlds which, for better
or for worse, have been interacting in such a way as to unleash a chain of
events whose consequences still form the warp and the woof of our everyday lives.

NOTES

1. See, for instance, the French Antoine Roselly de Lorgues, *Christophe Colomb, Histoire de
sa vie et de ses voyages, des d'après documents authentiques tirés d'Espagne et d'Italie*, Paris,
Didier, (1856), 2 vols.
2. See, for instance, the American John Boyd Thacher, *Christopher Columbus, His Life, His
Work, His Remains, Vol. III* (New York: The Knickerbocker Press, 1904), p. 461.
3. Gino Doria, "La letteratura colombiana", introduction to J.B. Charcot, *Cristoforo Colombo
visto da un marinaio*, Italian translation, Firenze (n.p., 1932) p. XIII; Paolo Emilio Taviani, *I
viaggi di Colombo, la grande scoperta* (Novara, Istituto Geografico D'Agostini, 1986), pp. 475-
6.
4. "Il faut aussi mentionner que Las Casas et [Ferdinand] Colomb assignent une quatrième
source au grand dessein de Colomb: l'inspiration divine. Mais c'est là un ordre d'idées qui ne
comporte aucune discussion critique et dans lequel, par conséquent, nous n'avons pas à entrer
ici; il souffit de l'avoir indiqué." In Henry Vignaud, *Histoire Critique de la Grande Enterprise
de Christophe Colomb*, Tome 1er (Paris: H. Welter Editeur, 1911) p. 8.
5. John Leddy Phelan, *The Millennial Kingdom of the Franciscans in the New World*, 2nd ed.
(Berkeley, 1970). The 1956 edition was published in the "University of California Publications
in History Series," 52:1-160.
6. Marianne Mahn-Lot, *Christophe Colomb*, Paris, Ed. du Seuil (Coll. Le temps qui court, No.
18, 1960).

7. Alain Milhou, *Colón y su mentalidad mesiánica en el ambiente franciscanista español*, Valladolid, Cuadernos Colombinos No. XI, (Publicaciones de la Casa-Museo de Colón y Seminario Americanista de la Universidad de Valladolid, 1983). It must be noted, however, that Milhou differs from Phelan in so far as he excludes that the mystical religiosity of Columbus were directly inspired by Joachim of Fiore.

8. Delmo C. West and August Kling, *The Libro de las profecías' of Christopher Columbus* (Gainesville: Univ. of Florida Press, 1991).

9. Alexandre Cioranescu, *Oevres de Christophe Colomb* (Paris: Gallimard, 1961), p. 20.

10. Milhou, *Colón y su mentalidad mesiánica...*, p. 199-203. For the definitions of "prophecy" and "mysticism," see Bernard Mc Ginn, *Visions of the End: Apocalyptic Traditions in the Middle Ages* (New York: Columbia Univ. Press, 1979), p. 4.

11. For an analysis in depth of this document, see Pietro De Leturia, S.J., "Gli ideali politico-religiosi di Colombo nella `Carta' del suo Maggiorasco: 1498," in *Humanitas*, Brescia, Editrice Morcelliana, No. 10, (1951), pp. 994-1015, which has been our main source in dealing with this topic.

12. See Cesare De Lollis, *Scritti di Cristoforo Colombo*, Vol. 1 (Roma: Ministero della Pubblica Istruzione, 1892), p. 311, quoted by Leturia " Gliideali...," p. 1009. In this document Columbus provided also for the construction of a hospital and of a church dedicated to the Immaculate Conception.

13. See De Lollis *Scritti...*, Vol. 1, p. 306, quoted by Leturia, "Gli ideali...," p. 996.

14. Cesare De Lollis, *Cristoforo Colombo nella leggenda e nella storia*, Firenze, 4a Ed. Sansoni Editore (1969), p. 199; translated by the author.

15. For this topic we have used: Antonio Ballesteros Beretta, *Cristobal Colón y el Descubrimiento de América* Vol. II (Barcelona-Buenos Aires: Salvat Editores, 1945), pp.676-700; and Bartolomé José Gallardo, *Ensayo de una biblioteca española de libros raros y curiosos*, Vol. II (Madrid, Imprenta y Esterotipía de M. Rivadeneyra, 1866), Columns 500-507.

16. Ballesteros, *Cristobal Colón...*, Vol. II, p. 695, translated by the author.

17. Ballesteros, *Cristobal Colón...*, Vol. II, p. 698. More recent studies have shown that this prophecy, known as *Vae mundo in centum annis*, is not Joachim of Fiore's. The author is Arnau of Villanova (1235-1311), a mystic and a follower of Joachim da Fiore's teachings. Arnau was a physician and a friend of James II of Aragon and of Frederick II of Sicily. For the text of the prophecy and its interpretation and analysis, see Milhou, *Colón y su mentalidad...*, pp. 375-83.

18. Ballesteros, *Cristobal Colón...*, Vol. II, p. 693.

19. Pauline Moffitt Watts, "Prophecy and Discovery: On the Spiritual Origins of Christopher Columbus's Enterprise of the Indie," in *American Historical Review* 90 (1, Feb. 1985), pp. 73-102. The incunabulum of the *Imago Mundi* which belonged to Columbus was published between 1480 and 1483 by John of Westfalia and comprised other writing by Cardinal D'Ailly and Jean Gerson. See Moffit Watts, "Prophecy and Discovery," p. 84.

20. Delmo C. West and August Kling, *The 'Libro de las profecías'...*, pp. 74

21. J. H. Elliott, *Imperial Spain 1469-1716* (New York: The New American Library, 1963), pp. 38 and 42.

22. Jeffrey Burton Russel, *A History of Medieval Christianity*, Prophecy and Order (New York, Thomas Y. Crowell Company, 1968), pp. 182-87.

23. Marinella Bovini Mazzanti, *1492: scoperta e conquista dell'America*, (Urbino, Argalia Editore [1978]), p. 40.

24. Marcel Bataillon, *Erasmo y España* (México, Fondo de Cultura Económica, 1982), p. 52.

25. Leturia, "Gli ideali...," p. 1000.

26. Leturia, "Gli ideali...," p. 1001.

27. Milhou, *Colón y su mentalidad...*, p. 165-166.

28. Leturia, "Gli ideali...," p. 1001; see also Taviani, *I viaggi di Colombo...*, p. 476.

29. Gerhart B. Ladner, "Homo viator: Medieval Ideas on Alienation and Order," *Speculum* XLII (2, April 1967), p. 259.

30. Moffitt Watts, "Prophecy and Discovery," p. 79.

31. Phelan, *The Millennial Kingdom*, p. 17.

32. Phelan, *The Millennial Kingdom*, p. 14. See also Marjorie Reeves, *Joachim of Fiore and the Prophetic Future* (London: SPCK, 1976), pp. 1-29.

33. Phelan, *The Millennial Kingdom*, pp. 18-19. Johannis of Rupescissa is with Arnau of

Villanova and Francesc Eiximenis one of the great figures who were inspired by the prophetic vision of Joachim of Fiore. In his prophecies Rupescissa extolled the messianic function of the Valois, the French royal family. Nevertheless he foretold that Spain would give the world a king that would defeat Islam, reconquer Jerusalem, and reform the Church. See Milhou, *Colón y su mentalidad...*, pp. 383-87 and Marjorie Reeves, *Joachim of Fiore...*, pp. 67-9 and 79-81.

34. Phelan, *The Millennial Kingdom*, p. 19.
35. Phelan, *The Millennial Kingdom*, p. 23.

3

CHRISTOPHER COLUMBUS, WHAT HAVE WE DONE TO YOU? THE RENAISSANCE PARADIGM

Harral E. Landry
Texas Woman's University

One of the more intriguing developments in the Columbus festival year was the explosion of moralistic judgmentalism in re-adjusting the ethics and worth of Christopher Columbus.[1] Perhaps it was due to the heat of the summer, although, in truth, there was some evidence of the coming re-evaluation during the cold of the previous winter months. Perhaps it represented the election year frustration of the American people who turned so quickly to a condemnation of both Columbus and his legacy, as if condemning him would be the first step to a quick solution to those societal problems. It seemed so easy to eliminate Columbus Day and, with it, the man himself.[2]

There are two major ideas with which this paper takes issue: the premise that Columbus can, or should, be judged outside the framework of his own time, the Renaissance, and, secondly, the conceit that he can be blamed for the conditions which have evolved in modern society since his discovery. We are being ordered, *a la* Josef Stalin, to re-write history.[3] To re-write, to re-interpret, the past in our own terms, from our perspective, is not the same as re-shuffling the past, with a memory frightfully selective, in order to please ourselves. It does seem that we like to think that *what* we like to think, is true.

To defend Columbus on moral, ethical grounds is to engage in combat on a dubious, shifting battlefield of artifice. Although both Blacks and Native Americans in their indigenous cultures did so, there is no defense for the enslavement of other peoples, for the destruction of other cultures, or for the conquest of American Indians. And yet, Columbus did not so much *do* these things, and certainly not on the scale for which we criticize him, as he did to provide others, including ourselves, with the opportunity to do them.[4] There is reason to consider that we can safely blame our own intolerance, our own ill treatment of our environment, our own societal problems, on a man unfortunate enough to be a dead Italian.

Viewing the past from the perspective as a descendant of French-Italian ancestors, with a heritable touch from the Creek Indians in Alabama, it is necessary to change, to improve, to learn, to adjust to the power of other cultures. Adaptation is quite different from merely shifting moral blame. Individual life, and the life of an entire culture or a nation, is a continuing readjustment. This message is one which the Indians of America could well give to a nation sometimes reluctant to learn, hesitant to change, and often slow to adapt, in a world where the only constant *is* the certainty of change.

Indeed, in many respects, Columbus and his legacy did leave the American Indians and their culture behind. Remarkably, one of our major current images of the Native American is an environmental group's television commercial. The TV picture is of an Indian man standing in the forest by a stream, presumably dressed exactly as he would have been 500 years ago, with tears running down his face. But the entire, unseen technology with which the image is presented, the cameras, the script, lighting, the television, the tangle of electric and audio cables, and the words and images which convey the thought, are of a culture different from his. If we must "blame" someone, do we blame the culture left behind, the culture that did not "progress," or the culture that did progress so much as to leave the other behind?[5]

We *can* defend Columbus when we judge him in terms of the values of his era rather than in terms of what we may believe to be our own present high peak of morality and ethical near-perfection. Admittedly, it can be documented that he was a man given to gross exaggeration, exceedingly secretive, quick to promise rewards which he could not in good conscience *know* he could deliver, untruthful in his official reports, a sloppy administrator, intolerant in religion, and not particularly sensitive toward the natives whom he "discovered" living in his new "India."[6]

But these human characteristics were qualities which his contemporaries both understood and practiced freely. It was an age of exaggeration, an era of secretive courts and hints of unspecific promises too vaguely given. It was a time of religious intolerance, and the phrase "human rights" was yet almost 500 years away from entering the lexicon of literary essays.[7] Not to accept, much less to understand, this era and its people for what it was and for whom they were, is to condemn the Renaissance to moral and ethical purgatory.

Although it can be argued that Columbus was no better than his contemporaries, it should be noted that he was no worse. A brief glance at some of the more prominent Renaissance leaders indicates that the era of his life was a time when aggressive individualism, the quest for ego-satisfying achievements, the forcible enculturation of other peoples with other religious beliefs, the acquisition of wealth—these were the drives with which Renaissance princes, merchants, artists, and explorers unabashedly challenged and changed the world both about them and beyond. These motives—often called the three "G's" of the Renaissance—glory, gospel, and gold—led them in an "age of giants" without hesitation and without fear of the moral and ethical plateau from which the world of the late twentieth century, particularly the United States, would judge them.[8]

To accept Columbus as another Renaissance leader, no better and no worse than his contemporaries, is to judge him, properly, in the terms of his own time. For him, and for most others of the era, the quest for glory, gospel, and gold were more than acceptable; they were ordained by their God and applauded by their peers. In studying the Renaissance, with the exception of Sir Thomas More and Desiderius Erasmus, it is exceedingly difficult to find even *one* major figure who did not fit the Renaissance pattern. Well-nigh no one had a halo.[9]

Renaissance heroes or heroines who fit the twentieth century paradigm are difficult to find; they fit the value system of the Renaissance, and to judge them from another era, from another culture, is intellectual arrogance. To attempt to force a different set of values onto Renaissance society, in the name of fuzzy revisionism, is to assume a moral superiority as offensive as that with which we charge Columbus.

The rulers in whose names he claimed these new lands provide two excellent humanistic examples of the era. Queen Isabella is often cited as a "good" person, and in some respects she was. Her original hope had been to become a nun at a convent; instead, she became Queen of Castile. But she carried with her a religious intolerance that could be virulent and oppressive. It should come as a surprise to realize that most of the Jews and most of the Moors in what we today call Spain lived in the area of or neighboring Isabella's Castile, not Ferdinand's Aragon.[10]

There is evidence to indicate that Ferdinand of Aragon accommodated both Jews and Moslems, but simply for money. It was Isabella who, in a religious zeal which would both justify and motivate, encouraged the persecution and/or death and confiscation of property of both Jews and Moors. It was Isabella, seven months pregnant and exceedingly short-tempered, who helped to lead from Castile the artillery assault on Grenada, an artillery barrage that for the first time in modern history would kill and destroy a city indiscriminately, justifying the assault on the mere basis that the people of Grenada were different — they were Moslems. One of the ironies of the time was that she refused to talk to the Italian seaman who wished to explore the Ocean Sea to the West until after Grenada had fallen, and Columbus had joined the artillery barrage.[11]

Ferdinand was an excessively vain king, with an overwhelming self confidence not in the moral *rightness* of his policies, but in the *efficacy* of his actions. In no way a religious man, any motivation he might have had for the gospel he transferred to both gold and glory. His life was an unfaltering, unwavering quest for those two goals. Tricky, lying, deceitful, conniving, he seems to be excused by modern judgementalists by the fact that he was a Spanish king, not merely an Italian explorer, and by the fact that he was quite successful.[12] Such an evaluation belies the fact that he laid waste far more of "Italy" than did the Italian in the New World.

Ferdinand was a cruel man, a father who locked away his own daughter, Juana. To be caught up in the argument of whether he locked her up *because* she was "la loca" —insane, or whether she became insane *because* he locked her up, is to beg the issue of his insensitivity and cruelty.[13]

It might well be expected that revisionists could cite the Pope, the Bishop of Rome, the head of the church "universal," as a role model of the era. But in 1492, His Holiness was Alexander VI, Rodrigo Borgia, who, like his predecessor Innocent VIII, of a noble Genoese family, openly recognized his children, Cesare and Lucretia Borgia.[14] Although Cesare is often cited as the inspiration for Machiavelli's *The Prince*, Ferdinand may well have been the model.[15]

Another potential role model of the era might well have been the King of England, Henry VII, of the new House of Tudor. But Henry was exceedingly stingy, constant in *his* quest for gold and glory, short and looking much like a dried prune, so overly suspicious that he approached paranoia, oppressive in his taxation, ruthless in his Court of Star Chamber, and quick to rid himself of potential rivals to the crown, whether they be of the royal York family or great nobility who could trace back their family trees much further than could Henry, and without the "flaws" which graced the early Tudor genealogy. While it is true that Henry VII did appoint John Cardinal Morton to the post of Lord High Chancellor, it must be noted that Bishop Morton was, and had always been, a scheming *political* leader, not a religious one. His appointment to a *political* benefice within the church was quite common for the era.[16]

There are two images of Henry VII that are especially relevant. One is that he appointed an Italian, Polydore Vergil, to re-write the history of England. And though stingy he was, Henry paid him well as the first revisionist in English history. Vergil wrote his history, beginning at the Garden of Eden, to please his paymaster, applauding and condemning the past according to Tudor standards, particularly praising Henry VII and condemning Richard III, whom Henry had killed to attain the crown.[17]

The other image is a particularly poignant one. Henry is usually pictured as "a family man." But, in truth, although he had promised to marry Elizabeth of York, he did not do so until after Parliament had urged the wedding for political reasons. Even after the birth of a child, Arthur, Prince of Wales, his father Henry VII did not name her as his queen. Eventually, bowing to public pressure, he arranged her coronation in the time of Columbus. Henry VII and his bitter mother, a vengeful woman, made sure her coronation was a shambles which they could enjoy watching from behind a lattice screen.[18] It is little wonder that *this* Queen Elizabeth is so seldom mentioned.

The king of France during the Renaissance era of Columbus is almost always accorded a judgment in terms of his own era. Louis XI, the "Spider King," which is about the worst thing noted of the man, had died. The new French king, at the time of Columbus, was Charles VIII, an incredibly stupid man, who became the foil for many of Ferdinand's plots. Probably the action for which he is most remembered was the invasion of Naples, two years after Columbus made the first effective discovery of America. Under Ferdinand's encouragement, neither Charles VIII nor his era saw anything amiss with using French artillery and cavalry, in a style *a la Grenada*, to take the city and crown himself king of Naples, beginning a half-century of wars for the control of Italy. But there is seldom a judgement of Charles VIII by twentieth century values. For his time his policies were judged to be normal.[19] The most that the late twentieth century could, or should, add, is that they were also stupid.

In revising the appraisal of noted writers and artists in the creative arts, it could be noted that most were no better nor no worse than the others, when seeing them in terms of a Renaissance value system. Giotto di Bondone, noted for his Assisi and Arena Chapel frescoes, was also noted in his time as a man hungry for fame and wealth; he set the standards not only in art but in a variety of profitable businesses—lending money, running a debt-collection service, and renting looms, at stiff fees, to poor woolen weavers in the Italian countryside.[20]

Margaret of Navarre, born in 1492, would press the parameters of social and moral ethics even further. For her, Giovanni Boccaccio's *Decameron* was too mild. As a queen married to Henry of Navarre, she would write the *Heptameron*, shock the Sorbonne, and preside over a miniature court in Southern France that would have enormous influence later.[21]

Contemporaries of Columbus saw little wrong with the activities of these creative artists. Leonardo da Vinci made his living as a military engineer in the service of the Sforza in Milan; Leonardo would both manufacture shrapnel for killing and help design the Cathedral of Milan, before moving to become the military engineer for Cesare Borgia and later for Francis I of France.[22] Michelangelo, an artist driven by his inner furies, was certainly not what the twentieth century would call "normal" in his personal life. Moreover, he could exhibit an argumentative quality almost equal to the grandeur of his artistic conceptions. He could be petty, placing Paul III's Master of Ceremonies in the sublime fresco "The Last Judgement" with the ears of a jackass to retaliate for the Cardinal's remark on the artistic quality of the work.[23] In addition, it comes as a surprise that Raphael, a young child of nine when Columbus first sailed to the West, a man known for his religious Madonnas, usually used his mistress, La Fornarina, the baker's daughter, as his model for the paintings of the Virgin Mary and Mother of Christ.[24]

Remarkably, the era of the Renaissance would praise Baldassare Castiglione for *Il Cortegiano*, his book on manners and courtly etiquette written for an increasingly powerful professional middle class who might best be described as uncouth and unschooled in courtliness. But the book has virtually nothing on the morals and ethical values of the Renaissance. Castiglione accepts the concept that life may be a quest for glory, gospel, and gold; he merely provides directions on how those who acquire these characteristics may be courtly, and mannerly, in their exhibition of them.[25] Equally remarkable is the fact that as late as the eighteenth century, Dr. Samuel Johnson would call it the greatest guide to courtliness in the history of the world.

In many ways, Giovanni Pico della Mirandola established the boundless parameters of Renaissance man. In his *Oration on the Dignity of Man*, written at the time of Columbus, Pico praised not so much the dignity of *all* men, and women, but rather the intellectuals, who would thus be angels and sons of God. Pico added what he envisioned as the new Renaissance commandments of God, who, having created the world, then created man and gave him, in God's powerful voice, a stirring, exuberant challenge.[26]

> Thou, constrained by no limits, in accordance with thine
> own free will, in whose hands we have placed thee, shall
> ordain for thyself the limits of thy nature. We have set thee
> at the world's center that thou mayest from thence more

easily observe whatever is in the world. We have made
thee neither of heaven nor of earth, neither mortal nor im-
mortal, so that with freedom of choice and with honor, as
though the maker and molder of thyself, thou mayest fashion thyself in whatever shape thou shalt prefer.

It might reasonably be doubted that Christopher Columbus read Pico's ex-
act words, but it might also be reasonably accepted that Columbus inherited
the spirit of an era which believed those words as a creed.

Nothing in this paper should be construed as condemning the Renaissance figures or judging them, outside their time, as either good or bad,
ethical or unethical, sensitive or insensitive. These few figures, chosen from
many, were interesting personalities, and they either fit or molded the value
system of their time, the Renaissance.

And yet, revisionists of the late twentieth century seem at times to
wish to re-write history, to spin it to fit some new idea, either passing or
permanent. Re-writing history is not in itself either good or bad; it has been
done repeatedly to please a new power. Henry VII of England, stingy, par-
simonious Henry, paid handsomely to have history re-written for himself.
Josef Stalin ordered that it be done in Russia, not only re-writing the history
but re-painting the artwork, re-editing the films, and re-naming some cities.[27]
But while we can passionately condemn Stalin for re-writing the past in terms
of his contemporary values, and for his own purposes in his own agenda,
there is a noticeable lack of hesitation at re-writing our own past.

The question then arises as to why, of all the early figures in American history, we should choose to denigrate Christopher Columbus and his
achievements. In truth, there are many others whom we might re-measure in
our value system and spin the past. George Washington was an exceptionally
cold, aloof, haughty man, often insensitive; a number of contemporary problems can be hung on his shoulders. James Madison, Thomas Jefferson, and
Lafayette, a French marquis with the first name of "Marie," would have a
share of modern problems, in not one but two countries. Benjamin Franklin,
once we toss out the mostly untrue *Autobiography*, carousing, "wine, women,
and song" Benjamin, would merit an entire separate category of problems so
numerous as to pile high around his statue.[28]

Conversely, Columbus had many qualities that we as Americans, even revisionist Americans, could applaud. He had an incredible patience, was a good father, a good sailor, he had vision, courage, leadership skills, tenacity, scholarship (adequate for his day), a good mind, some business sense (though certainly not enough), common sense (again not enough), and a sense of responsibility. We can admire particularly the persistence of his vision, his willingness to go where, apparently, no other European had gone before, and his unshakable belief in his own judgment. We can even admire his lying to his crews about the distances traveled each day, noting that he was using masterful psychology on men who had less faith, less vision, less persistence than he himself possessed. His historical period, the Renaissance, might well have admired these qualities. Certainly the Renaissance world accorded to Spain a note of respect for her contribution to the Renaissance, the *conquistadors*, in spite of the fact that many of them might not be "admirable" in a twentieth century system of values.

The new judgments of Columbus seem at times to have less to do with Columbus, especially if we judge him by the standards of his own era, than they do with the *results* of his discoveries. He did not begin the African slave trade; that would begin a hundred years later. He did not decree that native Indian cultures and Native American lives should be lower than those of European whites; in fact, it can be noted that the Spanish were far more considerate, or at least tolerant, of Native Americans than were the English.

While Columbus did not seek to preserve Native American cultures, Native Americans themselves have not preserved the original quality of that culture. Life was, and is, always changing; history exacts a terrible price from those who refuse to change, to adapt, and refuse to preserve the past with dignity.

We in America feel compelled, when facing some particular problem, whether it is an Native American, urban, African American, or societal problem, to seek someone other than ourselves whom we can "blame" for the problem. In his case, Columbus seems a likely candidate, since he was the one who "discovered" America in the first place. It matters less what we have done with this land in the past 500 years than that we can so easily point to the man who discovered it.

Such reasoning, carried to a logical (or illogical) extreme, could well be used in countless other ways, all designed, presumably, to make us feel better about having problems in the first place. Pornography could be blamed on Johann Gutenberg (after all, he was German) and Benjamin Franklin (he was the "wine, women, and song" man). Blood diseases, including many cases of AIDS, may be laid at the feet of the researcher who discovered blood plasma or the person who invented hypodermic needles. The blame for the pornographic Maplethorpe *et alii* photographs would have their villain in photography. Early chemists and arms manufacturers, including Alfred Nobel, would, in the re-writing, be roundly condemned. But to blame Columbus for the ills of today is equivalent to charging the Wright brothers with crowded skies and airport noise.

It might be well to consider giving back to Columbus his day of remembrance and restoring him to his dignity. Americans of all ethnic origins today may see the admirable qualities of courage and resilient dignity in Sioux Indian Chief Sitting Bull and in Chief Joseph at Wounded Knee Creek. At the same time, today, descendants of Native American Indians can respect Columbus in his time, admire his qualities, and emulate him. We can applaud Columbus in that he brought a vibrant, different, more powerful culture to these shores and opened the door to a new world, a world that would prove as new to those already here as to those who were yet to come to America. That this new world developed to a condition less than perfect after his life is not so much his fault as ours. At one time, at one point, he may have been "the enemy." But today, the enemy is as much ourselves as it is he.

In short, it can be argued that the personal influence of Columbus died before the man himself in prison, and that what we have done with his discoveries are *our* responsibilities, not his. If those who persist in re-writing the past must make judgments, must charge him with "what he has done to us," then he would ask for nothing more than to be judged by the standards of his own time, the Renaissance. It can be argued that, as a Renaissance man, he was no better, nor was he any worse, than anyone else, and that to "revise" his life in any terms other than those of their own time, is both unfair and intellectually offensive.

NOTES

1. The inspiration for this paper came when the author was invited to an annual conference of the American Studies Association. The theme of the conference, "Christopher Columbus, What Have You Done to Us?," sounded at once both interesting and depressing. In that particular American Studies Association conference, every paper in every session pilloried Columbus and heaped upon him blame for virtually every major social problem with the possible exception of abortion.

2. Surprisingly, very few persons protested either the elimination of Columbus Day or the contemporary re-adjustments of moral relativism with which it was done, apparently unaware that the re-adjustors may themselves be re-adjusted in yet another contemporary era.

3. See particularly the studies of Stalin in Carmichael, Joel, *Stalin's Masterpiece: the Show Trials and Purges of the Thirties - the Consolidation of the Bolshevik Dictatorship,* (1976); Wolfe, Bertram David, *Three Who Made a Revolution: A Biographical History* (1964); and Ulam, Adam Bruno, *Stalin: the Man and His Era* (1973).

4. There are a number of biographies of Columbus, among the more recent being Wilford, John Noble, *The Mysterious History of Columbus: An Exploration of the Man, the Myth, the Legacy* (1991); and Meltzer, Milton, *Columbus and the World Around Him* (1990). The biography generally acknowledged as perhaps the best is Morison, Samuel Eliot, *Christopher Columbus, Mariner* (1955). Morison, a yachtsman and Harvard history professor, actually sailed the route of Columbus' voyages.

5. One of the unusual characteristics of the commercial seems to be that the Indian leader would, or could only, respond with impotent tears, standing in the middle of the woods, surrounded by the unseen film camera crew. Perhaps descendants of the Native American Indians might well consider a better image.

6. De Lamar, Jensen, *Renaissance Europe: Age of Recovery and Reconciliation* (Lexington, KY: D.C. Heath, 1981), pp. 289-98. In a standard textbook used at many universities with courses covering "The Renaissance" in modern European history, De Lamar includes a long discussion of Columbus. Unfortunately, however, in a moment of unreconstructed language, he does refer to the Native Americans as "gullible savages." He will, no doubt, perhaps as a result of this published notation, politically correct his description in the next edition.

7. See especially the work of Durant, Will, *The Reformation: A History of European Civilization from Wyclif to Calvin, 1300-1564* (1957), and Davies, Stevie (ed.), *Renaissance Views of Man* (1979).

8. De Lamar, *Renaissance Europe,* p. 146. See also, Dunlap, Benjamin, *The Renaissance: the Origins of the Modern West: A Production of South Carolina ETV* (1993); and Trevor-Roper, H. R., *Renaissance Essays* (1985).

9. More, the outstanding scholar, would be executed by Henry VIII and become a saint; Erasmus, the illegitimate son of a priest in Rotterdam, would become the scholar known as the "Prince of Humanists" and a man of peace, although he would face hearings for his excommunication as a result of his translations. See also, Ferguson, Wallace Kippert, *The Renaissance in Historical Thought: Five Centuries of Interpretation* (1948); and Schwoebel, Robert, *Renaissance Men and Ideas* (New York, 1971).

10. See Kelso, Ruth, *Doctrine for the Lady of the Renaissance* (1956); and Thompson, James Westfall, *The Civilization of the Renaissance* (1929).

11. Mariejol, J. H., *The Spain of Ferdinand and Isabella,* tr. by Benjamin Keen (New Brunswick, 1961); and Miller, Townshend, *The Castles and the Crown: Spain, 1451-1555* (New York, 1963).

PART II
POLITICAL ISSUES:
AT HOME AND ABROAD

4

THE ITALIAN DEMOCRATIC LEFT AND WOODROW WILSON: A VENTURE IN POLITICAL COLLABORATION

CHARLES KILLINGER
VALENCIA COMMUNITY COLLEGE

The extended stalemate that turned World War I into a war of attrition, defeatism and revolution led belligerents to explore diplomatic solutions. While the Western powers remained locked in *impasse*, the withdrawal of Russia from the war triggered diplomatic movement on the Eastern front. Italy, locked into a gruelling struggle along the Isonzo River with troops from the Hapsburg Empire, thus became an object of diplomatic interest as the great powers anticipated an end to the conflict. After the Italian disaster at Caporetto in late 1917, an Italian emergency government headed by V. E. Orlando presided over a divided political system and a demoralized population.

As the war extended into its fourth year, American President Woodrow Wilson emerged as a diplomatic force, announcing his Fourteen Points as broad terms for a "peace without victory." Among them, Point 9 promised "to readjust Italy's frontiers along. . . lines of nationality." Wilson became a "prophet for a year."[1] Partly in response to an American propaganda campaign that promised democratic reforms in postwar Europe, Italians demonstrated greater enthusiasm for Wilsonian diplomacy than did any

European population.[2] And in Italian political circles, Wilson found his strongest support within the democratic left, particularly among reformist Socialists, democratic interventionists, and their journals. From the spring of 1918 until the spring of 1919, Wilson and elements of the Italian democratic left sought to cooperate. Believing that they pursued a similar vision, all parties hoped at the same time to augment their own domestic political influence.

Wilson's most prominent Italian supporter was Leonida Bissolati, Vice-Premier in the Orlando government. Bissolati was a respected reformist socialist who had left the P.S.I. to found a new party and had become a leading advocate of Italian intervention against the Central Powers in the Great War.[3] In the immediate postwar era, Bissolati forcefully advocated Wilson's "new" diplomacy of "peace without victory."[4] However, Bissolati did not reflect an official Italian position. In fact, on the most critical issue of postwar boundaries, there was not a *single* Italian position. Instead, the Orlando cabinet maintained overlapping and contradictory positions based the Fourteen Points, the Pact of Rome and the Treaty of London.

At Rome in April 1918, Italian and Slavic delegates had gathered at the Congress of Oppressed Austrian Nationalities. American authorities attributed the meeting primarily to the initiative of Bissolati, noting that he had persuaded Orlando to call the Congress.[5] The Italian delegation, divided in its views, had included democratic interventionists as well as nationalists. In the resulting Pact of Rome, the delegates had committed themselves to cooperate against the Hapsburg Empire and to negotiate boundaries on the basis of nationality. Bissolati, Gaetano Salvemini, and Luigi Albertini supported the agreement, while the nationalists opposed it.[6] Both the Pact of Rome and Point X of Wilson's war aims promised autonomy to south Slavs, a position largely incompatible with the Treaty of London.

In fact, it can be argued that sufficient ambiguity existed within Wilson's Fourteen Points to constitute contradiction as well. Point IX promised "A readjustment of the frontiers of Italy should be effected along clearly recognizable lines of nationality." Point X read: "The peoples of Austria-Hungary, whose place among the nations we wish to see safeguarded and assured, should be accorded the freest opportunity of autonomous development."[7] A policy of autonomy for Slavic nationalities threatened the extension of Italian borders, especially in areas of the Istrian peninsula with Italian majorities. Bissolati did provide a rationale for reconciling the contradictory positions of the Treaty of London and the Fourteen Points: "...The provisions of the Treaty of London would be used against Austria," he told Wilson, "but not against the nations which might arise from the wreck of Austria."[8]

The Treaty of London was the special cause of Italy's Foreign Minister, Baron Sidney Sonnino, committed nationalist and advocate of the conventional diplomacy of power politics. Sonnino, who overshadowed Orlando and Bissolati, had negotiated the Treaty of London with the Allies in 1915 as the premise for Italian belligerency, and he remained firmly committed to its full implementation. Orlando, with no apparent commitment to any of these diplomatic positions, searching at best for a politically feasible solution, did little to take a stand favoring either Sonnino or Bissolati.[9]

Woodrow Wilson had no such difficulty choosing between the polar opposites. In reaction to Sonnino, Wilson considered the Treaty of London, which the United States had not signed, to be the archetypal secret alliance, a contradiction of the spirit of the Fourteen Points and a violation of two of its provisions. Thus, Colonel Edward House, trusted adviser to Wilson, labeled Sonnino "an able man, but a reactionary" who "would never consent to any of the things necessary to make a beginning toward peace."[10] F. S. Nitti, Italian Treasury Minister and member of the Italian mission to the United States, contributed to this impression of Sonnino, portraying the Foreign Minister as "the principal obstacle to an Italian policy of conciliation."[11]

Sonnino's rigid commitment to the Treaty made him anathema to Wilson and pushed the President toward Bissolati and the democratic left.[12] In Italy, as in the rest of Europe, Wilson saw the moderate left as the political faction closest to his ideological positions and, more importantly, his best asset in developing a European popular base.

In early 1919, at the urging of some diplomats and advisers, Wilson made a bold play to win Italian public support. He hoped to build pressure on the Italian government to drop some of its territorial demands. This was the one point that would make or break the effort at transatlantic cooperation. The president and his Italian supporters enjoyed temporary success, but ultimately failed, not only to change Italian policy, but to sustain Italian popular support for the Treaty of Versailles. Ironically, among Wilson's Italian critics were some of the very democratic socialists he had considered his staunchest defenders. In light of the failure of the American president and leaders of the Italian democratic left to find a productive relationship, several issues emerge: First, what brought them together? What combination of motivation and circumstances explains the transatlantic coalescence of such very different political elements? Second, since they found enough common ground to mount what appeared to be a joint campaign, why did they fail? What were the dynamics of that brief, but promising, relationship that rendered their efforts futile, and what tactical mistakes did they make? Third, what were the costs of that failure? Can they in any way be blamed for contributing to the general demise of Italian democracy?

The Great War politicized diplomacy in a way never before experienced. Having utilized mass propaganda to mobilize backing for the war, governments found it necessary to continue to influence public opinion as they anticipated the postwar settlement. The energizing of mass political movements forced further integration of politics and diplomacy.

Woodrow Wilson, president of an emerging behemoth, was clearly the senior partner in this American-Italian affair. Amid the vast body of historical inquiry on Wilson are numerous references to his Italian venture. Arno Mayer's ideological interpretation, that Wilson was waging a propaganda battle to buttress the European democratic left against Bolshevism, has dominated Cold War era Wilsonian scholarship. Mayer also argued that Wilson attempted to use the same groups as leverage against the advocates of conventional European balance-of-power politics, especially Sonnino and Georges Clemenceau, as well as Orlando.[13]

Others stressed the influence exerted on Wilson by Colonel House, Walter Lippmann, the planning group called The Inquiry, and various intellectuals and diplomats. They argue that some of Wilson's advisers were more interested than he was in lending American opposition to European imperialism.[14]

Out of practical necessity and interest, this paper will focus not on

Wilson, but on the Italians he hoped to utilize as political allies in a high-stakes diplomatic initiative, those of the democratic left. They included, in this context, some reformist socialists, especially Claudio Treves and Filippo Turati, who had begun to support the war after Caporetto and had further distanced themselves from the P.S.I maximalists in 1918; a number of labor organizations; several newspapers, including the influential Milanese paper, *Il Secolo*, and the major national daily, *Il Corriere della Sera*; its liberal editor, Luigi Albertini; Gaetano Salvemini, editor of *L'Unità*; and, most prominently, Leonida Bissolati. This somewhat disparate group shared a commitment to social and economic reform through the democratic process, shared in their criticism of the electoral methods of the Giolittian Era, and mutually opposed Italian Bolshevism and nationalism. Within this group, Wilson's diplomatic advisers focused on Bissolati, Salvemini, and Albertini, who had been the leading voices of democratic interventionism and were now the leading advocates of Wilsonian diplomacy.

Leonida Bissolati was a sincere idealist whose vision of a postwar world largely coincided with that of Wilson. Even his critics admit that this man of reason represented the best of the political tradition of the Liberal State. On the specific issues of postwar boundaries, Bissolati had consistently argued that Italy should renounce the Treaty of London, and with it the Dalmatian coast (except Zara), the Brenner frontier, and the Dodecanese islands. In particular, he succeeded in reenforcing Wilson's belief that the Dalmatian coast was unnecessary for postwar defense of Italy, offsetting Sonnino's efforts to make that case. In each instance, Bissolati invoked the principle of national self-determination in the name of Mazzini and Wilson, argued the specific strategic and economic merits of his case, and attempted to align Italy with Wilson's peace initiative.[15]

Thus the motives of Wilson and Bissolati converged. They hoped to adjust boundaries, not as a matter of convenience or to reward the war's victors, but "in the light of justice for all people."[16] As advocates of the "new diplomacy," they also recognized mutual enemies: militarism, imperialism, authoritarianism, and Bolshevism. The cry of the moderate left became: "Either Wilson or Lenin." Thus the effort of Wilsonian and Bissolatian elements to cooperate was, in part, also an ideological campaign to build a social democratic consensus to counter the winds of European extremism.[17]

In late 1918 and early 1919, the American president and the leaders of the democratic left made political moves designed to capitalize on their mutual interests. In September, Bissolati defeated his arch-rival Sonnino in a cabinet vote to recognize Yugoslavia, thus achieving the high water-mark of official Italian endorsement of Wilsonian policy. This vote, in essence, reaffirmed the Rome Pact of April.[18]

However, after the celebrated Italian victory at Vittorio Veneto, the political climate changed. Within a week, Italian troops took Trieste and Fiume. Victory brought a resurgence of nationalist pride and, at the same time, a breakdown of the patriotic unity to which Italians had rallied after the humiliation of Caporetto. In a politically charged setting, the maximalist socialists still hoped the war would bring revolution, and the nationalists clamored for even more territory than Sonnino. Salvemini sounded the cry from the near left, criticizing Sonnino and the nationalists for their blustering, and demanding that the government renounce its grand ambitions in the Adriatic. The nationalists, in turn, labeled Salvemini and Bissolati "*rinunciatari*." In Parliament, Turati and Treves generally advocated Wilson's positions over those of Sonnino, and Orlando rode out the storm by remaining non-committal.

In Paris, Wilson continued to hear of his popularity in Italy. Ray Stannard Baker wrote to Colonel House that, of all the European allies, none was "more fluid, more open to our leadership than Italy, or more willing to accept Mr. Wilson's program or to follow him to the end."[19] Writing three weeks later from Turin, Baker reported to House that "President Wilson's popularity seems to have grown enormously." He recounted cries of "Viva Wilson," "indescribably whole-hearted" enthusiasm, a great demand for pictures of the president, and a request to name "a street or square after him."[20]

While the American Ambassador in Rome pled for a Wilson visit, the president heard that four of Orlando's left-of-center cabinet members had resigned in protest, hoping to force Orlando to send Bissolati to Paris to counter-balance Sonnino.[21] Encouraged by the reports, Wilson decided to take his case to the Italian people in a bold new initiative. On December 6, assuming now that Wilson would travel to Italy, Baker advised House that

Wilson should avoid the trap of Italian "officialdom" that had ensnared Samuel Gompers and meet with leaders of "radical, labor and socialist groups."[22] A week before Wilson departed, Bissolati lost a cabinet vote and made his own dramatic exit from government.[23]

On January 3, 1919, Wilson took his message to the Italian people, who greeted his visit with wild enthusiasm. Over the next two days, the president met with Bissolati and Albertini. In Milan, reformist Socialist mayor Emilio Caldara endorsed Wilson's diplomacy while cheers of "Viva Wilson!" rang through the piazzas. Wilson returned to Paris, moved by his popular support. Two weeks later the Peace Conference opened.[24]

However, neither Wilson's campaign, nor Bissolati's resignation, nor repeated criticism from the democratic left could change the position of the Italian delegation at Paris, dominated by Sonnino. In April, Wilson gave final rejection to Italy's demands for possession of Fiume and the Dalmatian coast and published in Italy an extraordinary appeal to the Italian people to join him in opposing their own government. On that same day, Orlando and Sonnino left Paris in protest.[25]

Wilson's new propaganda initiative failed. As quickly as his popularity had materialized, it now dissipated. For a number of reasons that Wilson did not anticipate, his bold political initiative not only failed to sustain Italian support, but it proved counterproductive. In the same cities where Italians had shown him adulation, Wilson was now the target of angry epithets. By summer, Orlando's government fell; but his successor, F.S. Nitti, had no better luck winning Wilson's endorsement for Italian annexation of Fiume.[26] In September, Gabriele D'Annunzio and his nationalist followers seized that city. Wilson remained adamantly attached to his position even as he was stricken during his futile campaign to win American popular endorsement for "his" treaty.

It was in the turbulence of early 1919 that cracks first appeared in the relationship between Wilson and the Italian democratic left. Soon it was shattered beyond repair. In retrospect, the failure of this experiment in transatlantic cooperation can be attributed to several causes. It was unbalanced, unrealistic, subject to various political mistakes, and, ultimately, overwhelmed by circumstances.

The most fundamental problem in this relationship was the diplomatic context in which it developed. In spite of the common idealism and ideology of Wilson and the Italian democratic left, progress was unlikely because of the low American regard for Italy. The United States was primarily interested in the Western front and in Germany, and held a huge preponderance of power *vis-à-vis* Italy. In addition, The Inquiry lacked Italian expertise. Because the United States had its own agenda, and considered Italy a second-rate power, historians have generally concluded that official disregard for Italy was based on ignorance and indifference. One historian has described Italian-American relations in this period as based on a "vicious cycle of mistrust."[27] Italians, aware of being snubbed, thought of the war as "la nostra guerra," with war aims detached from those of the "Big Three" at Paris.[28]

Partly because of this imbalance, productive cooperation between Wilson and the democratic left was, from the outset, unrealistic. Based on exaggerated reports from American diplomats in Italy, and encouraged by his staff, Wilson overestimated his support. Ray Stannard Baker advised Wilson to go directly to the people, "over the heads of the government." Baker suggested to House that "when the time comes [Wilson] may have to make or threaten to make an appeal direct to the people over the heads of the obstructors."[29] Baker and George Creel suggested a meeting with Turati. Colonel House urged visits to Milan and Turin.[30]

The relationship failed also because Wilson and his advisers misread the relative strengths of Italian political factions. Baker, writing from Turin in late 1918, saw great promise in the realms of the labor and socialist organizations. He also advised House that returning soldiers would "come back newly radical." Baker regarded organized labor as "this force which believes vitally in Mr. Wilson's program, and upon which, if we have to go down into the sawdust of the arena in the final struggle, we will have to depend."[31]

In reality, the democratic left was far too weak to provide Wilson the power he needed to negotiate successfully with the Italian government. It appeared stronger than it was because of an active press with a clear Wilsonian message. What it lacked was organized strength, leadership in

Parliament, and, most notably, a mass base. In contrast, Sonnino's dogged adherence to the Treaty of London, the indirect boost given him by the growing nationalist sentiment, the emergence of mass political parties, and growing political violence rendered the moderate left even weaker.[32]

Within this troublesome context, it is now also apparent that both Wilson and Bissolati had made mistakes. In the case of Wilson, his inflexibility cost him the opportunity to settle the Fiume issue through negotiation, packaged with the Brenner frontier and the Dalmatian coast, and thus to defuse its political volatility. As a result, even in his dominant position, he managed to throw away his advantage and alienate some of his closest Italian allies. Salvemini asked the question: Why does Wilson impose "absolute justice" on Italians, while making exceptions from the Fourteen Points for the British and French.[33]

As for Bissolati, he had enough experience in politics to avoid the tactical mistakes he made. But he remained the idealist, convinced that he could win on the strength of ideas alone. His futile campaign of manipulation inside the cabinet to counter Sonnino was probably necessary. However, resignation was a mistake. His idea was to force a showdown with Sonnino, to force Orlando to make a choice that he did not wish to make. The result was, according to one source, that Bissolati only succeeded in embarrassing Orlando and playing into the hands of Sonnino who, silently as usual, won another round.[34] Sadly, Bissolati, this voice of reason, did not even succeed in making his moral stand. As he attempted to give his resignation speech at La Scala in Milan, spelling out his Mazzinian-Wilsonian policy positions, he was shouted down, his meeting disrupted, by a raucous mob of annexationists and nationalists. Benito Mussolini and Filippo Marinetti were among the participants.[35]

When, one week later, Mussolini appeared again at La Scala as the Arditi scuffled with democratic interventionists, expelling an editor of *Corriere della Sera* and producing one hundred casualties, it was clear that the postwar crisis was escalating. Both extremes, right and left, became more active, and the moderate center further weakened. That same week, under pressure from nationalists and conservatives, Orlando accepted Nitti's resignation and shuffled the cabinet to the right. The moderate left was caught

within the European postwar swing toward conservatism, overwhelmed by
the groundswell of Italian nationalism, and victimized by the first wave of
Fascist violence.

In the final analysis, the inability of Bissolati to cooperate effectively with Wilson must be considered within the context of the general failure of the democratic left. It was primarily a political, not an intellectual failure. In this crisis, they generated a set of ideas, Mazzinian and Wilsonian, that
provided a framework for a diplomatic solution. Their biggest political fault
was the lack of an effective campaign. They failed to build an effective organization, failed to put forward a convincing program of domestic reform,
and failed to make a convincing case for embracing their postwar diplomacy.

Without an effective mass political organization, the Bissolatians
missed their best opportunity to forge a compromise with Wilson, giving up
Dalmatia, while keeping Istria and possibly Fiume. Defusing the nationalists
on the Fiume issue would have served the interests of Wilson as well as the
democratic left.

Ultimately, the failure of this cooperative venture may have been
intellectual in one sense. Neither party understood the impact of war on Italian politics. For example, they clearly underestimated the Fiume issue. The
democratic left did not understand that the Giolittian system of orchestrating
voting blocs was obsolete, and so continued to attempt to play by the rules
of the Liberal State, something they had never done very well. They did not
understand the social psychology of 1919 and did not anticipate the triumph
of irrational political forces. In the end, they were too insulated from mass
politics. Their failure was the failure of European democracy.

NOTES

1. The phrase "prophet for a year" is quoted from Riccardo Bacchelli, *Oggi, domani, mai*, by
Louis John Nigro in "Propaganda, Politics, and the New Diplomacy: The Impact of Wilsonian
Propaganda on Politics and Public Opinion in Italy, 1917-1919," PhD dissertation, Vanderbilt
University, 1919, p. 8.
2. On the American propaganda campaign for democratic reform, see Nigro, "Propaganda." A
portrayal of the European response to Wilson is found in Stefan Zweig, *Tides of Fortune* (New
York: Viking, 1940), 263 ff.

3. Sources on Bissolati include his own *La politica estera*; Ivanoe Bonomi, Leonida Bissolati (Milan, 1929); Raffaele Colapietra, *Leonida Bissolati* (Milan, 1958); Ugoberto Alfassio Grimaldi and Gherardo Bozzetti, *Bissolati* (Milan, 1983); O. Malagodi, *Conversazioni della guerra 1914-1919* (Milan, 1960), Vol. II, pp. 451, 460-6 and 713-715; Dino Cofrancesco, "Democrazia, socialismo, nazionalizzazione delle masse: La vicenda di Leonida Bissolati," *Storia contemporanea* 17 (1986): 667-94.

4. The most original and influential study of the "new diplomacy" is found in the work of Arno J. Mayer, *Wilson vs. Lenin and Politics and Diplomacy of Peacemaking: Containment and Counterrevolution at Versailles, 1918-1919* (New York, 1968). For a statement of his Wilsonian views, see Bissolati's speech of July 5, 1918, "Gli Stati Uniti e la guerra" in *La politica estera dell'Italia dal 1897 al 1920: Scritti e discorsi* (Milan, 1923), pp. 378-83.

5. American authorities noted that "Bissolati devoted himself actively to the so-called `policy of the oppressed nationalities'" and persuaded Orlando to hold "a Congress of the Opressed (sic) Races in Rome." "Translation of a Confidential Statement Obtained from Hon. Leonidas (sic) Bissolati," December 30, 1918, Woodrow Wilson Papers, Series 5B, Reel 387, Library of Congress, Washington, D.C.

6. Seton-Watson, *Italy*, pp. 494-5.

7. Rene Albrecht-Carrié, *Italy at the Paris Peace Conference* (New York, 1938), pp. 36-47. Texts of the Treaty of London and the Pact of Rome can be found in Albrecht-Carrié, *Italy*, pp. 334-9 and 347-8; see also Colapietra, *Bissolati*, pp. 252-3.

8. "Translation of a Confidential Statement Obtained from Hon. Leonidas (sic) Bissolati," December 30, 1918, Woodrow Wilson Papers.

9. On Sonnino, see his own *Carteggio 1914-1916* and *Carteggio 1916-1922*, in Pietro Pastorelli (ed), (Bari, 1974 and 1975); Sonnino in Pastorelli (ed), *Diario 1914-1916* and *Diario 1916-1922* (Bari, 1972); H. James Burgwyn, "Sonnino e la diplomazia italiana del tempo di guerra nei Balcani nel 1915," *Storia Contemporanea* 16 (1985): 113-38; Rodolfo Mosca, "Autunno 1918: Sonnino, La Francia e la vittoria da spartire," *Storia e Politica* (1976), pp. 49-69; Alberto Monticone, "Salandra e Sonnino verso la decisione dell'intervento," *Rivista di studi politici internazionali* (January-March, 1970): 64-89; Brunello Vigezzi (ed), "I problemi della neutralità e della guerra nel carteggio Salandra-Sonnino (1914-1917)," *Biblioteca della Nuova Rivista Storica* (Milan, 1962); Benjamin F. Brown, "Sidney Sonnino: The Stranger in Two Worlds," PhD dissertation, Harvard University, 1966; Geoffrey Arthur Haywood, "Sidney Sonnino and liberal Italy, 1847-1901," PhD dissertation, Columbia University, 1990. See also H. James Burgwyn, *The Legend of the Mutilated Victory: Italy, The Great War, and the Paris Peace Conference, 1915-1919* (Univ. of North Carolina Press, 1993).

10. Charles Seymour. *The Intimate Papers of Colonel House* (New York, 1928), Vol. III, p. 283.

11. Albrecht-Carrié, *Italy*, p. 55.

12. On Wilson's opposition to Treaty of London, see Albrecht-Carrié, *Italy*, p. 90 ff.

13. Mayer made his basic ideological interpretation in *Wilson vs. Lenin: Political Origins of the New Diplomacy* (Cleveland, 1964). The point about Clemenceau, Sonnino and Orlando is found in Mayer's *Politics and Diplomacy of Peacemaking*, p. 212.

14. N. Gordon Levin, Jr. *Woodrow Wilson and World Politics: America's Response to War and Revolution* (New York, 1968), p. 66, argues that House, Lippmann, et al hoped to "accommodate the American war effort to the values of radical anti-imperialism."

15. Telegram, Ambassador to Italy (Page) to Secretary of State (Lansing), January 21, 1918, *Foreign Relations of the United States* (hereafter *FRUS*), *1918, the World War*, supplement 1, I (Washington, D.C., 1933), p. 35; Confidential Digest of the President's Conference with On. Bissolati, Thomas Nelson Page to Wilson, January 7, 1919, WWP, Series 5B, Reel 388, LC.

16. Bonomi, Carteggio, *Bissolati*, p. 220.

17. On the issue of ideological motivation, see Mayer, *Political Origins, prologue and passim*;

David F. Schmitz, "Woodrow Wilson and the Liberal Peace: The Problem of Italy and Imperialism," *Peace and Change* XII (1987): 29; Inga Floto, "Woodrow Wilson: War Aims, Peace Strategy, and the European Left" in Arthur S. Link (ed), *Woodrow Wilson and a Revolutionary World, 1913-1921* (Chapel Hill, 1982), p. 128. The phrase "O Wilson o Lenin" was used by Turati, Salvemini and Bissolati on various occasions in these months.

18. Mayer, *Political Origins*, p. 198; Albrecht-Carrié, *Italy*, p. 46; "Translation of a Confidential Statement," p. 2.

19. Ray Stannard Baker to E. M. House, November 1, 1918, Ray Stannard Baker Papers, Library of Congress (hereafter Baker Papers, LC).

20. Baker to House, November 22, 1918, 856.00/213, Record Group 59, National Archives, Washington, D. C. (hereafter RG 59, NA).

21. Mayer describes this Parliamentary debate in *Politics and Diplomacy*, pp. 202-3.

22. Baker to House, 6 December 1918, 856.00/214, RG 59, NA.

23. Vivarelli explains Bissolati's resignation in *il dopoguerra in Italia e l'avvento del fascismo (1918-1922)*, I (Naples, 1967), p. 211 ff., as does Colapietra, *Bissolati*, pp. 265-71. U.S. Ambassador to Italy, Thomas Nelson Page, attributed Bissolati's resignation to apparent "differences with Sonnino over Adriatic and disapproval over alleged half-heartedness in real application [of] Wilsonian principles to Italian national and international problems." Page to Ammission, Paris, December 30, 1918, Woodrow Wilson Papers, Series 5B, Reel 387, Library of Congress (hereafter WWP, LC).

24. Mayer describes Wilson's trip to Italy in *Politics and Diplomacy*, pp. 212-15. See also Bruno Tobia, "Il partito socialista italiano e la politica di W. Wilson (1916-1919)," *Storia contemporanea* V (1974), p. 295.

25. See Schmitz, "Wilson," pp. 32-3; Floto, "Wilson," p. 142; Albrecht-Carrié, *Italy*, pp. 142-9.

26. For a summary of Italy's official position on Fiume as stated at the Paris Peace Conference, see Albrecht-Carrié, *Italy*, pp. 98-103. See also Vivarelli, *Il dopoguerra*, p. 195 ff.

27. Albrecht-Carrié, *Italy*, p. 85.

28. See also Schmitz, "Wilson," p. 33; Floto, "Wilson," p. 131.

29. Baker to House, November 1, 1918, Baker Papers, LC.

30. Floto, "Wilson," p. 133; Mayer, *Politics and Diplomacy*, pp. 211-12; Renzo De Felice, *Mussolini il rivoluzionario* (Turin, 1965), pp. 446-8.

There are, however, examples of more realistic, less exaggerated estimates of the impact of Wilsonian ideals in Italy. One month before Wilson's visit, while confirming "deep-seated popular support" for Wilson and quoting a Turati Parliamentary speech of "unstinted praise" for Wilsonianism, Ray Stannard Baker warned Colonel House. Baker anticipated radicalism, discontent with the government, "petty bickerings" in Parliament, "the spectacle of discredited political leaders (like Giolitti) jockeying in the old pre-war way for political power." He also noted a "disquieting outlook." Most importantly, he communicated his "impression of the growth of a great imperialistic spirit" and "a great deal of anxiety as to whether Wilson will or will not support the Italian claims. If he does not," Baker projected, "his popularity among many of these nationalists will quickly evaporate." Baker to House, 6 December 1918, 856.00/214, RG 59, NA.

In his telegram of January 21, 1918, U. S. Ambassador T. N. Page gave a similar warning. Page described his conversation with "an intelligent Italian general of standing just arrived from the front" who had reported that "the Italian army is asking now, `What are we fighting for if Trent and Trieste are not to be Italy's?'" Telegram, Page to Lansing, January 21, 1918, *FRUS*, supplement 1, I, p. 35.

31. Baker to House, November 22, 1918, 856.00/213, RG 59, NA.

32. Mayer, *Politics and Diplomacy of Peacemaking*, pp. 208-12; De Felice, *Mussolini il rivoluzionario*, p. 448; Floto, "Wilson," pp. 120-35; Colapietra, *Bissolati*, pp. 270-1.

In support of the more realistic American estimate, Ambassador T. N. Page reported five weeks later from Rome that "press backing of Bissolati is considerably censored" and that "Bissolati's actual following in the country is not believed very large." At the same time he noted that "the propaganda for Italian expansion along Eastern Adriatic shore is tremendous." T. N. Page to Ammission, Paris, December 30, 1918, WWP, Series 5B, Reel 387, LC.

33. Salvemini's well-known statement on "absolute justice" appeared in *L'Unità* May 3, 1919, and was partially censored. Salvemini, *Opere*, III (vol. 2), Carlo Pischedda (ed), (Milan, 1964), p. 509. See also Schmitz, "Wilson," p. 36; Albrecht-Carrié, *Italy*, 95: 146; Mayer, *Politics and Diplomacy*, p. 205 ff; De Felice, *Mussolini il rivoluzionario*, pp. 449-56; Vivarelli, *Il dopoguerra*, p. 159 ff.

34. Gino Speranza, Entry of December 29, 1918, *The Diary of Gino Speranza*, Italy, 1915-1919, Florence Colgate Speranza, ed., Vol II (New York, 1941), pp. 232-3. See also Albrecht Carrié, *Italy*, pp. 82-4.

35. De Felice, *Mussolini il rivoluzionario*, p. 449. See also Mayer, *Politics and Diplomacy*, pp. 194-204; Albrecht-Carrié, *Italy*, 46:71-82; Bissolati, *La politica estera*, p. 432; Bonomi, *Bissolati*, p. 209; Giuseppe Borgese, *Goliath* (New York: Viking Press, 1938), pp. 139-49.

5

THE FASCIST / ANTI-FASCIST STRUGGLE IN SAN FRANCISCO

Rose D. Scherini

It is well known that Mussolini's fascism had considerable impact on immigrants in this country, perhaps even making them feel "Italian" for the first time. But it is less well known that the fascist/anti-fascist struggle in this country was a factor in contributing to the severe, often tragic outcomes suffered by some Italian Americans who were considered "subversive" at the time of U.S. entry into World War II. With the war's outbreak, a convergence of anti-fascist and anti-immigrant forces resulted in the undermining of San Francisco's Italian community. This unintended effect of the anti-fascist movement, and the war itself, contributed materially to the dissolution of a formerly cohesive ethnic community.[1]

Past analysis of the influence of fascism and anti-fascism among Italian Americans has focused on the East Coast. There were some major differences between the situation in New York and that in San Francisco; one was the size of the respective Italian populations on the two coasts.

San Francisco's Italian population peaked in 1930 with 27,300 foreign-born and a total of 58,000 including the first generation born here — what the census calls "foreign stock." The Italian foreign stock was 9.2% of the city's population. When the war began, foreign-born Italians numbered 24,000, with half already naturalized as citizens. Six thousand foreign-born Italians lived in North Beach, the district that is still the center of the Italian community with its ethnic restaurants and shops, social clubs, a cultural center (Casa Fugazi), and a national church (Saints Peter and Paul's).[2]

The New York area, by contrast, had an Italian population nearly ten times as large as that in San Francisco. Furthermore, East Coast "Little Italys" tended to be relatively homogeneous; i.e., the majority in a given community had migrated from two or three adjacent provinces in Italy. The San Francisco community, on the other hand, represented many provinces, with an approximate 60/40 split between the North and the South. Situated on a sheltered bay with ocean access, the city had attracted both Genoese and Sicilian fisherman, would-be gold prospectors, and others from throughout the "boot."[3]

But the significant difference between these two communities for our present purpose is found in the political role of the anti-fascist emigrés. The *fuorusciti* congregated in the New York area and formed the nucleus of the anti-fascist movement in the United States during the 1920s and 1930s. In San Francisco, by contrast, there were few anti-fascists to speak out. The primary spokesman was Carmelo Zito, the socialist editor/publisher of *Il Corriere del Popolo*, whose masthead read "The Only Italian Labor Newspaper on the Pacific Coast." In 1931, Zito had moved to San Francisco from New York, where he had worked on several anti-fascist publications. He became the leader of the local anti-fascist protest and a founder of a Mazzini Society chapter in 1940. Another group that was unofficially anti-fascist was a Masonic Lodge, *Speranza Italiana*, founded by immigrants in 1871. Two anti-fascist publications, *La Critica*, and *Cultura Popolare*, appeared irregularly in the 1930s, but had disappeared by the end of the decade.[4] Other than Carmelo Zito, there were no anti-fascist leaders in the West with the influence and power comparable to New York's Congressman Vito Marcantonio, the anarchist Carlo Tresca with his newspaper, *Il Martello*, or the labor organizer, Luigi Antonini.[5]

During the Spanish Civil War, anti-fascist activities in San Francisco were publicized in *Il Corriere*, including notices of fund-raising dinners and dances sponsored by the *Donne Anti-fasciste per la Spagna Repubblicana*, and even an item about a North Beach physician who appended this notice to his office-hours sign: "Active in the anti-fascist movement." It was also during the mid-thirties that Zito launched an attack on the Italian language schools whose pro-fascist books and teachers were financed by the Italian Consulate. As a consequence of this publicity, the American Legion passed a resolution and sponsored legislation (which did not pass) to place the language schools under the supervision of the State Board of Education.[6]

Unfortunately for the anti-fascists, any opposition to Franco was deemed to be communist and anti-Catholic. Similarly, Mussolini was generally characterized as the defender against the bolshevik menace, leaving his opponents with little support either from the U.S. government or from Italian Catholics. Zito, however, extracted his *quid pro quo* in 1941 when he accused Ss. Peter and Paul's, the Italian national church, of aiding the fascist cause through its drive to collect clothing and other personal items for Italian sailors interned at Fort Missoula, Montana. The pastor, Reverend Joseph Galli, was subsequently transferred to a "less strenuous post" in a smaller city.[7]

The absence of a major anti-fascist movement on the West Coast has led some researchers to claim that San Francisco Italians were more pro-fascist than those in other parts of the country, and even more than Italians in the homeland. There were, of course, many pro-Mussolini immigrants among Italian Americans, but the San Francisco community was probably not any *more* pro-fascist than other Italian American communities. In fact, there is substantial data that pro-fascism in the New York area played a much more prominent role among the Italians there.[8]

What *did* take place in San Francisco—as in most other Italian communities in the 1920s and 1930s—was an eruption of nationalistic fervor in support of Mussolini. Added to that was the linguistic tendency (that suffers in translation) to exaggerate, sensationalize, or glorify, so that Mussolini, for the anti-fascists, was the devil incarnate. Zito called Ettore Patrizi, publisher of the pro-fascist *L'Italia*, a "Fascist pirate." And Patrizi wrote glowingly that "the Roman Eagles have landed on Lake Michigan" when an Italian Air Force squadron visited Chicago in 1929.[9]

Consequently, when the United States entered the war in December, 1941, prewar statements by individuals in support of Italy and often-innocent activities undertaken out of altruistic motives and emotional ties to the homeland came to be seen as "subversive" from an Allied military perspective. Thus began a series of tragic events that changed the lives of North Beach community leaders and many ordinary Italian Americans, even some naturalized citizens.

Beginning the night of the Pearl Harbor attack, approximately 250 Italian immigrant aliens throughout the country, then "enemy aliens," were arrested and later interned in military camps, with perhaps fifty or more being from the San Francisco area. Eventually, about 2000 Italians were arrested, some for curfew or travel violations, and most were released within a short time. Government documents show varying numbers of internees, but most often the number of Italian Americans interned for the duration of the war with Italy is reported as 228.[10]

Why were these Italian aliens interned? Because their names were on a list—the Custodial Detention List. Since 1939, the FBI, Army G-2, and Naval Intelligence had been compiling a list of persons allegedly associated with communist, Nazi, or fascist organizations or activities, and considered "potentially dangerous" in time of war. The list was made up of organization membership records, foreign-language newspaper staffs, and names provided by informants, such as American Legion members, who reported to the FBI names of persons "Primarily interested in another country."[11]

The intelligence agencies also had a list of "dangerous" organizations, e.g. the Federation of Italian War Veterans (*Ex-Combattenti*), the Dante Aligheri Society, the Italian language schools, and the Fascist League of North America (a short-lived group, defunct since 1929). On December 7, 1941, the U.S. Department of Justice wired lists of names to FBI field offices around the country. In San Francisco, all of the non-citizen members of the *Ex-Combattenti* were apprehended and interned. These men were veterans of World War I in Italy when the United States and Italy were allies.[12]

A second blow to the North Beach community came several months later, in the Fall of 1942, when the Army issued exclusion orders to another twenty or so Italian Americans, all naturalized citizens. At this point, the anti-fascist and anti-immigrant forces converge. Immigrants had come to be seen as radicals or subversives, leading the Department of Justice into an egregious travesty of justice. The excluded persons were on the FBI list and had also been named in hearings held by the State Legislature's Un-American Activities Committee (the Tenney Committee). The Committee had held hearings in the city earlier that year in pursuit of its mission to investigate communist, Nazi, and fascist activities in the State. The hearings were held in the Borgia Room of the St. Francis Hotel, a double irony.[13]

Zito, a prime witness, named several *prominenti* as pro-fascists. His testimony led the Committee to conclude that the "Italian Fascist Movement in California" was directed by three North Beach community leaders: Ettore Patrizi, publisher of *L'Italia*; Sylvester Andriano, attorney, former member of the city's Board of Supervisors, and then-chair of a draft board; and the third, Renzo Turco, another attorney active in several Italian American organizations. All three were naturalized citizens: Patrizi since 1898, Andriano since 1912, and Turco since 1928.[14]

Besides Zito, three other Italian anti-fascists had testified before the Committee that fascist propaganda was being disseminated through *L'Italia*, Italian language schools, the Italian Chamber of Commerce, Italian-language radio, the Sons of Italy's publication (*Il Leone*), and by the *Ex-Combattenti*—in short, by most of the organized Italian community.[15]

Even California-born Angelo Rossi, then the city's mayor for twelve years, came under attack at these hearings, first by Zito, then by Harry Bridges, the labor leader. These two witnesses reported that Rossi had supported both German and Italian causes and claimed that the mayor had been seen giving the Fascist salute at public meetings. Rossi cried openly during his own testimony before the Committee while vehemently denying the accusations. According to his daughter, Rossi died of a "broken heart" a few years later, having lost his bid for re-election in 1944. Apparently all that Rossi had been guilty of was the receipt of two medals which the Italian government regularly awards to persons making extraordinary contributions to immigrant communities abroad. Rossi also had a photograph of Mussolini in his City Hall office along with photos of other world leaders. It had been Guglielmo Marconi who had given Mussolini's photo to the Mayor on a visit to San Francisco in 1933. But even medals and photographs were suspect during the first year of the war.[16]

Within months of the Tenney Committee, the Army's Western Defense Command issued exclusion orders to the three men named as leaders of the "fascist movement" and to another twenty naturalized citizens in the city. The area of exclusion covered much of the populated area of the state, so an exclusion order virtually meant resettling outside of California. Excluded persons had to leave within ten days. Many moved to Reno, Nevada, the nearest large city where they might find work. Others moved to Salt Lake City, Denver, or Chicago. It is important to realize what having to find housing and work in a strange city meant to these men and women at this point in their lives. Patrizi was 77 years old and hospitalized when he received his exclusion order.[17]

The anti-fascists could not have realized that their attacks on the *prominenti* would affect many others, even some working-class men, innocent not only of subversion, but also without any strongly-held ideology. Some who were interned or excluded were publicly known as anti-fascist; others were simply apolitical. Zito himself wrote to the enemy alien hearing board attesting to the loyalty of an internee who had been a drama critic for *L'Italia*; still the man was interned for almost two years before he was "exonerated" and released. Incidentally, the name of Carmelo Zito was also on the Custodial List—probably because anti-fascists were earlier suspect as pro-Communist.[18]

The hearings had seriously damaging effects on the North Beach community. Italians had testified against Italians, who were then deemed to be "subversive" without any evidence of subversion. At the most, they had been overzealous in their support of Mussolini, and yet innocent men, women, and children were traumatized by the exclusion orders. They did not know what the charges were; they did not know what was going to happen to the accused. Patrizi "American" sister-in-law—admittedly a subjective informant — said that his only fault was that he had "loved Italy too much." The organized life of the community was badly fractured by the exclusions and internments and never fully recovered. Twenty years after the hearings, there was still fear of begin "too Italian" and of belonging to any group receiving funds from the Italian Consulate. A woman community leader, who had been subpoenaed by the Tenney Committee, remembered sorrowfully that "the best people had been sent away" and that, consequently, many Italian Americans no longer participated in promoting language classes or other ethnic activities.[19]

Even more disturbing, in recent years, many family members of internees and excludees still refuse to talk about this experience. Both anger and shame seem to be the reasons for their silence. The betrayal was not only perpetrated by the *paesani*; it was carried out by the U.S. government. And they do not even know today why their spouses or parents were singled out. The fact that the government has never publicly acknowledged what happened to Italian Americans (and German Americans, too)—nor have the families even received private acknowledgment—has made it difficult for some to fully support the reparations and apology given to Japanese Americans for their wartime internment. The Japanese evacuation was, technically, a different case in that it affected an entire racial group including those born in the U.S.; but that is little solace to the spouses and children of the Italians and Germans.[20]

This episode began the dissolution of a lively ethnic community. North Beach never fully regained its prewar vitality. The Italian War Veterans never met again. The Italian Athletic Club changed its name to San Francisco Athletic Club. There is no longer an Italian-language newspaper published in the city. Of course, many other factors contributed to this community's decline: the post-war exodus to the suburbs; the influx of "beatniks" into North Beach in the fifties and, later, the overflow of Asian immigrants from adjacent Chinatown; and, finally, the diminished emigration from Italy to the West Coast.[21]

Finally, the anti-fascists are not to be indicted for their struggle against the fascist ideology. If blame is to be assigned for the tragedy of these unfair internments and exclusions, it should be directed at the government agencies whose policies ignored the Bill of Rights and fostered ancient prejudices against foreigners. Those policies enabled organizations like the American Legion, the FBI, and un-American activities committees to accuse and stigmatize individuals without due process of law. A major lesson of this bit of history is that Italian Americans must vigilantly guard against any infringements on the civil rights of all groups and individuals. For, if this could happen to them when they were the largest immigrant population in the United States, it can happen again—to *any* group.[22]

NOTES

1. There has been no comprehensive study of fascism on the West Coast, but several researchers have dealt briefly with this subject: Marino DeMedici, "The Italian Language Press in the San Francisco Bay Area from 1930 to 1943," Master's thesis, Univ. of California, Berkeley, 1963, pp. 230-35; Sebastian Fichera, "The Meaning of Community: A History of the Italians of San Francisco, Ph.D. dissertation, UCLA, 1981, pp. 193-215; and Dino Cinel, *From Italy to San Francisco: The Immigrant Experience* (Stanford Univ. Press, 1982) pp. 247-55. For an analysis of the work of the California UnAmerican Activities Committee, see Edward L. Barrett, Jr., *The Tenne Committee* (Ithaca: Cornell Univ. Press, 1951).
2. U.S. Census of the Population, 1940, v. II, Pt. 1, Table 24; U.S. Immigration & Naturalization Service, "Report on Alien Registration," February 1, 1943, Tables 2, 3.
3. Population data for New York is drawn from 1940 Census, v. 11, Pt. 5. Literature on East Coast settlements is numerous. I have drawn from Virginia Yans McLaughlin, "Like the Fingers of the Hand: The Family and Community Life of Five Generations of Italian Americans in Buffalo, 1880-1930", Ph.D. dissertation, SUNY, Buffalo, 1970; Virginia Yans McLaughlin, *Family and Community: Italian Immigrants in Buffalo, 1880-1930* (Ithaca: Cornell Univ. Press, 1977); Carla Bianca, *The Two Rosetos* (Bloomington, IN: Indiana Univ. Press, 1974); and Francis A. Ianni, "The Acculturation of the Italo-American in Norristown, Pennsylvania, 1900 to 1950," Ph.D. dissertation, Pennsylvania State Univ., 1952. On the make-up of the San Francisco community, see Paul Radin, "The Italians of San Francisco, Their Adjustment and Acculturation," (San Francisco: SERA Project, 1935), and Cinel, 1982, p. 32.
4. This paragraph is based on DeMedici, 1963, and Andrew M. Canepa, "Profila della Masonneria di Lingua Italiana in California," *Studi Emigrazione* 27 (1990):97. My understanding of anti-fascist in San Francisco owes much to discussions with Andy Canepa. For an Italian scholar's view of Zito, see Gabriela Facondo, *Socialismo Italiano Esule Negli USA (1930-1942)* (Foggia: Bastogi, 1993), v. 54, pp. 41-50.
5. See John P. Diggins, *Mussolini and Fascism: The View From America* (Princeton: Princeton Univ. Press, 1972); Ventresco, Fiorello, "The Struggle of the Italian Anti-Fascist Movement in America (Spanish Civil War to World War II)," *Ethnic Forum* 6 (1-2, 1986):17-48.; and Cannistraro, Philip V., "Luigi Antonini and the Italian Anti-Fascist Movement in the United States, 1940-1943," *Journal of American Ethnic History* 5 (1, 1985):21-40.
6. *Il Corriere del Popolo*, January 14 and 21, March 25, and April 8, 1937; DeMedici, p. 59. The American Legion also passed a resolution in September, 1941, proposing that all foreign-language newspapers, periodicals, and broadcasts be translated into English or be banned (Sullivan to Biddle, June 17, 1942, File #148-303-14, Box 76, RG60, Dept. of Justice, National Archives).
7. *Il Corriere*, June 1, 1941; Baccari, A., V. Scarpaci, and G. Zavattaro, *Ss. Peter and Paul's: The Chronicles of the Italian Cathedral of the West, 1884-1984* (San Francisco, 1985), p. 175. Father Galli's name was also on the Custodial Detention List, perhaps because he was pastor of an Italian national church; Shinto Buddhist priests were detained because of their religion's of their religion's allegiance to the emperor of Japan.
8. Writers who posit that the San Francisco community was more pro-fascist include Patrizia Salvetti, "La Communita` Italiana de San Francisco tra Italianita` e Americanizzazione negli

Anni `30 e `40," *Studi Emigrazione* 19 (65, March, 1982):3-39; and Cinel, pp. 274-55. On East Coast fascism, see writings of Gaetano Salvermini and Philip Cannistraro.

9. DeMedici, pp. 13-13; *Il Corriere*, May 18, 1937; and *L'Italia*, April 1, 1929.

10. FBI, Custodial Detention Files, "1521 Italian Aliens Taken Into Custody by FBI," June 30, 1942; Dept. of Justice, October 7, 1942 (press release), Univ. of California, Bancroft Library, JERS 67/14c, D 2.03.

11. See Rose Scherini, "Executive Order 9066 and Italian Americans: The San Francisco Story," *California History* 70 (4, 1992):366-77; and Stephen Fox, *The Unknown Internment: An Oral History of the Relocation of Italian Americans during World War II* (Boston: Twayne Publishers, 1990).

12. See Scherini, 1992.

13. California Legislature, *Report of the Joint Fact-Finding Committee on Un-American Activities in California*, 1943, pp. 309-14.; *San Francisco Chronicle*, May 28, 1942; *San Francisco Examiner*, May 28, 1942.

14. On Patrizi, see War Relocation Authority records, RG210, Box 10, A-7, October 14, 1942; On Andriano, Giovanni Vigo (ed.) *Italian American Who's Who*, v. 19 (1962), p. 14; and on Turco, FBI HQ file 100-6-471, March 25, 1941, p. 3.

15. California Legislature, pp. 309-14.

16. California Legislature, p. 298; *San Francisco Chronicle*, May 8, 1942; interview of Eleanor Rossi Crabtree by Phylis C. Martinelli, San Francisco, August 1, 1974 (on cassette). For a slightly different view of Rossi, see Salvetti, p. 20, and Fichera, pp. 219-27.

17. Scherini, 1992, pp. 369-71.

18. For the Custodial Detention List, see microfilm files of the Wartime Relocation and Internment of Civilians, 24: 25780-85; Zito's letter is in Guido Trento's FBI HQ file 100-61-677.

19. See Rose Scherini, *The Italian American Community of San Francisco: A Descriptive Study* (New York: Arno Press, 1980), pp. 194-5.

20. For a different, but related, discussion of Italian American silence in the face of social problems, see Robert Viscusi, "Breaking the Silence: Strategic Imperatives for Italian American Culture," *Voices of Italian Americana* 1 (1, 1990), pp. 1-13.

21. A fuller discussion of the factors in this post-war decline is in Scherini, 1980, pp. 25-30, 209-17.

22. For more on the role of the American Legion, see Athan Theoharis, "The FBI and the American Legion Contact Program, 1940-66," *Political Science Quarterly* 100 (2, 1985).

6

ITALIAN DEMOCRATIC CHIEFTAINS AND THE MAKING OF A DEMOCRATIC MAJORITY AMONG ITALIAN-AMERICANS IN PITTSBURGH

STEFANO LUCONI
UNIVERSITY OF ROME I: LA SAPIENZA

This paper is a first attempt to shed some light on how the presence of ward and precinct heelers of Italian ancestry in the machine of Democratic boss David Lawrence contributed to the hold of the Democratic party on the Italian-American community in Pittsburgh during the so-called New Deal realignment.[1]

Before the Depression and Roosevelt's relief policy turned Pittsburgh into a Democratic stronghold, the city had been a bailiwick of the GOP.[2] Republican bosses usually employed Italian-American chieftains, because ethnic matching between party workers and potential voters facilitated the political mobilization of Italian immigrants who could hardly speak English and usually lived segregated in their own neighborhoods.[3] Italian-American precinct captains offered their constituents aids and services ranging from free buckets of coal and baskets of food to jobs in the municipal administration. In return they asked their fellow-ethnics to vote for the candidates of the machine on election day.

The Depression not only hit Pittsburgh's Italian-American community hard, but also drained the traditional sources of Republican political
power. In 1932, the businessmen who had been the financial backbone of the
GOP withheld their contributions when the reelection of Hoover became a
forlorn cause.[4] Without the usual influx of money from the County Committee, Italian-American Republican workers found it more and more burdensome to supply their community with political services. The economic crisis also destroyed the image of Italian-American Republican captains as job-
providers. Even GOP heelers themselves found it difficult to make ends meet.
Deprived of their traditional means to influence the vote and worried less
about the outcome of the election than about their own plight, Italian-American Republican workers failed to keep their fellow-ethnics in the GOP column, and Roosevelt carried the community with 62% of the vote in 1932.[5]

The sources of the patronage of the Republican organization further
shrank when the GOP lost its grip on most of the county and municipal jobs
following a Democratic victory in the 1933 local elections. The new balance
of power in Pittsburgh particularly affected the Republican henchmen because the GOP machine began to lack for the political plums through which
it had usually rewarded its workers.

An analysis of the occupation of Pittsburgh's Italian-American
members of the Republican and the Democratic County Committees and of
the Republican Ward Executive Committee highlights the role of patronage
in the political experience of the Italian-American community. A perusal of
the election returns for these bodies has provided the names of their members
and a name check conducted on the lists of candidates has made it possible
to single out the committeemen of Italian ancestry. In addition, *Polk's Pittsburgh Directory* has offered information about the occupation of both the
committeemen and their relatives.

No election returns for the Democratic and the Republican Committees are available before 1934. That year 12.5% of the Italian-American
Republican committeemen were on the public payroll. If their relatives are
also considered, the percentage of the Italian-American Republican workers
who took advantage of patronage opportunities jumps to 37.5%. In 1934 the
GOP still enjoyed a share of patronage because a Republican administration

was in power in the State House. Moreover, Democratic Mayor William McNair refused to cooperate with the leaders of his own party and was willing to deal with the GOP as for political appointments.[6]

These figures were to slump in the following years. In 1934, Democratic George Earle became Governor of Pennsylvania, and two years later a Democratic stalwart replaced the maverick McNair as Mayor. Therefore, by Roosevelt's reelection in 1936, Pittsburgh's Democratic party had wrested control of patronage out of the hands of the GOP. Indeed, in 1938 no Italian-American Republican committee-person could be identified as a political jobholder.

In the meantime, patronage became a real bonanza for Democratic workers. In 1934, 9.7% of the Italian-American members of the Democratic County Committee were on public payroll, and 12.9% of them had a relative who benefitted from a political appointment. In 1936, the first percentage did not change, but the ratio of kinfolks who were political jobholders rose to 15.9%. The percentages of both groups grew respectively to 13.8% and 16.9% in 1938.

The chance of enjoying a share of the winner's spoils induced Italian-American Republican workers to go over to the Democratic party, especially in 1934. After an unsuccessful campaign for the GOP gubernatorial nomination, Charles Margiotti, a prominent lawyer based in Pittsburgh, came out for Earle, and was later rewarded with the appointment as State Attorney General.[7] Margiotti brought John Verona, the political leader of the Italian-American community, over with him. Patronage was the main reason for Verona's bolt. In 1933, Republican Mayor John Herron refused to appoint John Scorza, Verona's nephew, to a vacancy in the court of police magistrates. Moreover, Verona hoped to make some money with the new Democratic administration after Earle's likely election.[8] Several other Italian-American Republican workers followed Verona's lead. Indeed, at least 9.7% of the Italian-American Democratic committee-persons elected in 1936 had served in the Republican party two years before.

It is likely that the shift in allegiance of the Italian-American GOP chieftains strengthened the Democratic sentiment in their community. In a city where the influence of any boss within the party in power was related to the size of the vote he could deliver, people were well aware that the best chance to obtain more political services was when the candidates of their ward and precinct heelers came out on top.[9] After Republican Mayor Charles Kline gave ward chairpersons complete control over the distribution of patronage among the voters of their own districts in the late twenties, the personal power of ward leaders became even more effective.[10] As a matter of fact, Verona cashed in on Kline's policy to become the political boss of the Italian-American community.[11]

It has been suggested that Verona's bolt from the GOP in 1934 accounted for the establishment of a Democratic majority in the 3rd Ward almost overnight.[12] Moreover, the Democratic vote increased by nearly 7% among Pittsburgh's Italian-Americans between 1932 and 1934.

After the Democratic party lost the 1938 gubernatorial elections in Pennsylvania, the state reverted to Republican domination through 1954. Following this voting trend, several Italian-American communities began to gravitate again toward the GOP, especially in the years after World War II.[13] Yet the percentage of the Democratic vote among the Italian-Americans in Pittsburgh never fell below 68% until 1952.

The balanced-ticket strategy did not play a major role in fostering the Democratic sentiment in Pittsburgh's community. Indeed, the year 1938 saw the reduction from three to two of the places allotted to Italian-Americans on the Democratic ticket for the State House of Representatives.[14] In addition, from 1939 to 1951 the Democratic organization slated no member of the community for any municipal or county office except for judicial seats.[15]

Conversely, it seems that the distribution of political spoils was instrumental in cementing the Democratic majority in the community. The New Deal was all but the "last hurrah" for machine politics in Pittsburgh. Indeed, benefiting from Roosevelt's relief policies and from the Democratic hold on local patronage, boss David Lawrence managed to build up a powerful organization which was pivotal in electing him Mayor in 1945.[16]

The growing number of Italian-American Democratic workers and of their relatives on public payroll together well illustrates the increasing dependence of the Italian-American community on the patronage controlled by Lawrence's machine. The percentage of Italian-American Democratic officials who lived on political jobs nearly tripled, jumping from 13.8% in 1938 to 38.2% in 1942. In 1946, after Lawrence himself had taken office as Pittsburgh's Mayor, 40% of the Italian-American precinct heelers worked for the municipal, the county or the federal administration, while 23.2% of those chieftains had a relative on the public payroll.

The high proportion of Italian-American Democratic committeepersons holding political jobs can also help to account for the persistence of Democratic majorities in workers deeply involved in elections and more active in getting out the vote because, under the spoils system, they faced layoffs in case of defeat of their party.[17] In addition, ethnic communities usually perceived the political appointments of their members as collective benefits for their group, and were likely to use their votes to reward the party which granted them this kind of recognition.[18]

Besides providing nearly half of its workers of Italian descent with a job, Pittsburgh's Democratic party also gave the Italian-Americans political recognition through the accommodation of their fellow-ethnics in Lawrence's machine. The Democratic organization endorsed Verona for the leadership of the 3rd ward after he had defected from the GOP.[19] When Verona died in 1937, the Democratic Party replaced him with another member of the community.[20] By 1952 the number of the Italian-American Democratic ward captains had grown to three, representing almost 10% of all the ward leaders of the party.[21] The rise of the Italian-Americans in the Democratic organization occurred also at a lower level. In 1936 5.1% of Pittsburgh's members of the Democratic County Committee were of Italian descent. This percentage grew to 9.7% by 1954. Conversely, in that very year, Italian-Americans made up only 5.7% of the Republican County Committee.

It might be assumed that party officials of Italian ancestry are a representative sample of Pittsburgh's Italian-American community and, hence, that their political experience mirrored the voting behavior of their fellow-ethnics. Therefore, the previous date might lead to the conclusion that, since there were more Democratic than Republican Italian-American committeepersons, the Democratic party received larger support than the GOP in

Pittsburgh's community. This theory may be plausible especially for such years as 1938, when the Democratic party polled 74.6% of the vote in the community, while in several precincts the GOP could not even find candidates for the County or for the Ward Executive Committee or both.

It is also likely that, besides reflecting voting patterns, the disproportionate number of Italian-American Democratic workers directly affected the partisan alignment of their fellow-ethnics. As Cornwell has suggested, parties can win the vote of immigrant groups also through the accommodation of ethnics in their own political organizations.[22] Moreover, Leuchtenburg has argued that some ethnic groups joined the Roosevelt coalition not only because they benefitted from the New Deal relief, but also because they received recognition from the Democratic party in terms of political offices.[23] Such arguments establish a link between the number of Italian-American chieftains in Lawrence's machine and the size of the Democratic vote in their community.

The 1951 Democratic primary well illustrates the strength of the personal following of Italian-American party workers among their fellow-ethnics. Charles Papale, the leader of the 12th ward, where the largest Italian-American neighborhood was located, refused to endorse Loran Lewis, the candidate of the Lawrence machine for the District Attorney nomination.[24] As a result, Lewis' opponent carried the community with 92% of the vote. It can easily be suggested that such an outcome primarily resulted from the personification of partisan loyalty in the figure of the ward leader. Indeed, Lawrence did not change Mayor Kline's way of handling patronage, and left ward chairpersons in charge of the distribution of political spoils at the grassroots level.[25] To the average voter, therefore, the very provider of jobs and services was the flesh-and-blood ward leader rather than an abstract and far-off party organization.

A brief analysis of the 1952 and 1954 election returns highlights how the presence of Italian-American chieftains in Pittsburgh's Democratic machine influenced the political behavior of their fellow-ethnics. In 1952, for the first time since 1934, the Democratic vote in the community dropped below 68%. This relatively disappointing performance was the aftershock of a reshuffle of political power in the 12th ward. A few months before the presidential election, Papale was fired from his job in the municipal administration and replaced as ward chairperson.[26] Exploiting personal connections, Papale managed to marshal his stalwarts to Eisenhower's side.[27] In two years, however, the new ward leader, Victor Martinelli, was able to build up his own political following and recapture the vote of the 1952 switchers.[28] As a matter of fact, in 1954 the community cast 76.9% of their ballots for the Democratic nominee for governor, despite the fact that he was regarded as a "throw-away candidate."[29]

In conclusion, this paper has suggested that although Pittsburgh's Italian-American community turned Democratic before its own party workers, Italian-American Democratic chieftains played a key role in keeping their fellow-ethnics in the Democratic fold after Pennsylvania relapsed under Republican control. Of course, the distribution of patronage through committeemen was only one of the many facets of ethnic politics. Nonetheless, political spoils were pivotal in strengthening the hold of Lawrence's machine on the Italian-Americans.

NOTES

1. The periodization of this paper draws upon the two-stage theory elaborated by Sundquist, who has placed the years of Pennsylvania's New Deal realignment, i.e., the process of the end of Republican dominance and the formation of a Democratic majority, between the early 1930s and the election of George Leader as Governor in 1954. See James L. Sundquist, *Dynamics of the Party System: Alignment and Realignment of Political Parties in the United States*, rev. ed. (Washington, D.C.: The Brookings Institution, 1983), pp. 252-56.
2. Parker, H. Sheldon, Jr., *The State of Allegheny: The Republican Party in Pittsburgh and Allegheny County from 1930 to 1961* (Pittsburgh, 1965), pp. 2-7.
3. For scattered information on the Italian-American community in Pittsburgh see Bodnar, John, Roger Simon, and Michael Weber, *Lives of Their Own: Blacks, Italians, and Poles in Pittsburgh, 1900-1960* (Urbana: Univ. of Chicago Press, 1982).
4. *Pittsburgh Sun-Telegraph*, Nov. 6, 7, 1932; *Pittsburgh Press*, Nov. 6, 1932; Williams, Thomas E., "Will Pennsylvania Go Democratic?,"; *Nation*, Nov. 9, 1932: 452.
5. It has been assumed that the election returns of the voting divisions which contained at least 52% of Italian-American registered voters are representative of the vote of Pittsburgh's Italian-American community. The ethnic concentration of voting divisions has been identified through a name check conducted on the few *Street Lists of Voters* held by the Archives of Industrial Society, University of Pittsburgh, and supplemented by census tract data and *Polk's Pittsburgh Directories*. The row votes by division have been obtained from either *The Pennsylvania Manual*

(Harrisburg, PA: The Commonwealth of Pennsylvania) or the official election tabulation sheets held by both the Archives of Industrial Society and the Office of the Prothonotary of Allegheny County.

6. Stave, Bruce M., *The New Deal and the Last Hurrah: Pittsburgh Machine Politics* (Pittsburgh: Univ. of Pittsburgh Press, 1970), pp. 84-91.

7. Harris, Chester, *Tiger at the Bar: The Life Story of Charles J. Margiotti* (New York: Vantage Press, 1946), pp. 320-29.

8. *Pittsburgh Sun-Telegraph*, Apr. 18, 1933; Dec. 4, 5, 1939.

9. Souza, Milanie, "The Social Background of Political Decisions Makers: The Ward Chairmen of Pittsburgh," (Tutorial thesis, Chatham College, 1960), p. 3.

10. *Pittsburgh Press*, July 25, 1931; *Pittsburgh Sun-Telegraph*, Mar. 27, 1933.

11. *Pittsburgh Post-Gazette*, June 10, 1926; *Pittsburgh Press*, Dec. 5, 1927; Jan. 12, 1937; *Pittsburgh Post-Gazette*, Nov. 7, 1930.

12. *Pittsburgh Press*, Nov. 22, 1939.

13. Grifo, Richard D., and Anthony Noto, *Italian Presence in Pennsylvania* (University Park, Pa.: The Pennsylvania Historical Association, 1990), p. 22.

14. *The Pennsylvania Manual* (1937), pp. 195-6; *ibid.* (1939), p. 167.

15. *Pittsburgh Press*, Nov. 5, 1939; *Pittsburgh Sun-Telegraph*, May 11, 1951.

16. Stave, *The New Deal and the Last Hurrah*; Weber, Michael P., *Don't Call Me Boss: David L. Lawrence, Pittsburgh's Renaissance Mayor* (Pittsburgh: Univ. of Pittsburgh Press, 1988), esp. pp. 65-85.

17. Kurtzman, David Harold, *Methods of Controlling Votes in Philadelphia* (Philadelphia: Univ. of Pennsylvania Press, 1935), pp. 43-4; Key, V.O., Jr., *Politics, Parties, and Pressure Groups*, 4th ed. (New York: Thomas Y. Crowell, 1958), p. 371.

18. Dahl, Robert A., *Who Governs? Democracy and Power in an American City* (New Haven, CT: Yale Univ. Press, 1961), p. 53.

19. *Pittsburgh Sun-Telegraph*, Apr. 29, 1936.

20. *Pittsburgh Press*, Sept.

21. *Pittsburgh Post-Gazette*, June 19, 1952.

22. Cornwell, Elmer E., Jr., "Party Absorption of Ethnic Groups," *Social Forces*, 38 (Mar., 1960): pp. 205-10.

23. Leuchtenburg, William, *Franklin D. Roosevelt and the New Deal* (New York: Harper & Row, 1963), pp.184-5.

24. *Pittsburgh Post-Gazette*, June 19, 1952.

25. Donaghy, Thomas J., *Keystone Democrat: David Lawrence Remembered* (New York: Vantage Press, 1986), p. 197; Weber, *Don't Call Me Boss*, p. 68.

26. *Pittsburgh Press*, June 18, 19, 1952.

27. *Ibid.*, Nov. 2, 6, 1952.

28. *Pittsburgh Sun-Telegraph*, June 19, 1952.

29. Testimony of George Leader, in "Pennsylvania Politics and Government, 1950-1970: A Round Table Discussion," *Pennsylvania History*, 59 (Oct., 1992): p. 298.

PART III
ECONOMIC LIFE: RESOURCES AND ANALYSIS

7

ITALIAN AMERICAN MERCHANTS IN THE NINETEENTH CENTURY

LUCIANO J. IORIZZO
STATE UNIVERSITY OF NEW YORK – OSWEGO

Some years ago when I was completing my dissertation on Italian immigrants, my mentor at Syracuse University suggested to me that in the future I should look at the R.G. Dun Collection in Baker Library at Harvard University. The collection contained 2500 manuscript volumes dealing essentially with merchants' credit reports (from ca. 1840s–1890s) and might be revealing of the business dealings of Italian-Americans. Many years later, while visiting my daughter who was doing graduate work at Harvard, I finally had an opportunity to look into that collection. I was intrigued by the possibilities, but put off by the sheer massiveness of material and logistical problems. This helps to explain why such a valuable collection has been so little used by researchers of the Italo-American experience. The toughest, most experienced researcher might be intimidated by the sheer volume of paper, to say nothing of the faded, difficult to read handwriting that often presents itself on the pages. Questions immediately came to mind. What kind of material is in the collection? How does it relate to the Italian-American experience? Will the finished product be worth the effort? In business terms, what is the bottom line? Will it pay off? Not in dollars and cents, to be sure. They are not the currency of historians. Rather will the initial results encourage further research? What can this probing reveal about Italian-Americans in general? Their character? Their habits? Their behavior? Their lifestyles? Their personalities? Their patterns of migration? Their dreams? Fulfilled? Shattered? Their willingness to interact with the larger community? To intermarry? Will the broader quest bring us to a more accurate portrayal of the Italian-Americans' saga? Did Italian-Americans have anything to offer that was different or better than American merchants? Coming just before the Civil War, in an age that has been described as a take-off period of sustained growth, did the immigrants from Italy play a significant role in that dynamic period? Will concerted research efforts add something new to the body of knowledge on Italian-Americans? Will their place in American History or Business History be any different? All of the above is predicated on the fact that one can identify the Italian-Americans in the collection. The question arises: how does one identify an Italian American?

The situation was similar to my efforts in researching Italian immigration. Little had been done on the topic. I could not find in any one source where and how many Italian immigrants there were at any given time. I proceeded to compile statistics and eventually produced a chart which detailed the number and place of existence of Italian-Americans in the United States. If I were to study a group in America, I thought it only logical to first identify that group as much as possible, to place it specifically in time and place. The same principle seemed to apply in the case of Italian-American merchants. It was essential to begin my study of Italian-American merchants by finding out how many there were and where they were located. These are two simple questions to which we may never know the answers. If we can find them, we enhance the value of the collection and open it up to widespread use. If not, the collection remains valuable for those who have a specific merchant in mind who can be located in its pages.

A sabbatical enabled me to start a serious inquiry into the R. G. Dun Collection. With the help of my wife, Martha Marilee Bridges, we sought to uncover as many Italian-American merchants as possible and to present them in a systematic fashion so as to furnish a coherent body of information that could attract scholars to the study of Italian-American merchants.

How does one identify an Italian-American in the collection? We started by carefully going over the manuscript indices and marking for further examination those names which seemed most likely to be Italian-American. Having done that we proceeded to the entries and read the comments. They often identified the subjects by nationality. Sometimes the individual turned out to be Hispanic, or French, or some other nationality. But enough of the times our selection proved to be Italian. This gave us the encouragement we needed to continue on with the study. The goal was to catalogue and index as many Italian-American names as we could find.

To date, we have examined the data for selected cities and counties in five states: California, Illinois, Louisiana, Missouri, and New York as well as the Western Territories. We found in this sampling of thousands of names that most merchants were male (93%), averaged 38 years of age, were usually married (75%), were in business from one to fifty-five years (averaging 10 years), and carried credit ratings from worst to best. Overall, a majority of Italian merchants had positive credit ratings. A minor portion was negative and the balance was mixed. Additionally, the Italian-Americans' financial worth ran the gamut from bankrupt to millionaire. That lofty latter status was attained by the Grasselli family which made its fortune in chemicals and by the merchant firm of Viosca and Piaggia who had migrated from Genoa.

Done by field agents who signed their reports in code, ratings were confidential (even today, their use is subject to restrictions) and based upon a number of factors. They reflected the judgment of these agents who often played detective and ferreted out by observation, investigation, and conversation with business associates, neighbors and even their clients the information by which to evaluate and offer some opinion as the viability of their subjects' businesses. On the positive side, agents looked for business acumen, good character, a record of prompt debt payments, the ability to operate within one's means and talent, sources and amounts of revenue, and any other signal that boded well for success. On the negative side, they sought evidence of excessive drinking, gambling, womanizing, an inclination for high-living, an inability or unwillingness to pay one's debts, a tendency to overextend oneself so as to jeopardize an otherwise profitable venture, and any sign that would signal compromising one's chance of success in business. The end result was usually a mix of tangible evidence relating directly to the economic factor and to other aspects which gave a broader picture touching upon not only the business issues but also whatever social/racial/ethnic considerations might be involved.

Preliminary inquiries reveal the data to be especially useful in many ways. Particularly striking is the spatial and occupational mobility demonstrated by many of these merchants. A number of merchants went from one type of business to another. More than a few traveled back and forth between the United States and Europe or South America on business or for health reasons. Also, uncovering sources of capital was especially instructive. Italian fishermen in California, for example, were not reluctant to invest in the undertakings of their ambitious countrymen. Whether this is an isolated case of ethnic cooperation or a theme to be found elsewhere in Italian-American business communities is not yet known. Other merchants were sponsored by wealthy parents or married into money. Still others began on a shoestring. Agents often reported on the investments of their clients and how the movement of interest rates affected their business decisions. Today, when real estate is often a sure way to upward mobility, one learns that it once had many pitfalls in a century subjected to wide swings in the economy which included deep depressions. The agents' reports told us whether or not merchants lived behind or above their shops. If they owned their buildings, its value was generally listed. If they paid rent, a figure was given. Customers were often identified by class and race. Thus, one could determine if an Italian-American merchant's trade was mostly from his/her own kind, or largely from Blacks, Asians, Hispanics, or a mixture, or whatever.

Reading through a minor portion of the entries one might conclude that the reports were not very critical. There is a tendency for some agents to use the same convenient phrases often abbreviated: "Young man of gd char & habits;" but appears to be conducted correctly;" "Gd character. In gd standing;" "gd for any obligation he is likely to assume;" "cr gd for his wants;" "a gd risk: "His credit is good, considered safe;" " doing a gd little bus, has some means." But, if one reads enough of these reports, it is clear that agents were not reluctant to call them as they saw them: "is a worthless fellow, a hard drinker and is barely making a living:" (One need not add that the unfortunate merchant was not a good credit risk); "gd cr but spends as fast as he makes it." Remarks on a printer included "Has a few types and sets up a card or sm order & hires the use of a press. Is worth nothing;" "has many judgements against him. Is a deadbeat."

Typically, the entries described the Italian-American merchants as being modest in means and active "go ahead" fellows. That they took full advantage of the opportunity that was America comes through clearly in these reports. One such example is that of Giuseppe Ginocchio who in 1873 was identified as an Italian, single, and 33 years old. He came to California in 1856 when he was 16 years old and sought his fortune in mining for two years. He then opened a general store but failed. After clerking for a few businesses, he started his own commission house in San Francisco in 1870 on a shoestring. By 1877 Ginocchio was worth close to $50,000 net. Industrious with good habits and fair ability, he often moonlighted as a speculator with job lots of merchandise and met his obligations promptly. He fared better than most Italian immigrants. He did well! But more impressive is the fact that so many Italian merchants started with little and accumulated thousands of dollars in a relatively short time.

There is not time to go into detail on the extraordinary stories of people like Domingo Ghirardelli, of chocolate fame; Carlo Barsotti, the editor and publisher of Il Progresso Italo-Americano in New York City, Eugene Grasselli, of Grasselli Chemicals which eventually merged with DuPont and the like. Nor of other famous Italian-Americans whose stories can be found in the collection. People like Giovanni F. Secchi DeCasali, a teacher who came to the United States in 1843, started *L'Eco d'Italia* (the first important Italian-American newspaper) in 1849, and was worth about $5,000 in 1860; the political exile, General Giuseppe Avezzana, Judge Charles A. Rapallo (possibly the first Italian-American justice in New York City). And on and on. To dat, we have found more than 1,300 likely Italian-American merchants in Brooklyn and Manhattan. New Orleans has close to 350 names including Beltramo, Pellegrini, Sbarboro, Stella, Vigo; and San Francisco contains over 75 merchants with prominent names such as Cuneo, Fontana, Fugazi, and Ghirardelli. Chicago has close to 200 entries which are likely Italian-Americans with some familiar family names such as Brizzolara, Cuneo, Rolle and Sbarboro. St. Louis also has close to 200 entries with names such as Anselmi,

Devoto, Rossi and Solari. And in the Western Territories, names are liberally
sprinkled with Italians who served as miners and farmers, but mostly as operators of general stores and saloons frequented by a diverse frontier population.

What I have tried to do is whet the appetite of scholars. I will gladly
share my list with them. But, more importantly I would hope that they would
make their own lists from the collection. What will emerge, I am convinced,
is that the story of Italian merchants is one that reflects the interaction of
diverse peoples, the bringing together of people of different ethnic groups and
faiths. It is the story of an Italian-American business network often rooted in
family, but also inter-ethnic cooperation. Anyone who looks through the indices in the R. G. Dun Collection cannot fail to see that a diverse ethnic community was a vital part of grassroots frontier America as well as of an emerging urban nation. It gives us a clearer realization, indeed a mosaic detailing,
of the pluralist features that have shaped America.[1]

NOTES

1. Material in this paper was drawn from the R.G. Dun Collection, Baker Library, Harvard
University. See entries by state and city. It should be noted also that, in addition to individuals,
institutions like the Italian-American Bank are listed. Moreover, for those interested in broader
ethnic history, the same kinds of material are available for other ethnic groups. See, for example,
the City of Chicago and entries such as Gazet Polska Catoliche, German-American Publishing
Co., Scottish-American Mortgage Co., Scandinavian Printing Co., Swedish Lutheran Publishing Co., etc.

Author's note: Since this paper was delivered, an article which expands on this material and
contains documentation has been accepted for publication. See Luciano J. Iorizzo, "The R.G.
Dun Collection's Assessments of Merchants: A Neglected Source for Italian-American Studies," in Tomasi, Lydio, Piero Gastaldo, and Thomas Row (eds.), *The Columbus People Perspectives in Italian Immigration to the Americans and Australia* (New York: Center for Migration
Studies, forthcoming), pp. 509-22. In addition, a research note containing additional information is slated for publication in *Italian-Americana* in 1994.

     I would like to thank the staff in Special Collections at Baker Library for enthusiastic
and caring assistance, SUNY and the College at Oswego, which granted a sabbatical, allowing
me time to undertake this project, and Dun and Bradstreet for permission to publish the findings.

8

VENGO PER FARE L'AMERICA: THE SOJOURNER BUSINESSMAN

MICHAEL LA SORTE
SUNY BROCKPORT

"'Making America'. . . means that a nobody, a mere clodhopper, a good-for nothing on the other side, had contrived by hook or crook in this new, strange country, with its queer ways and its lack of distinctions, to amass enough money to strut about and proclaim himself the equal of those who had been his superiors in the old country."

Garibaldi M. Lapolla, *The Grand Gennaro* (1935)

Despite the prevalence of the sojourner during various phases of Italian emigration to the United States, the prevailing literature has given this type of immigrant insufficient analytic treatment. For the most part the sojourner has been generalized as a laborer who, forced by circumstances, left Italy temporarily for America to seek any kind of work to support himself and his family, left behind in the mountain village. Although there is sufficient reason to believe that many, if not most, sojourners did fit this profile, there were others who came not to earn a pittance, but with the intention of making much money over a short period of time. They included immigrant and work agents and other exploiters of Italian muscle. While these less savory immigrant capitalists have been documented, little has been said about the legitimate immigrant businessmen, those who comprised the emerging middle class in the Italian colonies. They gathered together sufficient capital to open and operate groceries, meat shops, a variety of service agencies (bankers, travel agents, undertakers), saloons, and other retail enterprises. Although the risk of failure was high and the economies of the Italian colonies were often depressed, some of these businessmen made substantial profits and returned to Italy in the full glory of their successes.[1]

This paper focuses on the most common immigrant retail establishment, the grocery. The grocery as it evolved in the late 1800s and into the 20th century will be discussed. Central to the paper will be an analysis of the unpublished life histories of two young immigrant grocers—one who did "make America" and one who did not.

Before 1870, in most large American cities, central land use was dominated by multi-functional warehouses. General retailing was unspecialized and widely dispersed throughout the city. Essential staples were provided by general stores and peddlers. Between 1870 and 1900, the downtown areas were developed into specialized retailing districts. Separate butcher, baker, cobbler, hat, dress, and grocery stores were built next to one another to form shopping centers.[2]

European immigrants brought with them from their native villages the same concept of retailing. Most immigrant retailers served the needs of their fellow countrymen, with some moving aggressively into the wider community to seek out a larger, more diverse clientele with greater purchasing power. Greeks opened groceries, confectioneries, coffee houses, and other small businesses. The Irish went into groceries, dry goods, and shoemaking. Many immigrant German industrialists began their careers as successful grocers. The saloon was a fixture in every Ukrainian neighborhood as was the grocery store. Syrians and Jews went from peddling into the food business and operated clothing, jewelry, and tailor shops.[3] By the turn of the century, the number of retail merchants per 1,000 employed men in the large cities was greater for the European-born than for natives.[4]

Of the immigrant retailing enterprises, the most common was the grocery. This was especially the case for the Italians, who quickly became highly visible in the grocery, fruit, and meat trades. In Utica, N.Y., in 1900, 27 Italian grocers and butchers accounted for over 16 percent of the town's businesses. The proportion of Italian grocers in New Orleans was 19 percent in 1900 and 49 percent in 1920.[5] Most of the first Italians to settle in Rochester, N.Y., in the 1880s and 1890s were fruit vendors. By 1900 there were at least a dozen fruit stands scattered throughout the city. The fruit men extended their businesses beyond their shops by hiring men to peddle fruit on the street and from door to door. During the next decade, with the rapid increase in the Italian population, Rochester saw the development of several Italian-owned businesses, especially the grocery store.[6] At first groceries, fruits, and meat were provided by separate establishments in the United States. By the First World War, these three businesses were in the process of being combined into one. The Italian food market came into being with the modernization of food retailing in the 1920s and 1930s.[7]

There are many reasons for the popularity of food retailing among immigrant businessmen. Since the Italians knew little English and preferred to deal only with *paesani*, they needed stores of their own. They were also partial to their own ethnic foods. With the creation of the immigrant colonies, therefore, came a variety of opportunities for food vendors. The grocery store was an easy-entry business because it required little capital. And that capital was quickly raised by borrowing from friends and relatives, who would charge no interest, as the Italian immigrant was as likely to borrow as to loan. (Banking among friends was informal; that man who at the moment was making the most money became the de facto loaner.) The money could also be borrowed from an Italian banker.

Thus, startup costs could be met, and overhead costs, although sometimes burdensome, could be kept low in one-man operations and family-owned shops. In addition, in many cases the owner needed no previous experience. He would purchase his goods wholesale at the lowest price, add a markup, display the food, and wait for the customers to come in and buy from him.[8]

Customer loyalty was crucial to success in a business that was overcrowded and very competitive. If the grocer failed to please his customers, and his friends and closest *paesani* did not frequent his shop on a regular basis, the business was in jeopardy. Expanding the range of clientele in an Italian colony was difficult and the small grocery was always at the mercy of customers with little money to spend and a local economy that was often linked to the fortunes of one industry, where most of the Italians worked. Those few grocers who were successful would often expand to a more profitable enterprise, such as a bar, liquor store or cigar shop. Such grocers, as they accumulated wealth and property, might quit the business entirely, leaving the field open to another enterprising immigrant, who was eager to work for himself rather than for others.

The grocer worked on a very close margin. His profits were more likely measured in pennies rather than dollars. The business had to be a model of economy to survive. A national study of meat markets in 1919 revealed that average net profits were only about two percent of sales. The cost of meat alone came to 81 percent of receipts. Half of the markets had gross receipts under $20,000 a year, a volume which could sustain only a one-man operation. To produce sufficient volume, therefore, it was necessary for the grocer to work longer hours than the immigrant factory laborer. The standard day at the turn of the century ran from early morning to at least ten in the evening each day except Sunday, when the shop would close at noon. Some men averaged 88 hours a week.[9] Despite this work pace, profit margins could still remain slim and the business could fail. But there was money to be made and in large amounts. There were those who were able to make substantial profit within the space of a few years. A percentage of those men would take their earnings and return to Italy, either for an extended stay or permanently, where the money was spent on improving living standards for themselves and their families.

We will now illustrate some of these general statements about the immigrant grocer and his business life through the utilization of case materials gathered on two sojourners who came to America prior to the First World War.[10] Like many of their compatriots, they believed America to be a land of opportunity for those with ambition and determination.

During the early 1900s more and more Italians were being attracted to Utica, New York, to work in the expanding textile mills. One of these immigrants was 20-year-old Giovanni Catucci who after spending a few weeks in the South Bronx went to Utica to work in the mills. Within a few months, he had become a grocery clerk and by late 1907 had begun to look to buy his own business. Needing a partner who was an experienced butcher to complete his combination grocery/meat store, he appealed to a friend in the South Bronx to recommend someone.

Vito Longo was twenty-one when he immigrated to the South Bronx in April 1907. After four jobless weeks, a friend found employment for him in a South Bronx piano factory as a polisher. He quit after a brief stay. In July, he took a job as an assistant in a butcher shop. Vito lived in a small room at the rear of the store and worked there until January 1908 when he heard about Catucci's search for a partner. Although from the same village in Italy, Longo and Catucci had known one another only by sight. Nonetheless, Longo wired Utica that he was on his way.

Longo was not happy working for someone else. His weekly wage of four or five dollars was well below what he had expected. Longo had come to America to make enough money to support both himself and his parents and siblings in Italy. Because his present position did not hold that promise, Longo wasted no time giving notice to his boss and the next day taking the early train for Utica.

Once in Utica, Longo worked out a "socio" (partnership) with Catucci. Each would take 50 percent of the business: Longo as the butcher would be responsible for the meat department, while Catucci would operate the grocery side of the store. Deciding that $155 was needed to put the business in good standing, Catucci put in 50 percent from his savings, whereas Longo had only $25 to invest. Longo would have to borrow the remaining $52.50 from his Bronx friends in order to claim a full partnership.

The store was open six and one-half days a week. The men worked from 5:30 a.m. to one in the afternoon, at which time they ate their main meal of the day, and then after a *riposo* would reopen the store until 10 p.m.

To these men who wanted to make money and return triumphantly to Italy with bulging money belts, the first few weeks were very disappointing. On some days, business was practically nonexistent. During one morning in particular, two customers came into the store and spent a total of eight cents.

From the beginning the partners were not compatible. Not only was there a clash of temperaments and work styles, Catucci kept reminding Longo of his outstanding financial obligation to the "socio." It took a few months for Longo's friends to send him money, and then it arrived piecemeal over the space of several weeks.

By the second month, business began to pick up and with that an increase in the cash flow. By late 1909, each partner was able to take money from the cash box for incidental daily expenses and draw a monthly salary of $13. An inventory showed a stock worth $175. The 1908 economic crisis was still being felt in Utica. The mills had been working reduced hours and some Italians who had not been able to find steady employment returned home. Regular customers were "put on the books" because they had no ready cash to pay for goods purchased.

By February 1910, the problems that had been brewing between the two partners became vocalized. When Longo openly accused Catucci of dishonesty, Catucci retaliated by suggesting that his partner did not know how to develop a smooth business relationship. After further discussion of their differences and a final decision that the "socio" could not endure, Longo sold his share to Catucci for one-half of the $188.50 in assets, $50 from the cash receipts and $100 from Catucci's account at the Italian bank. Longo remitted most of the money to his family and with the balance returned to his former "bosso" in the South Bronx for $6 a week and room and board.

The Utica store's business had been on the upswing and continued to prosper into 1911 when Catucci sold out to his new partner and returned to Italy with a clear profit of $2000. Meanwhile Longo, who had been looking for a butcher shop to buy, in April of the same year bought a "bottega" on 151st Street from a man who had decided to return home for an extended visit. After much bargaining, the men settled for $550. Longo gave the owner $420 in cash which he had gathered together from those who owed him and by cleaning out his bank account. The remaining $130 would be sent to the former owner in monthly installments.

After investing an additional $120 in repairs and new equipment, Longo had his grand opening and waited for his friends and *paesani* to buy from him. Business was good for the first few days and then went into an unpredictable pattern of good weeks and poor weeks. Some weeks would produce as little as $2 or $3 in net profit; during other weeks Longo would clear over $20. Although one or two of his unemployed friends helped out on occasion for no pay and he did hire a boy to work part time, the "bottega" was essentially a one-man operation. The long hours, small profits, and the apparent attempt by one of his competitors to keep the *paesani* women from shopping at his store by spreading false rumors about him soon took a toll on Longo's morale and endurance. When the former owner returned from Italy after six months and offered to buy the business back for $337, Longo took the cash and walked out.

That same day Longo invested $200 with a friend who had two large shops employing several clerks, one in the Bronx and the other in downtown Manhattan. Longo worked in both for a few months, earning $10 a week and a small return on his investment. The two shops did a very brisk business as they were able to draw on a clientele well beyond the confines of any one *paesano* neighborhood.

Longo's succession of jobs as a clerk and his business failures convinced him that he was not going to find his fortune in America, or at least the fortune was not going to come to him as dramatically as it had to others. His last job was with the brother of a friend who had recently purchased a store on 154th Street in the Bronx. Longo worked there long enough to earn passage back to his native village.

The immigrants had a saying: "Vengo per fare l'America," which can be understood to mean that there was money to be made in America. The proof was there for all to see whenever someone like Giovanni Catucci returned carrying more dollars earned in four years than an Italian farm laborer could earn in a lifetime. Catucci made it look easy and undoubtedly the success of men of his caliber caused many others to take the immigrant trail.

Compared to Catucci, Vito Longo was a failure. He had returned with little more than spare change and a record of lost opportunities. To be sure, Longo was able to support himself at a level above that of the immigrant laborer and at the same time fulfill his filial obligation by contributing to his family's finances—probably much more than he could have had he remained at home to work. But given Longo's expectations—his ambition to succeed through the accumulation of wealth and his desire to raise not only his status but also that of the other family members—he fell far below that which he expected of himself and that which others thought he ought to have achieved.

If the typical Italian immigrant had realizable goals in terms of monetary gain, men like Giovanni Catucci and Vito Longo were far from typical. They were more capitalistic than most native-born Americans. They also accepted without condition and perhaps somewhat naively that American society and its freedoms allowed anyone with enough gumption to move beyond the station in life to which he had been born. Both of these individualists had high achievement orientations, much too high for the Italian economy of the day and notably higher than those of the American working class. Such immigrant businessmen were not driven from Italy by misery and want. Rather they were pulled across the Atlantic by the lure of wealth far exceeding their boyhood dreams. But that wealth was not there for the taking; the streets were not paved with gold. The competition was fierce; the risk of failure almost a certainty; the opportunities for business in the immigrant community severely circumscribed; the essential personal characteristics of luck, pluck, greed, and deviousness in short supply, as were sophistication and education. Thus there were more Vito Longos than Giovanni Catuccis. Yet given the heavy burden of the immigrant status under which these men labored and lived, one might wonder how did it happen that there were as many of the latter.

NOTES

1. In the prevailing literature the term sojourner has received a number of applications. One application comes under the term "middleman minority" and refers to the businessman who plays a middle role between producer and consumer. Middleman minority has encompassed such groups as the Chinese and Jews. Although the terms sojourner and middleman have theoretical similarities, the former is less precise in meaning and the latter does not appear applicable to the Italian immigrant experience. Sojourner suggests a person who did not plan to settle permanently. He came to make money, not to spend it. To that end the sojourner sought easily liquidatable and transportable occupations.

A major problem with the sojourner concept is the question of subjective intention. It is difficult to determine whether any emigrating Italian could have been classified clearly as an immigrant or a sojourner without accurate knowledge of motives, which could have been vague initially and overtime subject to reexamination as conditions warranted. Some had no intention of settling and did not. Others wished to do so but did not. Many initially had no intention to stay but remained. And there were those who never consciously made a decision one way or another, but stayed tied emotionally to the home village, visiting often, and dying either in America or Italy. In the two case studies presented here, one man fits the first type and other the last. See George Anthony Peffer, "From Under the Sojourner's Shadow," *Journal of American Ethnic History* 11 (Spring, 1992): 41-67; Edna Bonacich, "A Theory of Middleman Minorities," *American Sociological Review* 38 (October, 1973): 583-94.

2. David Ward, *Cities and Immigrants* (N.Y.: Oxford Univ. Press, 1971), pp. 94-99.

3. The following sources were consulted: Michael La Sorte, "Immigrant Occupations: A Comparison," in Richard Juliani and Philip Cannistraro (eds), *Italian Americans: The Search for a Usable Past* (Staten Island: American Italian Historical Association, 1989), pp. 84-91; Dennis Clark, *The Irish in Philadelphia* (Phila.: Temple Univ. Press, 1973); Albert Faust, *German Element in the United States* (N.Y.: Steuben Society of America, 1927); Wasyl Halich, *Ukrainians in the United States* (Chicago: University of Chicago, 1937); Philip M. Kayal, *The Syrian Lebanese in America* (N.Y.: Columbia University, 1954); Theodore Saloutos, *The Greeks in the United States* (Cambridge: Harvard University, 1964).

4. Julian L. Simon, *The Economic Consequences of Immigration* (Cambridge: Basil Blackwell, 1989), p. 72. For a general discussion of immigrant entrepreneurs, see Alejandro Portes and Ruben G. Rumbant, *Immigrant America* (Berkeley: University of California, 1990), p. 57-93.

5. David Brody, *The Butcher Workmen* (Cambridge: Harvard University, 1964), p. 203; Andrew Sanchirico, "Small Business and Social Mobility Among the Italian Americans," in Dominic Candeloro, F. L. Gardaphe and P. A. Giordano (eds), *Italian Ethnics* (Staten Island: American Italian Historical Association, 1990), pp. 202-03.

6. Source: *U.S. Federal Manuscript Census*, 1910, for Rochester, N.Y.

7. Carl W. Dipman, *The Modern Grocery Store* (N.Y.: The Progressive Grocer, 1931).

8. A wholesaler: "I do not call a man a butcher who will start a meat market. Most of them just buy their meat here." The wholesale house would cut the meat to the customers' needs and preferences, and deliver. The retailer would then display and sell the cuts. Brody, op. cit, p. 9.

9. Ibid, p. 9-10; Dipman, op. cit, p. v, 3.

10. The material presented here was collected during the 1980s as part of an oral history project. The data derive basically from two sources: the collection of family histories and conversations with two relatives and a former friend of Giovanni Catucci and Vito Longo. (The names are fictitious.) Part of the research was supported by a generous grant from the Casa Italiana, Rochester, N.Y. The author is grateful for the valuable assistance of Michelle Palmiotto and Mary Di Muro.

9

LIGURIAN MERCHANTS: BETWEEN ITALY AND THE AMERICAS

ADELE MAIELLO
UNIVERSITY OF GENOVA

The purpose of this paper is to present a still ongoing research project that attempts to retrace the history of Ligurian emigrants to the Americas. The first part of the research, that which is already finished, has examined the emigration and its results on Ligurian society and has suggested some possible fields of investigation regarding the results of their settlements in the Americas.[1]

This paper expresses the conviction that only by means of a comparative study of the various situations established in different countries by the same community (national, ethnic or cultural) can historians understand the level of reciprocal interaction between immigrants and residents in the new country. One helpful result of comparative analysis could be in distinguishing aspects of the social behaviour of immigrants that derived from their original culture from other aspects that resulted from the impact between two cultures. Another result could be the possibility of reconstructing the way in which social classes were shaped in the new world, and seeing which parts of this process were the direct offspring of a previous culture and what the cultures involved were.

The present paper presents the first results of this research and some important suggestions coming out of it. To this purpose it is useful to focus the analysis on Ligurian merchants, their behaviour, and the values they communicated to the two societies they lived in. We shall see how they went to the new land with a strong sense of initiative and openness to risk, often behaving more as permanent settlers rather than as temporary emigrants. If in this way they succeeded in making a contribution of their own to building a new country, they did not, on the other hand, transplant there a comparable sense of social commitment in everyday life. In some exceptional cases, however, they also brought the contribution of their bravery to the political life of the new society.

Later on, when we examine their behaviour upon their return to the mother-country, we will also discover their strong commitment to the improvement of Italian social life. This seems to be the most important legacy they received from the new society they settled in.

The merchants were the most significant economic and social figures in the regional population abroad. Moreover, they possessed a strong attachment to their mother-country which they not only retained through their own lives but passed along to their children. As a result, the merchants came to represent a cultural bridge between the two sides of the ocean. Moreover, the choice of studying their presence in South and North America springs from the results of the research already mentioned, which suggests a comparison between their presence in much earlier settlements such as Argentina and California, where traces of them still exist today.

Their importance to the whole history of Italian emigration to the Americas relates to the image they communicated to their contemporaries. This image is totally different from the ethnotype of the Italian that has affirmed itself in the mind of most Americans.[2] Their importance also relates to the quality of their achievements that made important contributions to the receiving societies even though their numbers were small.

Another word on the period chosen: it is twofold, because in describing the American setting of the story it is necessary to go back in time to the beginning of the 19th century. At the same time to give the idea of how the image of this emigration returned to its mother-country, it is useful to concentrate on the end of the 19th and the beginning of the 20th century.

By then, Ligurians as a community had already settled for at least a century in the above-mentioned states and their influence there was a consolidated feature of the local societies. Meanwhile Italy had already felt the positive result of their American experience at a time when the rest of the national migratory experience was very poor.

The reason for the last characteristic of Ligurian emigration can be partly traced to its regional culture. In Liguria, in spite of the amount of suffering and trouble, which is suggested in any case by the mere idea of emigration, it does not seem to have had its origin in any traumatic uprooting. Moreover, in spite of the fact that most Ligurian families have relatives in many parts of the world, the local culture has not produced any dramatic epic of emigration as, on the contrary, has been the case of Southern Italy.

As it will be shown later, this is due to the timing of the exodus, the way it happened, and its protagonists; but it is also due to the diffusion of a sort of "migration culture" among the population of the region, including that part of it not immediately involved in the departure.

It must be remembered that Liguria occupies a very narrow and relatively long part of the Italian coast between steep mountains and the sea and that therefore a part of its population was involved in a very poor agriculture in which the integration of seasonal migration to work in richer places elsewhere was indispensable to achieving a minimum subsistence; but also the population involved in the sea-life on the coast had to accept, for obvious reasons, the basic rule of daily distance from relatives and friends.

The choice of emigrating did involve pain and sorrow for Ligurians; there is no question about that. If we consider that the parliamentary enquiry of 1876 into the traffic in children showed that 35% of Italian traffickers were concentrated in the narrow territory of the valleys around Chiavari (the Ligurian town famous for its chairs and slate), and that they did not steal the children, but just bought them from the parents involved in the "survival" economy already described,[3] we can easily recognize the underlying misery. In fact, these miseries were so familiar as to be considered part of everyday life.

Moreover, the very same familiarity was at the origin of the lack of interest in the subject shown by scholars, who for many years treated it as a non-existent theme. It not by chance that it was first studied by an economic historian, Giuseppe Felloni[4] and a geographer-demographer, Gaetano Ferro,[5] both while doing research of a general nature on the region. Even now that emigration has been analyzed in new studies following the "oral history" or the wider "social history" approach, and using a paradigm of the "history of subordinate classes," the Ligurian case has not been studied in itself, but only as a part of the history of Italian peasant migration, in the period for which private documents such as letters or interviews are still available.[6]

It is rewarding from the historical point of view to retrace the particular Ligurian contributions to the receiving societies because with the same values they were also able to cooperate in building a new society at home. To reconstruct all of this it is necessary to go back in time to a period when Ligurians were received into social and territorial contexts that were still sufficiently shapeless or malleable.

At the present state of the research it is only possible to proceed by inference. We can pick out those parts of their history already written and try to understand through the combination of American and Italian witnesses what kind of image of themselves they left out and what kind of influence they had on the collective mentality in Liguria.

In the long run, historical processes or accidental circumstances, such as the prevailing of the Atlantic routes of trade over the Mediterranean ones from the 16th century onward, or the Napoleonic occupation (1797-1799), or the absorption of the Ligurian Republic into the Sardinian-Piedmontese Kingdom in 1815, gave both incidental or structural impulse to the choice of Genoese and Ligurian sailors and merchants to leave their country seeking a new life and fortune elsewhere or just to settle after arriving at the port of destination of some chance trip. Consequently as already in the 18th century, the future republics of Plata (Argentina and Uruguay) in South America received Ligurians[7] and they spread all over the American continent, reaching California in the following years.

During the first part of the 19th century, sailors and merchants were joined by liberal or Mazzinian republican exiles. It is true that the latter had as their essential aim the political restoration of their country from outside, but nevertheless endowed by their new life with suitable economic means and with another culture, in many cases decided to settle permanently in the new country, after being disappointed in their political hopes.

LIGURIANS IN ARGENTINA

In places like Argentina or California, there was enough room for the Ligurians to assert themselves both as a group and as individuals. Here their inflow into the new world was part of a pioneering stage of the populating of these lands, and it was successful to the point of giving a basic imprint to periods of local history. An example of this is the case of Argentina in which historians have singled out a "Ligurian stage,"[8] when we find a Ligurian fighter, Manuel Belgrano, at the origin of its independence from Hispanic rule as well as another Ligurian, Giuseppe Garibaldi at the origin of its independence from the dictatorship of Rosas.[9] We continue to find Ligurians, sailors and merchants, offering the Argentineans the service of their ships and intrepidity for the indispensable transport of goods all over the country. The same people who were promoting manufacturing and industrial activities were connected with shipping.[10]

These Ligurians presented themselves as a community so homogeneous as to lead historians such as Mario Nascimbene to define them as a sort of ethnic group.[11] They were also occupied in similar professions with such skill and efficiency as to induce another of the first historians who studied them, Niccolò Cuneo, to describe even their political commitment in the following way:

> L'emigrazione italiana di questo periodo è costituita, in primo luogo, da esuli politici del 1848 e del 1849 e questi in parte provengono dell'Uruguay, dove hanno seguito il Mitre, che fu commilitone loro sugli spalti delle barricate; in parte giungono dall'Italia con biglietto pagato da parenti e amici che hanno talvolta costituito e consolidato in precedenza cospicue fortune. I primi, garibaldini romantici, sono in prevalenza lombardi; i secondi, lavoratori parsimoniosi, sono quasi tutti genovesi.[12]

The geographical concentration in Argentina, due probably to the kind of settlement chosen (the port of La Boca), accentuated their homogeneity. One sign of this is probably to be traced to a characteristic that in other historical contexts might mean the opposite: the lack of mutual aid societies. As it was, the presence of a compact and homogeneous group, interconnected in the way we have already seen, made this kind of association pointless. It would be further regional differentiation among Italians which rendered them necessary. The Ligurians perhaps behaved more as an interest group than as an ethnic group, according to the definition of ethnicity given by Breton[13] and referred to by Nascimbene, by the use among Ligurians of the same language, the Genoese dialect. In this case, however, the definition of this group must be supplemented by the use of a stronger category, that stresses its socio-economic behaviour, so united and similar did they appear to contemporaries as well as to historians.

Their "golden period" in Argentinean history came to a close in the 1850s. By the end of that period, they had established solid, collective as well as individual, positions, in Argentinean society. They were making fruitful matrimonial contracts with women belonging to the local establishment and organizing increasingly frequent partnerships with Lombards and Piedmontese in new economic activities.[14] Furthermore, they had been able to spread the image of their success.

We find important evidence for this point in an article published in 1868 by a newspaper in Friuli-Venezia Giulia, a region in northern Italy a long way from Liguria and with large scale emigration on the part of its own poor population:

> C'è una emigrazione, la quale nasce spontanea, cresce da
> sé ed è fruttuosa agli emigranti ed al paese dove và, come
> al paese donde parte. C'è una provincia dell'Italia, la
> Liguria, ch'è fatta ricca ed industre dalla stessa povertà del
> suo suolo. I brulli Appennini, accostandosi al mare,
> lasciano nella Liguria poco spazio ai coltivatori, i quali
> però di quel poco ne fecero tanti giardini, ebbene i liguri
> diventarono marinai... i liguri oltre a popolare il loro paese,
> oltre all'avere una numerosa marineria, popolano
> l'America meridionale. Centomila almeno si trovano già

stabiliti al Rio de la Plata dei quali circa ottantamila nella Repubblica Argentina e molti altri poi nel Chile, nel Perù, e via via. Il paese però dove abbonda l'emigrazione italiana è per lo appunto il Rio de la Plata. Colà quegli operosi ed industri emigranti arricchiscono con la parsimonia e col lavoro e ormai giovano a sé stessi e alla madrepatria.[15]

"Industrious", "frugal", and "hard-working" are the attributes singled out by these contemporary accounts; "thrifty workers" is the definition chosen by Cuneo. Such qualities, which sprang from the hard life they lived at home, impressed the Ligurians on the attention of their contemporaries.

Interestingly enough, this well-structured community presented another feature with parallels to the community found in California, namely the social division. On one hand, the great majority of Ligurians were often of low social origins, held liberal or Mazzinian republican ideas, and were therefore also antimonarchic and antipiedmontese. A smaller group, with higher social backgrounds, included diplomats, ship-owners and traders. At first very deeply divided by political as well as economic differences, the differences between these two groups faded as sailors and merchants began to climb the social ladder.[16]

It is to the Ligurian community in Argentina that historians give the credit for the high social position later shared by the whole north-west Italian community, which prevailed in the following period. In any case, the attenuation of the economic factor as a source of distinction within the community in the Argentinean case did not involve the decline of the Ligurians, who continued to succeed, but more as individuals than as a community. In this later period community values were safeguarded through the founding of regional mutual aid societies, which also exercised an important function in promoting young people's education. Besides the "Societé des Genois" of which virtually only the name is known and which belongs to the earliest period of the Ligurian settlement in Argentina,[17] the first mutual aid society, the 'Società di Beneficenza per l'Ospedale Italiano', was founded in 1853, as the result more of the politics of the Regno di Sardegna, which wanted to provide the national community abroad with a hospital, than of local initiative.[18] It was not until the 1870's that regional mutual aid societies became important and they mostly represented communities of the northern regions of the Italian peninsula.[19]

LIGURIANS IN CALIFORNIA

The story of the Ligurian presence in California shows, in a different context, some important similar characteristics. The first immigrants to arrive from a still divided Italy were Genoese sailors, usually coming from South America, either in the period of Hispanic or of Mexican dominion.[20] It was still before the time of the Gold Rush, that exiles of the uprising of 1830 arrived, sometimes via London or South America, whereas the exiles of the 1848 uprising arrived at the same time as the gold diggers.

Until 1848, California belonged to Mexico as a region, an almost empty land, where immigrants and settlers had to create the very possibility of living in that territory, and where there was no predominance of any particular ethnic group. As a consequence of this "lack of predominance" they had the greatest possibility of creating a state according to their own ideas, which were much nearer to European examples than to the American one.[21]

From the economic point of view too, the possibilities in California were greater than in Argentina, both as a result of this lack of predominance of one ethnic group and because its nature and climate recalled the Mediterranean coasts.[22]

Even though concentrated in some areas of the large territory, the Ligurians were more spread out than in Argentina. Therefore over the years and especially after 1848 they were able to occupy economic fields such as agriculture and fishing, not only as merchants, but also as producers. Exceptionally too, they were also able to buy land from the very beginning.[23] The result of all this was that the foundations were laid for the large entrepreneurial fortunes that partly followed and partly created the evolution of the economy and society of California.

We can find the first traces of similarities between these settlers and the ones in Argentina reflected in the report of Federico Biesta, acting Sardinian consul in 1856:

> But what I can say. . .with a feeling of national pride is that
> the Italian population is one of the best, most active and
> hard working in California. Strong, industrious and accus-
> tomed to suffering and toil, our nationals tend to run their
> own affairs without taking part in those regrettable disor-
> ders that the heterogeneous people of the State give vent
> to from time to time.[24]

The majority of that population had come from Liguria. It seems unnecessary to point out that they are here described with similar attributes to the
ones seen in the preceding context: industrious, accustomed to sufferings and
toil, active and hard-working.

They were also alike in another important characteristic, i.e., the social
division within the community, which here was even more marked than in
Argentina. As we have already seen—since the times, the people and the
culture were the same—the exiles went to the Americas with no idea of stay-
ing but with the fundamental aim of promoting political change at home and
then coming back. The result of this attitude was a lack of commitment to the
public life of the community, which as in Argentina was split between merchants, sailors and countrymen on the one side and the exiles, who usually
belonged to the upper classes and were frequently of the nobility, on the other
one.[25]

The latter group and a part of the former (especially those who arrived
before the Gold Rush) came with enough money to start trades of their own.
They suffered great embarrassment at the presence of that mass of people of
humbler backgrounds who had arrived with the sole aim of finding gold and
who more frequently found only disease and bad luck and, as a result, did not
show any sign of solidarity with them. To sum up, the richer Ligurians did
not show themselves as leaders in the public life of the community, but they
were involved in another kind of 'solidarity' on a village or regional basis in
private as well as in the economic matters.

This situation meant, for example, that after occupying the field of
vegetable and fruit merchandising as well as production Ligurians did not
want to share control of these activities with other groups. We find evidence

for this conclusion in other consular reports written in 1868 and 1872 by the
first Italian consul in San Francisco, Giovanni Battista Cerruti, not by chance
a Ligurian:

> Molti agricoltori provengono da Genova. Sono efficienti e
> bene organizzati; e soprattutto intendono esercitare un
> monopolio sul loro settore. . . I Genovesi non intendono
> dividere il loro utile con altri Italiani. Se è necessaria
> manodopera agricola, i Genovesi fanno arrivare un parente
> o un amico dall'Italia, piuttosto che offrire un lavoro ad un
> italiano da un'altra regione.[26]

However, they did accept the sharing of a part of the marketing with Tuscans
from Lucca.[27]

The same thing happened in the field of fishing, where after a long fight
they were forced to accept the Sicilian presence after a long fight, but in both
cases they realistically compromised at a moment when they could still keep
the best part of the field for themselves and were able to embark on new and
even more profitable activities such as banking.[28] Rapid growth and change
of the society[29] led to a loss of some of their cultural peculiarities or at least
of their regional loyalties though there has been a long and involved debate
among scholars from many disciplines about the reasons for this change.[30]

Regarding the experience of the entrepreneurial part of the Ligurian
community, it is valuable to analyze their economic behaviour and its social
consequences, even though it may not be possible to make generalizations
about their experience that can be applied to other Italian Americans. It reflects, nevertheless, the pragmatic and professional culture of the Ligurians
as a group, which was not yet really Italian. It was, in particular, their keen
sense of economic trends and industrial development which gave them the
key to change and to transforming their regional mentality in the way that has
been described as "national", but which should be called "American" for
reasons we shall see.

For example, in the settled industries, which were at first for the most
part in the alimentary field and producing for a restricted market, the work
followed seasonal rhythms and did not require the continuous presence of an

often unqualified labor force, which was mostly regional. At the end of the 19th century the enlargement of the market, the introduction of machines into the cycle of production, and the reorganization on industrial bases of the agricultural production led to two different results.

One was the reorganization of the productive cycle of the alimentary industries without seasonal interruptions, a situation that required a limited turn over of workers. To have only employees from the same region did not fulfil this need for stability, for the reason that regional loyalty did not promote the desire to stay permanently in the new country. For other reasons, too, regional loyalty kept the market restricted. So these industries started assuming Italians from any region, but only, I should say, because Italians at that time were "cheap labor", and not because of any change of loyalty in a "national" sense. As a matter of fact the same thing was being done by most of industrialists in the rest of the States.[31]

The other result was the need of the enlargement and definition of the function of banks.[32] When agricultural production industrialized, it needed a specialized form of distribution, that bought the products in advance. The necessity for these middlemen was such that it induced the producers, who for the most part came from Ligurian hinterland, to overcome their mistrust of these traders, called "commission merchants," who for the most part came from the Ligurian coast. The trust between the two types of operators, forged on practical bases and quickly overcoming ancient suspicions, gave rise to short term loans by the commission merchants to the farmers and it was this kind of loans that underlay the emergence of the Italian banks in California. The horizons of those banks quickly enlarged and they soon needed to collect capital from outside the regional or the national community.

Merchants, industrialists and bankers were all children of the practical Ligurian mentality, able to overcome any difference of class or region in the name of efficiency and a prosperity that to be such had to be shared by the greater part of the society they belonged to. For example, when they exploited other Italians they preferred to use the economic weapons provided by a mobile society, quickly abandoning the sentimental appeals which foreshadowed 'godfather' and mafia-like exploitation.

Probably the Ligurians, with the large net of all their economic activities, succeeded in leaving something enduring both to societies like that of the USA and to that of Argentina. In the USA they succeeded in creating economic institutions and a mentality totally congenial with Anglo-Saxon ones, so that they became a part of that society leaving an imprint in things bigger than the one left in people's imagination. At any rate, it is not by chance that the best known among them is a banker, Amedeo Giannini, the founder of the Bank of America.

In Argentina too they left a mark on the collective imagination, but in a different way. Some key men in Argentinean history, like Belgrano or Garibaldi, represented the kind of Ligurian who united the traditional economic characteristics of its people—professionalism and open-mindedness —with others more congenial to the Hispanic world of values, those of bravery and initiative.

In both cases they seem to have acquired a sense of the community at large, no more restrained to a social class—as were in fact the political exiles of the beginning of the century—or to a village or a regional community; and also to have emphasized the importance of co-operation in a modern society.

LIGURIANS ABROAD AND LIGURIA

The result of their work created a sort of myth around many of those emigrants that is witnessed by the very fact that, if Liguria lacks an emigration epic as a collective drama, it boasts probably the largest number of successful emigrants recorded by any regional collective memory.

The local annals written for Santa Margherita Ligure in 1915 and covering the entire local history provides evidence of how emigration was considered. These sources document the origin of the change of Santa Margherita from a very poor fishing village into an elegant and well known tourist resort.[33] And this happened because the Sanmargheritesi who had migrated sent back a rich flow of money. However the case of Santa Margherita was not the only one witnessed by local historians. The radical change in image and individual revenue shown at the turn of the century by Ligurian towns and families, whose citizens and relatives were abroad, is still apparent today in the buildings, churches, streets and enterprises of the region.[34]

The myth of the successful emigrant flourished all over Italy,[35] making real that myth of America for which people were leaving the country in masses. Liguria had, differently from other Italian regions, the privilege of counting on a high percentage of people who had migrated and who had made their fortune, partly through their own talents and partly because their numbers were small and the circumstances were propitious, as we have seen.

In any case, to flourish, the myth needed continuous contact and a rich flow of money, both conditions fulfilled by those emigrants. They contributed to improving the quality of life for their fellow Ligurians building infrastructure, such as roads or bridges, for small villages where the State was particularly absent. Moreover, by a contribution which came directly from their American experience, they insisted on the value of education, another field where the Italian State was lacking in initiative. Nursery, elementary, technical and commercial schools were founded all over the region, and the study of Spanish and English was promoted. But this is not all, because it was American money as well which provided the initial finance for local industrialization and for the most important regional newspaper.[36]

Interestingly enough, at this point of their collective experience in the Americas, these emigrants demonstrated more social values than they had in the past. These individuals include those who left at the beginning of the 19th century as well as emigrants who left later on. What was new was their relation with society, which showed numerous signs of greater involvement in public affairs and no longer only a private life.

Making good the defects of the State in the everyday life of their former country was the easiest way to link public with private interest, not to mention the rich support they gave to the Catholic church, in terms of grants and funding for the building, renovation and enrichment of churches and chapels or for parish projects. Wills, in particular, were the occasions when the emigrants would best show the sense of public and private spirit that had ripened abroad. As a matter of course, Ligurians assigned more or less important sums of money to their own final celebration, usually for their burial, but a part of the legacy frequently went to the Church or to public institutions. Moreover, sometimes their money went directly to their former fellow villagers.

A clear example of this practice was found in the case of the Saturno brothers, whose parents left a small village near Chiavari, San Marco d'Urri, to go to California with tickets paid for by money collected by their *"compaesani" (fellow villagers)*. The family made its fortune in the United States, and the two sons, when they died without heirs, left all of their own fortune to the heirs of those *"compaesani"* of their parents. When, in 1956, this money arrived at the Cicagna branch of the Bank of America, the director had to find all the heirs. They all accepted, except one, who maintained that "nobody gives anything for nothing."[37] He did not understand the deeper meaning of the Saturnos legacy, which lay in the overcoming the private logic of *"do ut des"* by a sense of belonging to a larger society.

But the most significant way in which Ligurian emigrants formally expressed an interest in politics and traditions of their former country (and thus their regional pride) was through the building of statues of heroes of national unity, like Mazzini or Garibaldi in South America and of Columbus in North America. The commemoration of Italian soldiers who died during World War I can be interpreted the same way.

Historians who have addressed the problem of the creation of a national mentality in Italy (and it is still an unresolved question) stress celebrations of this kind as significant moments in the process of national identification.[38] Those were moments in which the emigrants participated very actively financially or which they themselves created abroad. In this context it seems that the Italianness of these emigrants was increased by the fact of being abroad and that they drew from this experience the conviction that it was time to break down the narrow boundaries of the village and of the region in favor of a larger identity.

The Catholic Church also worked through its missionaries towards the goal of keeping alive the religious feeling which it considered essential to include among the national traditions, such as a national language or national identity, which were nevertheless necessary to invent.

Without overestimating the importance of the innumerable signs of patriotism given by the emigrants abroad, it is useful to remind ourselves here of the following consideration made in those Annals of Santa Margherita Ligure quoted above:

(la) dimostrazione di schietto sentimento italiano...
(mostra) come, col diffondersi e aumentare delle
ricchezze, fosse venuto crescendo nei sanmargheritesi
lamore della comune patria (onde non sarebbe troppo
stravagante paradosso il dire che in essi l'amore per l'Italia
è venuto dall' America).[39]

Patriotic feeling became even stronger because it was made up not
only of public pride, but also of the private hearts of people, who missed
families, friends, places, food, and everyday customs. In any case beside the
more explicitly political aims pursued by the emigrants, a general lesson
emerges from their experience and this is the one they preferred to emphasize. As a matter of fact, it is clear that all the sums sent home transcended
personal celebration and became the celebration of the best civic qualities an
individual could show in a liberal society.

In addition, in this way Ligurian merchants carefully built up an
image which emphasized their achievements abroad. It does not matter that
many who helped to build this image of success were of peasant origin: the
spirit and the mentality they had developed abroad were the same as that of
the sailors and merchants at the beginning.

There are many still unanswered questions that cannot be ignored.
All this happened at the beginning of the 20th century, when the bulk of the
Italian peasants arriving in both Americas did not give a good impression. For
this reason, Italians in Italy were ashamed by the misery and ignorance shown
abroad by these emigrants and were probably also led by this shame to ex-
alt that part of the earlier emigration that had only become Italian after departure, as in the Ligurian case. Yet, we find a very positive evaluation of
Ligurians in contemporary Italian books dedicated to the best Italians abroad
with titles such as *Volere è potere* by Mario Lessona, an Italian bible of "self-
help."[40] It is a book organized into chapters, each dedicated to a region, and
the chapter dedicated to Liguria stresses that most of the region's best sons
were emigrants. This is the unique case in the whole book.[41]

We cannot really say if these characteristics were inclusive of the
entire region, as well as all generations, or rather merely belonged to the first

wave of emigrants to leave their country and who organized the bases of the communities abroad, influencing the behaviour and attitudes of the peasants who followed. At the same time we cannot forget the role played in the shaping of this image by the sort of commercial skill used by the Ligurians to propagate their greatest achievements, in conjunction with the widely felt need for national heroes in Italy, in the first part of the 20th century. All these questions are still open and the history of this group is so stimulating as to be worthy of a future study.

The comparison between the Ligurian settlers and emigrants in California and in Argentina has been made here with the aim of showing what the social behaviour at the point of departure was for the Ligurians who migrated abroad. This comparison can be also useful for understanding which kind of modification they came to make in their conceptions of social classes and the relationship between individuals and society.

What the research done in Liguria makes clear is that they exported to Italy the figure of the *"social benefactor"*, a typically American figure, which requires an active role on the part of the 'doers of good'. He doesn't give money to others because he has been asked to give to further someone else's purposes (as does for example the *"patron of the arts"*) or at least not only for that reason. The *"social benefactor"* adds to others' purposes an aim of his own: the fulfillment of his feeling of gratitude towards the society that has allowed his social advancement. This kind of feeling in the American culture can involve a political commitment on the part of the individual. In those early times, the American dream was still bright and strong and so was faith in the reliability of liberalism. The same feeling came to involve the engagement of the self-made man to propagandize the idea that the origin of his own economic success relied upon the exercise of civic virtues, among which entrepreneurial skill and social behaviour were dignified.

Thus, we describe the difference between these Americans and the first Ligurians to emigrate, whether to California or to Argentina. The originally rich and politically committed Ligurians belonged to a traditional *"ancien regime"* upper class with no aspirations to social leadership of people belonging to different social *"couches"*, but in a context completely different from the European one to which they still felt tied. The life and the economic choices they had to make in the societies of the Americas allowed their membership to a social class whose boundaries were much larger and defined more by economic success than by other elements such as family history or professional standing. Therefore, they had a different relation with other social classes and with the society as a whole.

In the long run they became convinced that their social goal in life should be that of spreading the *"spirit of capitalism"* modified by the religious conviction of human brotherhood. The latter involved helping other people to reach the same position as themselves in the new society they had helped to build.

In any case their behaviour was quite in harmony with other characteristics of Ligurian culture inherited from the past. The familiarity with the difficulties of life meant that these were considered as real challenges to improve their life and not just settle for any kind of life. We can consider this as another feature of their belonging to the 'new' mankind which was creating itself in the 'new' world according to the *"spirit of liberalism"*, without forgetting its past in the 'old' one.

NOTES

1. Maiello, A., "I genovesi e l'emigrazione: un passato da pionieri," in *L'emigrazione nelle Americhe dalla provincia di Genova*, v. I, in G. Ferro (a cura di), *Questioni generali e introduttive* (Bologna: Patron, 1990), pp.11-32; Id. (a cura di), L'emigrazione, cit., v. IV, Questioni di storia sociale, 1992, passim.
2. Ianni, F.A., "Identità etnica o etnotipo? Preliminari a un discorso sull'identità collettiva, metaforica e personale tra gli italo-americani," in *Euroamericani* (Torino: Fondazione Agnelli, 1987), 3 vv., I v., La popolazione di origine italiana negli Stati Uniti, pp.201-215.
3. Ferrari, M.E., "I mercanti di fanciulli nelle campagne e la tratta dei minori, una realtà dell'Italia tra '800 e '900," *Movimento operaio e socialista*, (a. IV, 1983), n.1.
4. Felloni, G., *Popolazione e sviluppo economico della Liguria nel secolo 19ᵉ* (Torino: ILTE, 1961).
5. Ferro, G., *Movimenti di popolazione dalla regione ligure (1951-1971)* (Genova: Istituto di Scienze Geografiche, 1973).
6. Porcella, M., *La fatica e la Merica* (Genova: Sagep, 1986); Id., "Da birbanti a emigranti," in *La via delle Americhe* (Genova: Sagep, 1989).
7. Nascimbene, M., *Historia de los Italianos en la Argentina* (1835-1920) (Buenos Aires: CEMLA, 1983), pp. 23-8.
8. Cuneo, N., *Storia dell'emigrazione italiana in Argentina* (Milano: Garzanti, 1940), pp. 350-1; Nascimbene, "Storia della collettività italiana in Argentina (1835-1965)," in *Euroamericani*,

II v., La popolazione di origine italiana in Argentina, pp. 209-43.
9. Ruiz Moreno, J., "Inizio delle relazioni fra Italia e Argentina," in *Euroamericani*, II v., pp 1-12.
10. Kroeber, C.B., *The Growth of Shipping Industry in the Rio de la Plata Region* (Minneapolis-St. Paul: Univ. of Wisconsin Press, 1952), pp. 121-5.
11. Nascimbene, M., "Storia ...," p. 215.
12. "The Italian migration of this period is made up, in the first place of political exiles of 1848 and 1849 who came partly from Uruguay, where they had followed Mitre, who was with them on the barricades; and partly they came from Italy with passage paid by relatives and friends, who in some cases had previously amassed conspicuous fortunes. The former, romantic Garibaldinians, are mostly Lombards; the latter, thrifty workers, are almost all Genoese," in Cuneo, N., "Storia ...," pp. 350-1.
13. Breton, R.J.L., *Les ethnies* (Paris: PUF, 1983).
14. Kroeber, C.B., p. 125; Donghi, T. Halperin, "La integration de los inmigrantes italianos," in F. Devoto, G. Rosoli (eds.), *La inmigracion italiana en la Argentina* (Buenos Aires: Biblos, 1985), p. 92.
15. "There is a type of emigration, which is born spontaneously and grows by itself and is as fruitful to the emigrants and to the country it goes to as to the country it comes from. There is a province in Italy (n.b., at that time regions did not exist as administrative entities), Liguria, which is being made rich and industrious by the very poverty of its soil. The bare Appennine mountains, so close to the sea, leave too little soil to the farmers, who have in any case transformed this land into hundreds of gardens. So then the Ligurians become sailors... The Ligurians in addition to populating their land, besides having a numerous fleet, populate Southern America. There are at least a hundred thousand in Rio de la Plata, eighty thousand of whom in the Argentinean Republic and many others in Chile, Peru, all the other Pacific ports as far as California. The country, however, where the Italian emigration is largest is Rio de la Plata. There those hard-working and industrious emigrants have become rich through frugality and work and are by now bringing benefit both to themselves and to their mother-country." These evaluations were made by Pacifico Valussi, a politician from Friuli in 'Il Giornale di Udine e del Veneto," 13 febbraio 1868, quoted by M. Clotilde Giuliani Balestrino, L'Argentina degli Italiani, 2 vv., Roma: Istituto dell'Enciclopedia Treccani, 1989, v. 1, p. 82.
16. Nascimbene, M., "Storia," pp. 213, 226
17. Cuneo, N., "Storia," p. 92.
18. Ruiz Moreno, J.L., *Origines de la diplomacia Italo-Argentina* (Buenos Aires: Istituto Historico de la Organisacion Nacional, 1983), p. 25
19. The list of Italian societies in the Argentinean Republic in 1906 cites Ligurian societies dating back to 1885, like the Ligure di Mutuo Soccorso in La Boca and in Barracas North (1889) and the Trionfo Ligure in Buenos Aires (1897). See E. Zuccarini, *Il lavoro degli italiani nella Argentina dal 1516 al 1910, Studi, leggende e ricerche* (Buenos Aires: Compania General de Fosforos, 1910), pp. 152 and ff. The list, from a publication made for the Milan Exposition of 1906 by I. Martignetti (Istituzioni Italiane nella Repubblica Argentina, in Gli italiani della Repubblica Argentina all'Esposizione di Milano 1906) is also quoted by M. Nascimbene, *Historia ...*, pp. 56 and ff.
20. Patrizi, E., *Gl'italiani in California* (San Francisco: L'Italia Publishing Co., 1911); Thompson, W.S., *Growth and Changes in California Population* (Los Angeles: Haynes Foundation, 1955); Nicosia, F., et al, *Italian Pioneers of California* (San Francisco: Italian American Chamber of Commerce of the Pacific Coast, 1960).
21. Gumina, D.P., *The Italians of San Francisco* (N.Y.: Center for Migration Studies, 1978), p. 12.
22. The appeal of the description on California given by the first Northern Italian immigrants

is still traceable in the memories of one of them, who arrived there drawn by those very descriptions, E.S. Falbo (translator and editor), California and the Overland Diaries of Count Leonetto Cipriani, (Portland: Champoeg Press, 1853 to 1871), pp. 1-29.

23. Drennen, A.A., "Italians in California," in G.M. Tuoni, G. Brofelli (eds.), *Attività italiane in California* (San Francisco: Mercury Press, 1929), p. 42.

24. Falbo, E.S. (translator and editor), "State of California in 1856: Federico Biesta's Report to the Sardinian Ministry of Foreign Affairs," *California Historical Society Quarterly* 52 (Dec., 1963): 325.

25. Cinel, D., "Dall'Italia a S.Francisco. L'esperienza dell'emigrazione," in *Euroamericani*, v.I, pp. 329-30 (engl.: "From Italy to San Francisco: The Immigrant Experience," in *Italian American Communities in the United States* (Stanford: Stanford Univ. Press, 1982).

26. "Many agriculturers come from Genoa. They are efficient and well organized; and above all they intend to exercise a monopoly in their field... The Genoese have no intention of sharing their profit with other Italians. If agricultural labor is needed, the Genoese get relatives and friends to come from Italy rather than offer a job to an Italian from another region." In Rapporti Consolari da San Francisco, "Corrispondenza diplomatica e consolare," Archivi del Ministero degli Esteri, Roma, 27 Settembre, 1868, May, 27, 1872, quoted also by D. Cinel, Dall'Italia, p. 346.

27. Jackson, W., *The San Francisco Wholesale Fruit and Produce Market* (San Francisco: 1926).

28. Gumina, D.P., *The Italians*, pp. 81-4; Cinel, D., "Dall'Italia," pp. 349-353.

29. Ricciardi, G.. "Le condizioni di lavoro e l'emigrazione italiana in California," *Bollettino dell'Emigrazione* 8 (1904), pp. 248-51.

30. The first historical explanation for the diffusion of nationalism among Italo-Americans followed a traditional historical-political approach, according to which the main reason was the emergence of Fascism on the international scene. See M. De Medici, "The Italian Language Press in the San Francisco Bay Area from 1930 to 1940," M.A. Thesis, Univ. of California, Berkeley, 1953. It was proposed again by J. Diggins in *Mussolini and Fascism: the View from America* (Princeton: Princeton University Press, 1972).
In times when the most popular approach to history was the political one, a social approach to the problem of the fading of regionalism among the immigrants was adopted by two sociologists. They attributed this phenomenon to the disappearance of the first generation of immigrants. See Fishman, J. and V.G. Nahirny, "American Immigrant Groups, Ethnic Identification, and the Problem of Generations," *American Sociological Review* 13 (1965). Another anticipation of a socio-historical point of view has analyzed the possibility that religious feeling and the work done by the Catholic Church among the immigrants had the greatest impact on the overcoming of regional identity. See Tomasi, S.M., *The Ethnic Church and the Integration of Italian Immigrants in The United States*, and Tomasi, S.M. and M. Engel, *The Italian Experience in the United States* (New York: Center for Migration Studies, 1970). This thesis is not shared by D. Cinel, "Dall'Italia," p. 360, who prefers a more economic approach, isolating the influence of the labor market and the politics of Italian-American banks. In another study with a more socio-historical approach, the focus of the problem has been placed on the interaction between different groups within the Italian community such as the shared everyday life of the various regional groups, or the action of the ethnic press and of their political leaders. See McBride, P., "The Italian-Americans and the Catholic Church: Old and New Perspectives", *Italian-Americana I* (1975).

31. *A History of the Labor Movement in California* (Berkeley: Univ. of California Press, 1935).

32. Cross, I.B., *Financing of Banking in California*, 3 vv. (San Francisco: S.J. Clarke, 1927); Tuoni, G.M. and G. Brogelli (eds.), *Attività italiane in California* (San Francisco: Mercury Press, 1929); Dana, J.A.P., *Giannini: Giant of the West* (New York: Prentice Hall, 1947); James, M.

and B.R. James, *Biography of a Bank: The Story of the Bank of America* (New York: Harper Bros., 1954); Giovincio, J., "Democracy in Banking: The Bank of Italy and California's Italians," *California Historical Society Quarterly* 47 (Sept., 1968):195-212; Bonadio, F.A., *A.P. Giannini: Banker, Philanthropist, Entrepreneur* (Washington, D.C.: NIAF, 1983).

33. Scarsella, A.R., *Annali di Santa Margherita Ligure dai suoi primordi sino all'anno 1914 scritti per uso dei Sanmargheritesi colti*, 2 vv. (Rapallo: Fratelli Fedele, 1915).

34. Saracco, C., "Una rete indistruttibile di denaro e di gloria: il mito dell'emigrazione nel Chiavarese," in A. Maiello (ed.), *Questioni*, pp.169-89.

35. Mangini, M.R., "Il 'mito americano' nelle testimonianze degli emigranti: il caso della Val Trebbia," in *La Via delle Americhe*, pp.83-6.

36. This is the case of the newspaper *Il Secolo XIX* and of the local engineering company Ansaldo, principally owned at the end of XIX century by F. M. Perrone, partly with the money he initially made during his emigration experience in Argentina, P. Rugafiori, *Ferdinando Maria Perrone. Da Casa Savoia all'Ansaldo* (Torino: UTET, 1992).

37. From an interview by the author to Roberto Foppiano, former director of the Cicagna's branch of the Bank of America, Cicagna, febbraio 1981.

38. Isnenghi, M., *Le guerre degli italiani. Parole, immagini ricordi 1848-1945* (Milano: Mondadori, 1989), pp. 329-49.

39. "(the) demonstration of a pure Italian sentiment ... (shows) how, with the spreading and increase of wealth, love of common mother-land had grown in Sanmargheritesi (so that it would not be entirely too paradoxically to say that for them the love for Italy has come from America)," in A.R. Scarsella, *Annali*, II v., pp. 203, 237.

40. Verducci, G., *L'Italia laica prima e dopo l'Unità 1848-1876* (Roma-Bari: Laterza, 1981).

41. Lessona, M., *Volere è potere* (Firenze: G. Barbera, 1911), p. 381.

PART IV
CONTEMPORARY IMAGES
AND STEREOTYPES

10

THAT'S ITALIAN. . . OR IS IT?: (UN)POPULAR IMAGES OF ITALIANS IN AMERICAN MASS MEDIA

JOHN R. MITRANO
BOSTON COLLEGE

JAMES G. MITRANO
LEHIGH UNIVERSITY

Previously, researchers have examined popular portrayals of religious, racial, and ethnic groups in the United States. Two groups that have fervently scrutinized their portrayals by the mass media are African-Americans and Jewish-Americans; however, the forms of media that are most often analyzed and critiqued have been television shows and movies. Other elements of mass culture have been largely ignored for analysis of their content. These elements include popular music, television and print advertisements, product packaging and labels, magazines and weekly tabloids, and newspaper headlines and articles. Similarly, critical analysis of depictions of Italian Americans in any mediated form has been insufficient. The purpose of our paper, then, is three-fold. First, we examine depictions of Italian Americans in popular television shows and movies and identify themes surrounding these depictions. Second, we expand the analysis to other elements of mass culture, again identifying common themes. Third, we discuss how these portrayals of Italian Americans only selectively reflect their social and cultural world experiences. Such depictions aid in the reinforcement of symbolic meaning systems created by non-Italian Americans, and these in turn contribute to the gross generalizations and stereotypes of Italian Americans. For future consideration, in light of the popular images and identified themes, we question and examine why a watchdog organization (e.g., Anti-Defamation League of B'nai B'rith or the National Association for the Advancement of Colored People) has not been established for Italian Americans.

Todd Gitlin, expanding the work of Erving Goffman, demonstrates that the ways in which events are "framed" by the media affect the meanings that viewers construct from the events, be they political or social events. Gitlin defines frames as "principles of selection, emphasis, and presentation composed of little tacit theories about what exists, what happens, and what matters... [they are] persistent patterns of cognition, interpretation, and presentation, of selection, emphasis, and exclusion, by which symbol-handlers routinely organize discourse, whether verbal or visual."[1] As Goffman suggests, these frames are then used by people in an effort to interpret reality, come to understand reality, and cope with or negotiate reality in their everyday lives. These socially constructed meanings and interpretations, in turn, affect individual opinion, behavior, and action.[2] As Gitlin notes:

> The media bring a manufactured public world into private space. From within their private crevices, people find themselves relying on the media for concepts, for images of their heroes, for guiding information, for emotional charges, for a recognition of public values, for symbols in general, even for language... Of all the institutions of daily life, the media specialize in orchestrating everyday consciousness... To put it simply: the mass media have become core systems for the distribution of ideology. That is to say, every day, directly or indirectly, by statement and omission, in pictures and words, in entertainment and news and advertisement, the mass media produce fields of definition and association, symbol and rhetoric, through which ideology becomes manifest and concrete.[3]

That is not to say that individuals are merely passive dupes, absorbing and internalizing each and every mediated message thrown their way. Certainly, individuals filter out many symbols and actively engage in (to varying degrees) the creation of their "world view" (i.e. the Weberian *weltanschauung*). However, the media contribute discernable fragments of that vision.

Recently, a spate of researchers have applied framing concepts to specific world issues. For example, Gans[4] examines the power of the mass media in helping shape Americans' views of domestic and foreign policy, and Gamson and Stuart[5] explore how newspaper editorial cartoons frame U.S. and Soviet nuclear technology during the Cold War era.

The mass media have also come under scrutiny for their portrayal of many racial and ethnic groups.[6] The nature and content of such material, as expressed through popular mediated forms, largely determine the images we have of certain ethnic and racial groups, especially those with which we have little or no direct contact in our daily lives. As Giordano aptly notes:

> As a transmitter of society's values, the mass media have
> a tremendous impact on the shaping of our personal and
> group identities. Radio, TV, films and the print media can
> convey the rich textures of pluralistic society, or they can
> directly or indirectly (by omission) distort our perceptions
> of other ethnic groups and reinforce our defensiveness and
> ambivalence about our own....More than any other com-
> munications medium, television plays a key role in provid-
> ing information and entertainment. It shows us worlds we
> otherwise seldom see, determines which elements of those
> worlds to focus on, and presents them to us in a 'good' or
> 'bad' light. TV, in short, helps shape what we know, what
> we believe, and what we feel about the world.[7]

While researchers have thoroughly scrutinized characterizations of other ethnic and racial groups in an attempt to control stereotypes and biases, Italian Americans remain legitimate targets of such biases. This occurs despite U.S. Census data evidence suggesting that such stereotypes are no longer reflective of many Italian Americans. Furthermore, while some of these media characterizations are still prevalent in the Italian American population, the disproportionate portrayal of such characterization (i.e., the "stacking" of negative stereotypes and the "unstacking" of favorable depictions[8]) in the mass media is what we are particularly concerned with.

The Italian American experience in the 1990s, whether it is presented by fellow Italian Americans[9] or, perhaps more importantly, by non-Italian Americans, needs to be examined. Questions of who should be allowed to or who is most capable of depicting the lifestyle of certain ethnic or racial groups has come to the forefront in the movie industry, most recently with director/producer Spike Lee's well publicized assertion that only an African-American should be allowed to make a movie on the life of Malcolm X. Such reasoning could be used by other ethnic and racial groups who are displeased with their portrayal in mass mediated forms. For the purpose of this paper, however, we have chosen to ignore the issue of who is producing the depictions of Italian Americans and instead, to focus solely on the content of those depictions.

METHODOLOGY

The guiding principle in our methodology was experiencing and encountering depictions of Italian Americans as naturally as possible while still maintaining some systematic rigor. This naturalistic or "experiential method"[10] is one in which researchers

> acquire their knowledge from their involvement in natural settings. . . Experiential analysis is performed with minimal expectations of what will be created, rather than originating in the interest of supporting or proving a theory. Once the analysis has been conducted, however, its relation to other bodies of literature must be investigated so as to situate the analysis in the context of the shared community of scholarship.[11]

In the incipient stages of our research, we readily discerned that certain mediated forms of popular culture are more easily accessible to systematic scrutiny than others. Actively screening rented movies of Italian Americans is far more routinized and systematic than passively waiting for a particular commercial to be aired on television. We recognize the limitations of our research and do not claim to have been exhaustive and comprehensive in the gathering of data for our analyses. However, we aggressively sought out depictions in numerous mediated forms that most American pop culture consumers would encounter and believe our findings to be rather.

Methods Used to Examine Marketing/Packaging/Labeling
We each visited the most popular grocery store chain in the respective cities where we were based at the time of our research (Pathmark in Bethlehem, PA and Star Market in Boston, MA). Once in the grocery stores, a survey of every aisle was made and the products contained in the aisles were examined for how "Italian products" were marketed, packaged, and labeled. Typical items identified as "Italian-styled" or "Italian" included bread, salad dressing, pasta, pasta sauces, and pizza products, to name but a few (See Appendix 1). Print advertising for Italian products was collected from the *Boston Globe* and the *Easton Express-Times* for a three month period. This form included both store & manufacturers' coupons and product advertisements.

Methods Used to Examine Movies
Since we are concerned with (un)popular portrayals, we chose to examine those movies, containing Italian American characters, which are most accessible to the general public. Millions of American households own a VCR and regularly rent movies. Since the largest chain of movie rental stores is Blockbuster Video (over 2,000 locations in the United States), we chose to examine movies contained in Blockbuster's "Comedy", "Drama", "Classics", and "New Releases" sections, as these are among the most popular movies rented at any given time. Together we systematically read the synopses of the movie rental boxes for character names and movie plots. If we agreed that a character in the movie had an Italian surname or if the plot would involve Italian American characters, we recorded the name of the movie in a database. In addition, any movies that serendipitously were found

to have an Italian American as a character were also recorded. A list of 58 movies was compiled (see Appendix 2). We then divided the movies into two lists and each of us rented and reviewed movies over a three-month period, culling themes of the portrayals of Italian Americans in the cinema.

Methods Used to Examine Television Shows

A decade ago, the Lichters[12] examined over 250 television episodes and discovered that negative portrayals of Italian Americans outnumbered favorable portrayals by a two-to-one margin. Unlike the Lichters, we chose to examine television shows in a more naturalistic manner. Current television shows that we knew contained an Italian American as one of the main characters were singled out and general portrayals coded. However, we must acknowledge that scores of other TV shows which do not have Italian Americans as the main characters occasionally contain cameo appearances by Italian American characters. Analysis of secondary figures is just as important as for primary figures, as these supporting character portrayals often focus on Italian Americans as organized criminals or volatile individuals (e.g., a recent episode of *The Simpsons* contained a plot in which Bart works for a thinly-veiled "Godfather" crime syndicate).

Methods Used to Examine Commercials

As in the case of television shows, commercials are difficult to assess systematically; one does not know when a commercial will air featuring an Italian American character. For the purpose of this study, we chose to keep a logbook nearby whenever either one of us watched television. We concentrated on prime time weeknight television programming, as well as weekend sporting events. If a commercial aired depicting an Italian American character or an Italian product, we recorded the content of the commercial (See Appendix 3).

PORTRAYALS IDENTIFIED BY PAST RESEARCH

A panoply of other researchers have examined the portrayal of Italian Americans in popular culture. Iorizzo and Mondello's notable contribution traces the history of the portrayal of Italian Americans in film, television, and comic strips/comic books between the period 1900-1979.[13] Prior to that era, they discovered that Italian Americans were largely depicted as artistic or violent, citing that "[f]or most of the nineteenth century, the American stereotype of the Italians as an artistic people took precedence over the image of the Italians as rogues. By the end of the century, the reverse became true."[14] These two images competed well into the 20th century, with several new portrayals being added. They included Italian Americans as largely comical and ludicrous (epitomized by the Marx Brothers) or terrorizing and menacing (epitomized by gangster movies and comic books). Such images predominated in the 1920s and 1930s.

Iorizzo and Mondello note that until the 1940s (with the rise of Joe DiMaggio and Frank Sinatra), Italian Americans possessed a semblance of a positive media image and were looked upon somewhat favorably. However, soon after WWII, the Italian American was depicted as criminal again —an image that remained up until the early 1970s, epitomized by *The Godfather* movies. Those few Italian American males who weren't portrayed as criminals or buffoons were portrayed as "lower-middle class clods with little ambition, a caricature which remained popular in media portrayals of Italians well into the 1960s."[15]

Iorizzo and Mondello claim that not until the early 1970s did depictions begin to turn favorable again. Television shows such as *Columbo*, *Baretta*, and *Petrocelli* depicted Italian Americans as heroes and crimefighters. Sit-coms such as *One Day at a Time* (Ann Romano), *Happy Days* (Arthur Fonzarelli), *Welcome Back Kotter* (Vinny Barbarino) and *Laverne and Shirley* (Laverne DeFazio, Carmine Ragusa) depict Italian Americans as having the same "coming of age" problems as other characters on these shows. Even elements in more stereotyped movies (e.g., *The Godfather* and *Rocky*) emphasized positive traits (e.g., the importance of family values, honor, personal pride, and religion). Such a turn of events led Iorizzo and Mondello to conclude that "Rocky Balboa may be the last great stereotyped media Italian American. During the seventies, stereotyped Italian Americans began to disappear from our popular culture. The Italian American is now fully integrated into all aspects of American society as represented by the popular arts."[16]

In sum, Iorizzo and Mondello conclude that Italian Americans (and primarily Italian American males) were previously pigeon-holed into five main stereotypical categories for the vast majority of the 20th century: racketeer, lover, artist, showman, and family man.[17] They also declare the death of such stereotypes in popular media.

We argue, however, that such assertions are premature. We also disagree that Italian Americans truly are fully integrated into all aspects of American life as portrayed in the media. Where are the highly educated, well paid, good-looking, and powerful Italian American characters to be found in the 1980s and 1990s? Such characteristics were embodied in personalities found in the most popular television programs throughout the 1980s (e.g., *Dynasty, Dallas, Knots Landing, LA Law*). Instead, Americans were exposed to Carla Tortelli on *Cheers* and Vinnie DelPino on *Doogie Howser, M.D.*.

PORTRAYALS IDENTIFIED BY CURRENT RESEARCH

Product Packaging and Labeling

In examining product packaging, labels, and print advertisements, we discerned that marketers and advertisers tend to mimic one another in certain product lines (e.g., colors and graphics). No other ethnic or racial group comes close to Italian Americans in the sheer volume of goods that are what we term *ethno-labeled*, *ethno-packaged*, and *ethno-marketed* in one way or another. Nor are other ethnic and racial groups subjected to such gross stereotypes and caricatures as Italian Americans.

Ethno-labeling

We define ethno-labeling as attributing a specific product to a particular ethnic or racial group, regardless of the authenticity of the product or exclusivity of its use (e.g., grits for Southern Americans, soy sauce for Asians, pasta products and pizza for Italians, nachos and salsa for Mexicans, potato products for Irish, etc). The product may not have originated with the specific ethnic group perceived to be associated with the product, nor is the specific ethnic group necessarily the primary consumer of the product.

Ethno-packaging

We define ethno-packaging as ascribing cultural fragments to represent a complete ethnic experience (akin to synecdoche in languages). This is often manifested as specific colors and symbols, both linguistic and pictorial (e.g., shamrocks for Irish, sombreros for Mexicans, bullfights for Spaniards, etc.).

Ethno-marketing

This is accomplished through the use of both ethno-packaging and ethno-labeling. It includes both print and media images, encompassing music, hyperbole, and spoken language in addition to the aforementioned characteristics (e.g., "Vinny", dressed in a red, white, and green outfit, hawking pizza to the American masses in pigeon English).

In a systematic survey of products in the aforementioned supermarkets, no less than 80 products were ethno-labeled, ethno-packaged, or ethno-marketed (e.g., identified as "Italian", "Italian style", marked by the distinct "Red, White, and Green" color motif of the Italian flag, etc.). The following are packages and labels of products which are representative of how stereotypes of Italian Americans are used to sell such products. They include:

Mama Mia! Italian Bread (Features Red, White, and Green packaging [referred to as "RW&G" in future references] and the Italian flag.) While the packaging of this bread is not significantly different from many other products (i.e., emphasis on colors of Italian flag), what makes this product particularly offensive is the very name of it. Other ethnic groups are well known for their quality breads (e.g., Jewish rye and pumpernickel breads, French bread, Syrian pita bread, etc.), yet market such breads by emphasizing the quality of the ingredients or the breads' nutritional value and not with a brazenly stereotypical (and we might add, outdated and misspelled) expression.

Wonder Bread Italian (RW&G packaging, picture of a gondola, the Latin phrase "Qualitas Vera", ad copy that reads, "Baked the Old World way, Wonder Italian Bread brings the authentic taste and rich texture of bread from

Italy to your table....) This product contains prototypical elements of ethno-packaging and ethno-labeling.

DeCecco Spaghetti (Features a drawing of a buxom, dark-haired woman adorned with jewelry and sporting a bandanna. She is engaged in harvesting a crop of semolina. The excerpt from the advertising copy reads: "Since 1887 the DeCecco family name and peasant girl trademark have been internationally recognized guarantees of a traditionally made pasta of unmatched quality... Wheat for the family mill is selected by a DeCecco, personally, from the world's best durum grain wheat crops, giving our pasta its unique aroma and nutritional quality... DeCecco means 'al dente'! Responsible for this legendary quality is a family-patented drying process.... Buon appetito!") This package contains elements of several techniques marketers use for Italian products. Like others, this advertiser depicts Italians as secretive, for "secret recipes" or "family-patented processes" are to be kept "in the family" at all costs. This package also contains Italian words and phrases sprinkled throughout, even though far more Americans take classes in Spanish or French and fewer Italian Americans of the third and fourth generations speak Italian. As for the picture of the buxom, bandanna-covered peasant girl harvesting semolina by hand, we again challenge anyone to find semolina harvested this way; evidence indicates that Italian Americans are no longer "peasants", literally or figuratively. Even that venerable purveyor of waffles and syrup, Aunt Jemima, has shed her slave-era bandanna for a professional-looking blouse and hairdo. It is time for the peasant girl to do the same.

Michelina's Frozen Pasta (RW&G packaging, a photo of an old woman with a necklace looking wistfully skyward, underneath the name is a pronunciation guide: "Say 'Mick-Ah-Lee-Nah's'. On the back is a guarantee. The ad copy reads as follows: "This product is dedicated to my mother, Michelina, who used only the freshest ingredients and no preservatives when preparing her homemade sauces. These are her recipes.... I wouldn't sell a product with my mother's name on it unless it was good, pure, and the best possible value. [signed] Luigino Paulucci.") Again, emphasis on "mama" and secret homemade recipes. This package also contains a phonetic aide for proper pronunciation of a relatively easy Italian American name. We have yet to encounter such assistance for other ethnic food products, e.g. Manischewitz baked goods ("Say 'Man-Ah-Shev-Its'").

Bravo Frozen Pizza (RW&G packaging, photo of two dark-haired males, one flipping pizza dough in the air. The advertising copy on the front of the box reads: "Our pizza is made from a secret family recipe that is over 60 years old. . . —And on the back . . .We are proud of our premium-quality pizza, and personally watch over the way it's made, every day. . . [signed] Michael and David Tiscia.") Again, this product presents the tired motifs of secret recipes, colors of the Italian flag, and signatures of actual or mythical founders.

Celeste Italian Bread Pizza (RW&G packaging, a photo of an older woman with earrings. The advertising copy reads: "Mama Celeste has created a masterpiece of a pizza. . . Each loaf is individually baked, then topped with a zesty blend of Italian cheeses, flavorful toppings, the finest Italian spices— and Mama's specially seasoned sauce... is sure to please you with this abbondanza of authentic Italian taste.") In typical fashion, this product uses the tri-color packaging, a picture of the supposed founder, a story of the product's origin, Italian phrases, and references to "mama".

In sum, we discovered that a disproportionate number of Italian food packages were ethno-marketed in the following manner: 1) references to "Mama" and the family; 2) pictures of buxom dark-haired or old women lavishly bejewelled; 3) emphasis on "secret recipes or techniques" in the ad copy; 4) colors of or actual drawings of the Italian flag; 5) stereotypical symbols (e.g, gondolas, Leaning Tower of Pisa, Mt. Vesuvius, etc.); 6) Italian words and phrases; 7) ethnic names (e.g. Tony, Gino, Angie, Luigi, etc.); 8) photographs of an actual or mythical founder (often complete with his/her signature); 9) Roman medals, coins, heraldry, and Latin phrases; 10) anecdotal stories of the company's founding; 11) caricatures of mustached men often bedecked in comical garb; and 12) peasants toiling by hand in agricultural endeavors. The use of the Italian flag and phrases may be particularly pernicious to Italian Americans, as if to signify that no matter how far removed from Italy they are, they still have inseparable ties to the motherland (and even to ancient Rome!). Such is not the case with Germans, Jews, Poles, nor a multitude of other ethnic groups.

Ethno-marketing techniques are also prevalent in many television commercials. However, the ability to use live characters for commercials (rather than simple text and drawings for packages) elicits even more stereotypical images of Italian Americans. Four that are representative of contemporary television advertising include:

Boboli Pizza Shell (The characters speak with a heavy Italian accent, the scene takes place in the kitchen, the adult man's "mama" is talking in the background.) The main character of this commercial introduces his product in pigeon English while his "mama" exhorts his indiscretion of topping choices. The emphasis here is on food and family, with our Italian American character not being able to speak English with an American accent.

Old Spice After Shave (The main character, "Tony", is a greasy, dark-haired, unshaven individual who drives a sports car.) Our dashing young product-seller, Tony, drives along the streets of Italy in his Chevy Corvette in pursuit of American women. Machismo spared, his infatuation with American products leads him to purchase Old Spice, thus being able to impress the American women walking on the streets of an Italian city.

DiGiorno Pasta Products (Mustached, dark-haired men, Italian restaurant and street cafe.) A broken-English speaking waiter and *maitre de* encounter one of their loyal customers who is surprised to discover that the waiter's surname is "DiGiorno". This assumption is made via the client's discovery of "authentic" pasta products he recently saw in his local supermarket. As is often the case, this commercial uses mustached men speaking with Italian accents in an attempt to purvey a food product.

Cappio (Caricatures of dark-haired Italian men with razor stubble, dark-haired women sunbathing on the Mediterranean.) The makers of Cappio implore us to indulge in "refreshment Italian-style." Stereotypical images and caricatures of dark-haired, buxom women basking in "sunny" Italy abound. In viewing television commercials, we found the following qualities pervading numerous advertisements: 1) broken English and Italian accents; 2) razor stubble; 3) dark-haired men and women; 4) emphasis on "mama"; 5) slovenly dress and mannerisms; 6) incorrect grammar; 7) mandolin music; 8) red, white, and green background.

Movies and Television Programs

In examining current television programs and motion pictures, Iorizzo and Mondello's taxonomy remains a useful framework for categorizing media images of Italian Americans. From our list of movies, we randomly selected ten (see Appendix 4) and culled themes from each. When we analyzed the aggregate data, we discerned eight common themes in the portrayal of Italian Americans: 1) religious/ superstitious; 2) family oriented; 3) enamored with food; 4) use of Italian or broken English; 5) uneducated/ anti-intellectual; 6) violent (often tied to crime); 7) non-committal men; and 8) submissive women. Television shows fared similarly (see Appendix 5). Almost all of the characters examined are portrayed as lower-class buffoons with little ambition (e.g., Carla Tortelli, a waitress on *Cheers*; Tony Masselli, an ex-baseball player turned housekeeper on *Who's the Boss*, and Vinny DelPino, a comical, aspiring young film-maker overshadowed by his *wunderkind* friend, Doogie, on *Doogie Howser, M.D.*). Those with any ambition or status within their communities have achieved their positions (or aspire to) through illegal channels. The scripts are replete with broken English, malapropisms, and profanity. Men live and die by the sword. Women exist to sexually and gastronomically please men. Thus the message from Hollywood is lucid: Italian Americans are a lower-class group who can not improve their status via socially acceptable means (i.e., education). This depiction directly contradicts reality, as indicated by U.S. Census Bureau data.

ACTUAL CHARACTERISTICS OF ITALIAN AMERICANS

With all of the mispronunciations and malapropisms, as well as the plethora of swearing, one would think that Italian Americans were an uneducated, surly group of people. Femminella[18] finds Italian Americans to be quite the contrary. As compared to other ethnic groups, the percentage of Italian Americans enrolled in the nation's colleges (29.5%) is greater than all but Poles (33.5%), exceeding such groups as Germans, Irish, French, and English. Nelli[19] also notes that education among Italian Americans is highly valued, as many parents insist that their children attain more education than they themselves were able to attain.

In addition, many forms of media emphasize the importance and size of the family in Italian American households. The stereotype of a large, extended family living under one roof persists to this day. However, Femminella[20] debunks this myth as well, demonstrating that the number of Italian Americans living in group quarters is not significantly different from any other ethnic group of Americans. Nor is the percent of persons living in families significantly different either. A couple of aberrations Femminella discovers, however, are that the percentage of married Italian Americans is slightly less than other ethnic groups and that Italian Americans have a lower divorce rate than all other groups except for Poles. When Italian Americans do marry, Femminella finds they are increasingly apt to marry outside of Italian ancestry. In addition he notes that, contrary to media portrayal, Italian Americans (and, once again, Poles) clearly have lower birth rates than the other white ethnic groups.

The media often depict Italian Americans as either very wealthy (as in many of the Mafia movies, where money flows freely) or as lower and working class. Bonutti[21] examines the economic characteristics of Italian Americans over time and discovers that, while Italian Americans were at or near the bottom of the economic scale in 1910, significant changes occurred in subsequent years. Bonutti concludes that Italian Americans are an ethnic group

> which is consistently well above average, not only when comparing it with the total U.S. population but also in relation to the white population.... With the exclusion of the Jewish American community, no other major ethnic group has achieved a higher level of upward mobility than the Italian Americans. Moreover, available data clearly refute

the prevailing stereotypical perceptions of the Italian Americans. . . From the available census data, the perception that Italian Americans are heavily involved in crime... is not confirmed by census data. In fact, the number of prison inmates of Italian extraction is about 50% below the national average.[22]

Bonutti also found that

based on the 1980 census data, Italian Americans have clearly shown upward mobility from lower paying blue collar and craft positions to middle and upper class occupations: managerial and professional . . . . there is a declining participation rate of Italian workers in lower paying jobs with limited or no skills or prestige like laborers, machine operators, assemblers and private household positions. On the other hand, increasing numbers of Italians are found in upper level, well-paying professions: attorneys, doctors, engineers and accountants.[23]

As evidence of this upward mobility among Italian Americans, Bonutti cites recent census data on income levels. He asserts that no matter how one calculates median income, Italian Americans have anywhere from a 15-25% higher income than the national average. Nelli[24] cites similar examples of this economic success. However, Bonutti also points out that despite a higher income than the national average, Italian Americans still lag behind in the upper income levels. As Bonutti poignantly reminds us, "Evidently, one hundred years of presence in America has not been sufficient enough to produce a competitively large upper class among Italian Americans."[25] By the same token, however, he finds that the poverty level of Italian Americans is well below the national average.

What does all of this mean? While Italian Americans are not wealthy, they are not poor either. They are comparable to or slightly exceed many other white ethnic groups in educational and income levels. Thus, any popular depiction of Italian Americans that emphasizes extreme poverty or extreme wealth or inadequate education is guilty of "stacking" negative stereotypes/ "unstacking" positive ones.

A NEW GENERATION OF ITALIAN AMERICANS

We reject many of the cultural forms depicting Italian American life and call for new "cultural entrepreneurs" to create and disperse a more accurate portrayal of Italian American life in the 1990s. This would include greater emphasis on education, wealth, family, and acceptance of outsiders. It must also include a thorough examination of the eclipse of ethnicity and the effects of this eclipse on new generations of Italian Americans.

Vecoli[26] notes that "by 1980 the great majority of Americans of Italian descent were of these (3rd and 4th) generations. With them, we have embarked upon a new phase in the search for an Italian American identity." Vecoli claims that the younger generations are more apt to suffer an identity crisis, given the amount of intermarriage, divorce, and sheer distance between the time grandparents and great-grandparents immigrated and today:

> The making of an ethnic identity has become a complicated business for Italian Americans. . .the American born generations have choices . . . the ingredients which they have at hand from which to assemble the Italian part of their identity are varied and incongruous. . . . Folk, popular, and high cultures all meld in the miniature melting pot of the Italian American identity. Italian Americans, in greater or lesser degree, hold these discordant elements in their psyches, and it is the need to reconcile, to synthesize them which energizes their search for identity.[27]

Alba, also recognizing the impending "twilight of ethnicity" and subsequent "identity crisis", espouses an ethnogenesis interpretation of ethnicity "which stresses that ethnicity is not some fixed form handed down by tradition, but that it is continuously regenerated, and hence altered, in the process of adjustment to American society."[28] Alba continues:

> The essence of the ethnogenesis position can be summarized by three linked statements. First, the original form of

> ethnicity, brought by the immigrants, does not survive for
> long in America, because it is generally not compatible
> with American life.. . . . Second, the immigrants from any
> group, along with their children and grandchildren, come
> to share many commonalities of American experience that
> set them apart from other groups... The immigrants and
> their children choose certain possibilities over others that
> are open to them because of the propensities inherent in
> their values... Third, and finally, this common American
> experience provides a basis for transformed ethnicity. . .
> The group's culture is filtered through this experience;
> many elements are rejected, while others must be reshaped
> in order to fit.[29]

We contend that the potential for this "regeneration" and "transformation" of Italian American identity and ethnicity is being stifled by media
and popular culture in America. It is not occurring at an appropriate pace and
when it does occur, Italian Americans often are not the architects of such
transformation. They are rather passive in defining who they are, allowing
our "surrogate mothers" on Madison Avenue, Wall Street, and Hollywood
Boulevard to merely spoonfeed each of them an inadequate dose of
Italianness. The formula use by the media is inappropriate for Italian Americans' needs as growing and maturing Italian Americans, opting rather to feed
them the same mush for years, devoid of any nutrients.

Television, movies, commercials, and other mediated forms increasingly do not reflect what we consider to be "typical Italian American experiences" in the 1990s. This is especially true for increasing numbers of fourth
and even fifth generation Italian Americans. What marketers, writers, and
producers fail to realize is that these generations are quite distinct from those
of the first, second, and even third generations. Frank Sinatra does not sing
their songs. Many of them were not born yet when *The Godfather* first de-
buted. The few movies or television shows and characters that exist do not
speak to them, and those intelligent shows or shows geared toward their generation rarely, if ever, have Italian American characters. Such inadequacies

need to be redressed and the creation of a strong watchdog organization (similar to the Anti-Defamation League or the NAACP) needs to be established to prevent unfavorable "frames" and negative "stacking" from being produced in the future. Stephen Hall notes that "until recently, Italian Americans have not been particularly united nor particularly vigorous in pressing their case about perceived mistreatment. . . . If Italian Americans believe they are being unfairly portrayed in the media, it's about time they started getting seriously noisy about it."[30] We wholeheartedly agree and view this paper as our initial contribution in pressing for more favorable and salient portrayals of Italian Americans in the future.

NOTES

1. Gitlin, Todd, *The Whole World is Watching*. (Berkeley: Univ. of California Press, 1980), pp.6-7.

2. Goffman, Erving, *Frame Analysis* (New York: Harper and Row, 1974).

3. Gitlin, pp. 1-2.

4. Gans, Herbert, *Deciding What's News* (New York: Random House, 1979).

5. Gamson, W. and Stuart, D., "Media Discourse as a Symbolic Contest: The Bomb in Political Cartoons," *Sociological Forum* 7 (1, 1992): 55-86.

6. Morsy, S. "The Bad, the Ugly, the Super-Rich, and the Exceptional Moderate: U.S. Popular Images of the Arabs," *Journal of Popular Culture* 20(3, 1986): 13-29.

7. Giordano, J., "Italian Americans and the Media: An Agenda for a More Positive Image," in L. Tomasi (ed), *Italian Americans: New Perspectives in Italian Immigration and Ethnicity* (New York: Center for Migration Studies of New York, 1985), pp. 67-77).

8. Morsy, 1986.

9. Pane, R., "Italian American Experience through Literature and the Arts," in L. Tomasi (ed), *Italian Americans: New Perspectives in Italian Immigration and Ethnicity* (New York: Center for Migration Studies of New York, 1985).

10. Reinharz, Shulamit, *On Becoming a Social Scientist* (New Brunswick, NJ: Transaction Publishers, 1988).

11. Reinharz, 1988, p. 364.

12. Lichter and Lichter, Linda and Robert S. Lichter, *Italian American Characters in Television Entertainment* (New York: Commission for Social Justice, Order Sones of Italy, 1982).

13. Iorizzo, L. and Mondello, S., *The Italian Americans* (Boston: Twayne Publishers, 1980).

14. Iorizzo, L. and Mondello, S., 1980, p. 265.

15. Iorizzo, L. and Mondello, S., 1980, pp. 277-8.

16. Iorizzo, L. and Mondello, S., 1980, p. 283.

17. Although this last stereotype can be lauded as positive, they point out that this portrayal came about during the 1950s, a time when such a value was incongruous with the popular rise of individualism and freedom.

18. Femminella, F., "Italian Americans and Education," in G. Battistella (ed), *Italian Americans in the 1980s: A Sociodemographic Profile* (New York: The Center for Migration Studies, 1989).
19. Nelli, H., "Italian Americans in Contemporary Society," in L. Tomasi (ed), *Italian Americans: New Perspectives in Italian Immigration and Ethnicity* (New York: Center for Migration Studies, 1985), pp.78-87.
20. Femminella, F., "Italian American Family Life," in G. Battistella (ed), *Italian Americans in the 1980s: A Sociodemographic Profile* (New York: The Center for Migration Studies, 1989).
21. Bonutti, K., "Economic Characteristics of Italian Americans," in G. Battistella (ed), *Italian Americans in the 1980s: A Sociodemographic Profile* (New York: The Center for Migration Studies, 1989).
22. Bonutti, K., pp. 63-4.
23. Bonutti, K., pp. 64-5.
24. Nelli, H., 1985.
25. Bonutti, K.
26. Vecoli, R., "The Search for an Italian American Identity: Continuity and Change," in L. Tomasi (ed), *Italian Americans: New Perspectives in Italian Immigration and Ethnicity* (New York: Center for Migration Studies, 1985), p. 101.
27. Vecoli, R., 1985, p. 106.
28. Alba, R., *Italian Americans: Twilight of Ethnicity* (Englewood Cliffs, NJ: Prentice-Hall, 1985), p. 9.
29. Alba, R., 1985, pp. 9-10.
30. Hall, Stephen, "Italian Americans: Media Perceptions," in L. Tomasi (ed), *Italian Americans: New Perspectives in Italian Immigration and Ethnicity* (New York: Center for Migration Studies, 1985), pp. 61-6.

APPENDIX 1A: FOOD PRODUCTS FOUND IN BETHLEHEM, PA

Cardini's Original Caesar Dressing
Pfeiffer Fat Free Italian Dressing
Wishbone Robusto Italian Dressing
Progresso Red Wine Vinegar
Mancini Roasted Peppers
Morabito Italian Bread
Hatfield Sweet Italian Sausage
Medaglia D'Oro Espresso Coffee
Corrando Pepperoni
Centurion Genoa Salami
Ed & Joane DeLuca Mini Cheese Ravioli
DiGiorno Pasta Products (assorted)
Stella Asiago Shredded Cheese
Colonna Romano-Pecorino
Tempo Italian Meatball Mix
McCormick Chicken Cacciatore Sauce
Ragu Chicken Tonight
Berio Olive Oil-Limited Edition
Rienzi Tomato Puree
Columbus Commemorative Tin
Aunt Millie's Spaghetti Sauce
Francesco Rinaldi Tomato Sauce
Sauce Arturo

Seven Seas Italian Dressing
Lawry's Italian Dressing
Wishbone Italian Oil Blend Dressing
Pope Italian Style Vinegar
Michelangelo Pane
Appetito Hot Italian Sausage
Lawry's Pizza Pepper
Melitta Coffee
Tallarico's Steak Sandwich Sauce
Herakles Sweet Pepper Strips
Contadina Marinara Sauce
DiGiorno Sauce Products (assorted)
Rienzi Provolone
Progresso Italian Style Zucchini
Pasta Prima Tomato Basil Pasta Sauce
Hamburger Helper Zesty Italian
Betty Crocker Recipe Sauces -Filippo Cacciatore
Rienzi Crushed Tomatoes
Prego Tomato Sauce

Spatini Spaghetti Sauce Mix
Ferrara Clam Sauce

Rienzi Italian Pasta Sauce
Hunt's Pizza Sauce
D'oro Bread Sticks
Montini Crushed Tomatoes
Enrico Caruso Oil
Rienzi Salsa Sorrentina
Rienzi Salsa Di Pomidoro
Progresso Italian Style Bread Crumbs
Spigadoro Macaroni
Contadina Spinach Linguine
Pope Olive Oil
San Giorno Macaroni
Paesano Ravioli
Quaker Maid Italian Meatball Sandwich
Totino's Party Pizza
Three Tavern Cheese Pizza
Kraft Romano Cheese
Wonder Italian Bread
D'Italiano Real Italian Bread
Heluva Good Mozzarella
Frigo Part Skim Mozzarella
Supreme Mozzarella
Auricchio Provolone
Boboli Pizza Shell

Ragu Sauces (assorted)
Hunt's Classic Italian Spaghetti Stella
Sauce
Furmano's Italian Style Spaghetti
Sauce
Tuttorosso Tomato Puree
Shake and Bake Chicken-Italian Herb
Ferrara Ziti
Spidari Macaroni
De Cecco Spaghetti
Ronzoni Pasta
Ellio's Pizza
Michelina's Fettucine Alfredo
Celentano Ravioli
Celeste Pizza for One
4C Romano Cheese
Capri Italian Bread
Maeir's Italian Bread
Maggio Ricotta
Polly-O Ricotta
Stella Provolone
Maggio Mozzarella
Frigo Ricotta

APPENDIX 1B: FOOD PRODUCTS FOUND IN BOSTON, MA

Wishbone "Robusto Italian" Dressing
Cains "Bravo Italiano" Dressing
Arnold Crisp Croutons
Most all Olive Oils
Alpine Lace Mozzarella Cheese
Dragone Mozzarella Cheese
Contadina Tomato products
Carando Pepperoni
Chef Boyardi Ravioli
Shake and Bake "Italian Herb"
LaBella bread crumbs
LaBella grated cheese
Country Kitchen Italian Bread
Sunbeam Lite Italian Bread
Boboli Italian Bread Shell
Stor Select Pepperoni Pizza
Betty Crocker Recipe Sauce
ICCO Grated Cheese
4C Grated Cheese
Star Grated Cheese
Star Olive Oil
Luigi's Italian Ice
Creamette spaghetti

Pasta DeFino
Hunt's "Angela Mia" Crushed Tomatoes
DelMonte "Italian Style" Stewed Tomatoes
McCain Frozen Pizza
Louise's Frozen Pasta
Cole's Frozen Garlic Bread Sticks
Mama Rosie's Frozen Pasta
Angie's Frozen Pasta
Totino's Pizza
Tony's Pizza

APPENDIX 2: MOVIES EXAMINED FOR CULTURAL DEPICTIONS

Simple Justice	Tango and Cash
Raging Bull	Jungle Fever
Do The Right Thing	The Godson
The Freshman	Married to the Mob
Goodfellas	True Love
Things Change	Once Around Oscar
Cousins	Doctor Detroit
Fatso	Me and Him
Mob Boss	The Pick-Up Artist
Stewardess School	Crossroads
Dog Day Afternoon	A Wonderful Life
Ellis Island	The Godfather I
The Godfather II	The Godfather III
Gloria	Saturday Night Fever
Staying Alive	Mona Lisa
Oxford Blues	Fast Times at Ridgmont High
Rocky I	Rocky II
Rocky III	Rocky IV
Moonstruck	Blackjack
Our Family Business	Paradise Alley
Boys in Company C	Chicago Joe and the Showgirl
The Untouchables	Gangster Wars
The Gumshoe Kid	My Cousin Vinny
Scorpio	The Sicilian Connection
Biloxi Blues	The Palermo Connection
Prizzi's Honor	Mean Streets
Blood Brothers	Breaking Away
Risky Business	Scarface
A League of Their Own	A Woman Under the Influence

APPENDIX 3: RECENT TELEVISION COMMERCIALS

DiGiorno Pasta Products
Boboli Pizza Crusts
Prince Spaghetti
Ragu Sauces

Prego Sauces
Gioia Pasta Products
Francesca Rinaldi Sauces
P&R Spaghetti
Old Spice Aftershave
Cappio Drinks
Kraft Cheese
Chef Boyardi Macaroni
Mueslix cereal
Carefree Sugarless Gum
Burger King "Italianfest"
Pizza Hut

APPENDIX 4: MOVIE SAMPLE

Do The Right Thing
The Freshman
Goodfellas
Cousins
Fatso
Moonstruck
Prizzi's Honor
Jungle Fever
True Love
My Cousin Vinny

APPENDIX 5: TELEVISION PROGRAMS

Cheers
Doogie Howser
Who's the Boss
Golden Years
Murphy Brown

11

WHERE IS NELLA SORELLANZA
WHEN YOU NEED HER?

ROSE ROMANO

As the editor of *la bella figura*, the first and only literary journal devoted to Italian-American women, with a special welcome for lesbians, and owner of malafemmina press, which is doing a series of chapbooks of Italian-American women's poetry, and as an Italian-American lesbian poet, I correspond with a lot of women of Italian descent, most of them lesbians, throughout the United States and in Canada and Australia. Sometimes I use the phrase "nella sorellanza" to close a letter. I once sent a handwritten note to an Italian-American woman and received a response addressed not just to me, but to Nella too.

I was born and raised in Brooklyn. My father's parents came from Naples and my mother's parents from Sicily. My mother died when I was very young and I was raised by my father's mother, a woman who was just a tad more Neapolitan than she actually had to be in order to qualify. Her method of discipline was emotional abuse and her idea of emotional abuse was to call me American whenever I did something wrong, something stupid or something she just didn't like. I spent my entire childhood trying to convince that woman that I'm good enough to be Italian. Then I grew up and finally got it into my head that the culture I was suddenly expected to fit into, and with very little preparation, considers Italians to be inferior.

After I went through a lot of stuff, I came out as a lesbian at the age of thirty. After I came out, my life made more sense and some things got a little easier. But being an Italian-American just got more difficult.

When I first came out, I was excited by all the emphasis on multiculturalism in the lesbian community. After growing up in a mixed neighborhood, I had suddenly, at the age of sixteen, found myself grandmotherless and relieved of the overwhelming task of trying to be Italian. All I had to do, I thought then, was figure out how to be American, which I found baffling, but not daunting, because American standards didn't seem to be as high as Italian.

By entering the multicultural lesbian community, which looked pretty much like a mixed neighborhood, I could relax and be Italian again. And this was without even having to worry about my grandmother's high standards. After all, what did these Americans know about being Italian?

It turned out they knew even less than I thought. I've discovered that when some lesbians say "Europe," they're thinking "England;" when they say "Christian," they're thinking "Protestant"; and when they say "white," they're thinking "wasp." Because my skin is so light and I speak English with a Brooklyn accent, I'm expected to be American—although nobody can tell me what that is. It's assumed that my culture is "Anglo;" my history is "British;" my linguistic heritage is "English;" and my literary heritage is "Shakespeare."

Although these are not the descriptive terms used, they do denote a convoluted set of subconscious assumptions that's very real and has only one result, for example, my being called racist because I refuse to feel guilty about the kidnapping and enslavement of Blacks in this country. When I remind lesbians that Italians didn't even begin to arrive in this country until twenty years after the slave days were over, they just look at me like I'm nuts. I've spent a lot of time trying to untangle two different conversations which I seemed to be having at the same time with politically correct lesbians who don't realize that you can't read someone's history in their appearance. I never even get up to the part where I'm supposed to remind them that making assumptions about me based on my appearance is racist.

Although most lesbians don't actually admit to these haphazard, but politically convenient re-assignments of ethnicity, one Italian-American woman who wrote to me from Albuquerque said that Italian-Americans are openly considered Anglo over there. Do you suppose they consider Austrians to be Germans or Swedes to be French? And where do you think they get the right to erase what we are?

I've tried telling these lesbians that, although my people came over on boats, they didn't quite make it to the dock in time to get on the Mayflower. But they don't want to listen. They've already decided what my history and culture is and they don't need some dumb wop to correct them.

Once I sent a poem to an editor who, I imagine, considers herself progressive. The poem was intended for an anthology of lesbian eroticism and was spoken by a woman who finds large women especially attractive. Mostly it tells about this woman's frustration when she discovers that the large woman she's just started dating is on a diet. The poem, which is actually meant to be a little funny, describes different parts of the large woman's body in terms that are complimentary in Italian-American culture; each body part is compared to a kind of food. One line describes the large woman's "multiple bellies" as "fettucine coming out of a pasta machine."

The poem was returned with the suggestion that I change that line. The anthology's editor found it offensive because it reminded her of pictures that appeared in a men's magazine which showed women coming out of a meat grinder.

I explained that a pasta machine is nothing like a meat grinder. It doesn't grind and destroy; it kneads and creates. I suggested that she should learn more about Italian-American culture and, instead of asking me to modify it to avoid offending her sensibilities, she should learn to judge all cultures by their own standards. That's no more than what white progressives pretend to be doing when they talk about people of color. I told her she was asking me to omit part of *my* culture because it reminded her of something in *her* culture that she found threatening.

She responded by asking me to suppose that a woman wrote that her lover is "finger-licking good." It might be true, she admitted, but it would crack her up to read it and spoil the mood of the poem. Obviously, such a line would have to be changed.

But what's just as obvious is that this editor is still refusing to understand the point—she's still using references and symbols from *her* culture to devalue *mine*—and now to ridicule it as well.

I guess what I'm supposed to learn from this experience is that my culture and heritage are of no more value than the jingle of a fast food restaurant and I should forget what I am and write poetry that meets the proper feminist criteria. Well, I guess I'm just a wop put in her place.

Here's something that might be a joke on another planet. Every time I write something that shows Italian-Americans in a positive light according to Italian-American culture, feminist editors tell me I'm "feeding into negative stereotypes." And every time I write something that doesn't go beyond the stereotypes that bigots feel comfortable with, feminist editors tell me I've created an honest and real portrayal of my people.

I sent a poem to the editor of a lesbian literary journal showing my old neighborhood's Italian, Black, Chinese, Jewish, and Puerto Rican grandmothers' cooking. They were doing other things, too, but cooking is the only thing this woman picked up on. The point of the poem was that these grandmothers were more real to me as an Italian-American child than the wasp grandmothers who were tall and thin, had short blue hair, didn't speak with a special accent, and whose cooking had no special smell, and also that, as an Italian-American, I was still an outsider, like the others, and found American culture baffling. I was accused of "feeding into negative stereotypes" because, the editor said, "grandmothers are more than just sweet little old ladies who do nothing but cook."

My grandmother was a bitch who did whatever the hell she dammed well pleased—and when that included cooking, all you could do about it was shut up, wash your hands, and sit down at the table.

I think what this woman really objected to was the comparison between Italian-Americans and people of color. I've been told that this is racist because it insults people of color. I'm still waiting for someone to explain to me why the suggestion that a non-Italian might have something in common with Italian-Americans is so insulting to non-Italians.

Later I suggested to this woman that her magazine do a special issue on Italian-American lesbians. To my surprise, she agreed and asked me to edit it. Then I found out why she'd agreed. She expected me to do all the typesetting for the issue—so that she could take the time off to work on her novel.

Although this is just not routinely done, I agreed because I thought the issue, if done well, would make a difference. But the more I worked with this woman, the more I realized she was ignorant of Italian-American heritage and insensitive to our situation.

To give one example: I attended an editorial meeting for an issue of her magazine and found out that she intended to print a patronizing piece of drivel that presents an Italian-American woman as a one-dimensional freak—and this was in spite of the fact that the story didn't even have any relevance in a lesbian feminist context.

She tried to avoid facing her anti-Italian bigotry by ignoring my arguments and pounding on the word "freak," saying that my calling this character, who is fat, a freak betrays my own "fat-phobia." But her accusation just proved her contempt for Italian-Americans, her ignorance of Southern Italian and Sicilian standards of beauty, and her own negative feelings about being fat herself. I called this character a freak because the author has her lift a car that was wedged into a fence so tightly no one had been able to drive it out. And her solution to this problem was to change the "nationality" (that is, the last name) of the character—but only if it didn't offend the author to do so.

When I asked the editor what she thought an Italian-American issue would be, after trying to avoid giving an answer, she said she thought it would be an examination of the difficulties of being a lesbian in an Italian family, and a celebration of our culture. But these are only two tired stereotypes—the ignorant homophobe and the happy, dancing, singing harmless little Italian—which exclude much more important issues—like the difficulties of being Italian-American in the lesbian community, and how our history has been rewritten by both Northern Italians and Americans, including lesbians.

When I told her I was no longer interested in doing the issue, she assigned it to two friends of hers—two women who had been friends of mine until I dropped the issue. But first she made them sign a contract giving her full and final editorial control of the issue—something that's never been done before with any of the special women's issues produced by this magazine or any other magazine in the progressive lesbian community that pretends to see the need for each group to define itself. Now, the closest thing the Italian-American lesbian has to a self-definition is a single issue of a magazine censored by an ignorant, anti-Italian bigot.

Before the earthquake in 1989, in the main branch of the San Francisco Public Library, you can find special displays of books relevant to almost any ethnic group. If I wanted to find something about Italian women immigrants, I had to go to the stacks and plow through a dusty book about European immigrants, find the two or three pages devoted to Italian men, and maybe there'd be a mention of a woman. Occasionally, I'd find a whole book about Italians. The copyright would usually be something like 1910 or 1920; sometimes the book was so old, it wouldn't have a copyright at all. And the last due date stamped in it might be 1957. This means that very few people are interested in actively seeking out information about Italians. Now, since the earthquake, the stacks are closed, so nobody's going to just happen across information about Italians. Censorship doesn't always have to be censorship in order to be effective.

So, I'm reading what white male historians have written about Italian women immigrants. Ask any politically correct lesbian and she'll tell you that the white male historian has rewritten everyone's history and redefined everyone's culture—except the Italians. The reason, she'll tell you, that Italian women didn't come to this country unless they had family to go to, is that Italian women are wimps. It's a commonly known fact that Italian women are oppressed by their men and are forced to stay at home. It doesn't seem to matter to these lesbians that United States immigration laws at the time forbid any woman to enter this country if she didn't have family to go to—whether she was a wimp or not. Yet, Italian women are called wimps while Irish women, for example, are nearly always noted for how bravely they came over alone and nobody wonders how illegally they came over alone.

This got me mad and when I get mad I write poetry. I put together the new facts I was reading with the ignorant white male interpretation of them and what I had learned about Italian culture at home and wrote a first person narrative spoken by a Sicilian woman who describes how she came to America. She's strong, brave, sure of herself, and lives her life as she chooses—using Sicilian ways.

The non-Italian woman editor I sent it to said that, when we leave our original culture to live in another, we change, we assimilate, and that's why, although the poem might have special meaning for me, it just didn't "ring true" as a poem. I sent the poem to an Italian-Canadian man and he not only agreed to publish it, he seemed very excited about it and wanted to know if the woman who tells her story in the poem is still alive.

So, how do you complain about being called an unliberated female and being encouraged to get out and live? After all, they're just saying that for my own good; it's not a negative stereotype.

I read an article about Italy in the lesbian press in which the author makes generalizations about Italy based on a visit to one Northern city. This woman, who had never been to Italy before, wasn't fluent in Italian, apparently doesn't know how to read a street map and was probably never a girl scout, found it difficult to find her way around the city. She concluded that the reason for this was that Italians just don't know how to plan cities properly.

She also mentioned that she was having difficulty finding Black people in Italy. Although she's not Black herself and couldn't have been seeking the reassurance of a common bond in a land that was different to her, she seemed to think that this lack of Blacks in Italy was a sign of something wrong. After all, in spite of the racism in the United States, there are a lot of Black people here and I guess she doesn't think it means anything that that situation never existed in Italy.

And maybe she was looking for Black people in the wrong places. She was looking mostly in bars and nightclubs and in the streets. I have an illustrated Italian language textbook at home which has a picture of the library at the University of Perugia.[1] There are nine students in the picture; three of them are Black. And when I went to Naples and to Sicily this past summer, I saw a lot of African immigrants selling African handicrafts in the streets, chanting "prego, prego," whenever I stopped near them.

What I've found in the lesbian community is pretty much what's in the rest of the country. I'm reading a book now about Italian prisoners of war in Texas during World War II.[2] The author mentions that the prisoners complained because, well, you know those overemotional Italians are always dramatizing. Even the Red Cross said you have to take into consideration that Italians are sensitive and find captivity hard to endure. Ordinarily, I'd say a generalization like that is bigotry, but I'm hesitating this time because it makes Italians sound so much like people.

The situation for Italian-Americans in the lesbian community is actually a lot like the situation for lesbians in the straight community—nobody wants to admit we have any real heritage or significant value as a people. Whenever we ask for respect, somebody tries to divert the discussion by screaming unisex public toilets or the Mafia. So, while the straight non-Italian community tells me I needn't be trapped in this negative stereotype about being overemotional because I'm good enough to be accepted as American now and I don 't have to be Italian anymore.

Once, after presenting, at a multicultural conference in San Francisco, a paper similar to this one, a lesbian told the organizer that I was obviously uncomfortable both with my sexuality and with my ethnicity. That's what they tell women who are tired of being just housewives.

But I am tired of being a queer and a wop and I'm damned tired of bigots. Now, I want to be an Italian-American lesbian and everybody's just going to have to like it, because I already am.

NOTES

1. Lazzarino, Graziana, *Prego! An Invitation to Italian*, 2nd Ed. (Random House, 1984).
2. Williams, Donald Mace, *Interlude in Umbarger: Italian POWs and a Texas Church* (Texas Tech Univ. Press, 1992).

PART V
ARTISTIC INTERPRETATIONS: FILM AND POETRY

12

SALVATORE GIULIANO: THE FACTS, THE MYTH AND CINEMA

MARIO ASTE

UNIVERSITY OF MASSACHUSETTS –LOWELL

Salvatore Giuliano has become a legend in the mind of many. Much fiction about his life has been combined with facts and any discussion about him requires a concerted effort to discern fiction from reality. His brief, violent and romantic career in Sicily during the last years of the 2nd World War and the early years of the Italian Republic has fascinated many, including journalists, novelists and film directors.

Giuliano was born in Montelepre, a small mountain town near Palermo. In 1943, in his early twenties he became an outlaw. He came from a poor background and he led a life not unlike other peasant boys his age. He had dropped out of school to help his family on the farm. Due to the bad economic situation, he began buying olive oil in one place and selling it at a slightly higher price in another. He had no criminal record and from this activity he quickly moved into the wheat black market. This was a profitable enterprise especially under allied military occupation and to a certain extent a "normal career" at that time. One day he got caught by the police, but in order to escape, he shot and killed a *carabiniere*. To avoid capture and a jail sentence, Giuliano ran to the hills and his life as a bandit began. He found a hideout in the Sagana Mountain and from there with a growing band of outlaws he was able to become an "enforcer" of justice and "benefactor" to his native town, and soon he was affectionately named the "King of the Mountain."

His activity as a local bandit garnered him a certain degree of respect from the citizens of Montelepre and years later from the populace of Sicily. His band was only one of many in Sicily, but what made him famous was the flair with which he conducted his brand of banditry. This distinguished him and catapulted him to a higher state of heroic form. His attitude was very similar to the behavior of Sardinian bandits who were considered by the people noble patriots and leaders in exile. Like them, Giuliano possessed *balentia* (strength and honor) and this led to the formation of legends and the existence of popular myths about him.

In the 1940s, especially during the allied occupation, Sicily was going through extraordinary times and many forces were at play in shaping the future of the island. These forces included the separatist movement; the need for land reform; the re-emergence of the rural Mafia, struggling to regain the power and influence that it had lost during the period of fascism.[1]

With the Allied invasion of 1943, several plots were underway to create an independent Sicily. The major players in this movement were Lucio Tesca, a landowner and a rightist; Calogero Vizzini, the island's best known Mafia boss; the Di Carcaci family under whose protection congregated a large group of conservative nobles; and Antonio Canepa, who led a double life, one as a scholarly professor writing about fascist political theories and the other, under the pen-name of Mario Turri, publishing anti-fascist and separatist literature like the pamphlet *Sicilia ai Siciliani*.[2]

The separatist movement received a great push in 1943 when all ties with the Italian mainland were severed under the Allied Occupational Government. On July 28, 1943, the movement received public acknowledgment and respectability when Andrea Finocchiaro Aprile assumed its leadership and began to operate in a new, although limited, climate of public political expression. The transformation of this movement into a political party, Movimento Indipendenza Siciliana, was accomplished in the Fall of 1944 at the same time as the Communist Party, the Christian Democratic Party and others. The great strength of the Sicilian Independence Movement was in the provinces of Palermo, Catania and Messina. By war's end, the separatists, many Mafia groups, several noble families and rightist groups all advocated the importance of returning Sicily to the Sicilians.

The Mafia was the weak link in this movement and in the political and military strength of the coalition. When in the late 1944 and early 1945, the prospect for Sicilian independence encountered difficulties, due to the Allies and Italian government's strong reaction to separatists' declarations, the Mafia increasingly looked with great favor toward the traditional parties. By this time, the leaders of the Movement also realized that military action was necessary to achieve their goal. Politics and diplomacy no longer seemed to be viable alternatives to their program; therefore, they began to recruit groups who were in possession of armaments. By responding to this call, Giuliano took a major step toward fame. After intense negotiations with all the interested parties, he was made a colonel of EVIS (Esercito Volontario per L'Indipendenza Siciliana). In a typewritten manifesto to the Sicilian people Giuliano proclaimed that the day for struggle is at hand:

> Sicilians! The solemn hour of the Sicilian revolution is ready to strike. Imitating the heroic moves of our forefathers ... who liberated us from the French yoke, we will sever this Italian chain which under the guise of protecting us oppresses and suffocates us...We will fight and inevitably win that independence for which we have yearned so long...at the shout of liberty take up arms and gather in the town squares where you will find   men to lead you in the realization of the highest aims of the Sicilian nation.[3]

Giuliano's activities after the publication of this Manifesto reflected his true commitment to the independence cause. He began by attacking police posts, kidnapping people in order to finance his military campaigns, and asserting military and judicial leadership over Western Sicily. The resolve was to achieve victory through armed revolt, but this was soon abandoned after the elections of 1946 when the leaders of the movement opted for a political victory. In fact, before the election, Lucio Tesca had agreed with the authorities on two conditions: 1) the renunciation of violence; and 2) the surrender of all armaments in possession of the Voluntary army. Giuliano was suspicious of any agreement and wanted assurance that he and his men would be granted amnesty before surrendering their arms.

The elections of 1946 saw the end of the Italian Monarchy, the establishment of the Italian Republic, and a mortal blow to the Independence Movement. The party led by Tesca had failed because it did not address the issues of land reform and the Mafia had opted to make separate deals with other conservative parties.

At this time the major parties offered, in collaboration with the central government in Rome, a much broader form of Sicilian autonomy, which was more palatable to a large number of the Sicilian population instead of independence. Giuliano, who delivered for the Sicilian independence movement through the ballot box, felt left out of the new emerging political reality and began to look for alternatives to his situation. Giuseppe Calandra and Cardinal Ruffino of Palermo offered him a solution: emigrate to America after repentance of his crimes, possibly in Church. Giuliano did not accept this deal and convinced his followers, especially those closest to him, not to abandon their way of life.

The newspaper *L'Ora* of Palermo on August 11, 1946, published a letter of Giuliano's in which he continued his appeal to the people of Sicily and to the *carabinieri* to join in the struggle for social justice and independence. Probably the letter was written by Pasquale Sciortino, a teacher and a friend, who joined the separatist cause and for a while became part of Guiliano's family, by marrying his sister. In 1946, a major split occurred in the Movement between Finocchiaro, who endorsed a monarchy under the House of Savoy, and Varvaro, who founded his own party, leaning toward a Republican form of government.

Varvaro received the warm support of Giuliano and the election results of 1947 showed that the area of Montelepre, as in the previous elections, heeded his advice, voting overwhelming for the Varvaro party. But at this time it was clear that the independence movement was experiencing a sharp decline of popular interest, and Varvaro decided to join the Communist Party. Giuliano was troubled by his friend's political choice because he was ardently pro-American and anti-Communist. The winners of the 1947 elections indeed were clearly the Communist and Socialists, with 30% of the vote. This victory raised the anger of the rightists who immediately plotted to turn the tables by intimidating the people through violence. Their choice for intimidation fell upon Giuliano, the only person with an organized and armed band, who could stop the threats of a possible Red revolution.

In the meantime Stern, an American journalist, was able to interview Giuliano. This played a large role in the formation of a popular myth about him. The Sicilian outlaw gave Stern a letter for President Truman in which he described his strong anti-Communist views and disclosed his needs for arms to stop the rise of Communism in Sicily and to make Sicily a bastion against Soviet expansionism by annexing it as the 49th State of the Union. The Stern visit and Giuliano's hopes for American military aid made his future attacks against the leftists a more acceptable alternative. The occasion presented itself on May 1, 1947, at Portella della Ginestra during a gathering of leftists.

In the days preceding the event, Giuliano was visited by Sciortino, who gave him a letter that was immediately destroyed after having been read. After the visit, Giuliano told trusted friends that the hour of liberation of Sicily was at hand and that there was a need to recruit young men for activities to be undertaken against the left. According to several sources, the nature of these activities was a bit unclear. The plan was to attack the gathering of leftistS at Portella della Ginestra from two sides and fire over the crowd to create confusion so a band led by Terranova would be able to kidnap LiCausi, the Communist leader of Sicily, but the plan failed because LiCausi was not present at the demonstration. Giuliano's people were confused and a young man fired at the crowd instead, killing several people, among them women and children.

> After the incident Giuliano was remorseful over the deaths, but he was also angry over its failure. On other occasions he was more candid, as when he talked with the Italian journalist Jacopo Rizza in 1949. Giuliano told him that he had been deceived at Portella. A promise of liberty was given to him that was never kept, and other than for that promise, he never would have made the attack. He would not tell Rizza from whom the promise came, although he

talked in general terms of his association with the monarchists, especially with an unnamed one at the heart of the movement. As he did at other times, he affirmed that at the proper moment he would reveal the full story. Giuliano never made his promised revelations, at least in so far as is publicly known. One might still hope for the discovery of memoirs in his handwriting that tell all. Short of that unlikely event, the best answer to the central question of Portella della Ginestra rests on the statements of the police and residents of the area, Pisciotta's accusations, the Ramirez letter, and Giuliano's own limited admissions.[4]

After this action against the left, Giuliano confirmed his anti-Communist crusade in a new manifesto. The decisive hour has already struck! He who does not want to be easy prey to that baying pack of reds... must today decide. Those people who want at every cost to throw us into the lap of that terrible Russia, where liberty is an impossible fancy and democracy a legend ... must be fought without ceasing. And I have assumed this responsibility .... To the superficial chronicler of events it may seem strange that it would be I who gives life to this Crusade.... Resolutely many have wanted to falsify my positions .... For nearly four years I have fought unceasingly... for a rich, flowering, and prosperous Sicily, and to make it become, as before, the garden spot for Europe. For this I have fought and will continue to fight .... He who feels truly Sicilian ... and wants to cooperate in this great anti-Bolshevik battle let it be known that there is an estate called SAGANA where I have established my general headquarters .... I am certain that many will join me there.[5]

Giuliano's alliance with the right continued in 1947, but his activities tarnished his reputation and led him into greater difficulties especially after another attack to leftist offices and the killing of Giuliano's friend Ferreri, who had become a *carabinieri* informant. The massive military search for Giuliano continued. His response, in order to support his band, was to have more abductions, extortions and run-ins with the police, usually provoked by him.

In 1948, trouble surfaced again after the killing of two *carabinieri*. In the elections of 1948 Giuliano supported the rightist parties. He did so in order to combat communism. He also hoped by his action to see fulfilled a promise of pardon and amnesty made to him and his men by the central government. After the elections, Scelba, the Minister of the Interior, gave a negative answer to the request of pardon and amnesty and Giuliano's only viable choice was to emigrate to Brazil and find refuge in a farm owned by the Alliata family. Giuliano opted instead to remain in Sicily and to vent his frustration and anger with appropriate retaliation against those who betrayed him. The first victim of his anger was the mafioso Santo Fleres killed July 17, 1948, on Partinio's public square. The following months were very grim because Giuliano had exhausted all avenues of amnesty and felt destined to remain a bandit until either his freedom or his life would end.

After a last visit with his mother, Giuliano gave serious consideration to emigration, especially since Sciortino had already left for America. The police forces were relentless and acted quickly by arresting the members of his family. This action was followed by more violence and repression. The band began to break apart and some of the members left for Tunisia, other were either arrested or killed, one victim of this crackdown was one of his trusted friends, Passatempo. At this time Giuliano had an interview with the Swedish female journalist, Cyliakus, and another for *Oggi* in early 1949 with Jacopo Rizza. Both interviews were important, the first one because it gave a personal, emotional and sentimental account of Giuliano deeds; the second because it published in *Oggi* a series of photographs which gave a visual and personal account of Giuliano's life to the rest of Italy.

In August 1949, Giuliano attacked the *carabinieri* at Bellolampo. The results included eight fatalities and twelve wounded, all of them *carabinieri*. Giuliano in a letter published in *L'Ora* bragged, "Had I wanted to, I could have destroyed the entire column." Before the end of the month two more *carabinieri* were killed at Cipirello. Given the very tense situation, contacts and negotiations were established through intermediaries between Giuliano and the police to resolve the situation by negotiating on such issues like honor, amnesty, respectability, and law and order.

In December 1949, Giuliano had a second meeting with the police commander Vidriani about these issues. The purpose of the meeting was to arrange for the release the members of his family and a possible emigration and amnesty for himself and his band. To a certain extent, the meeting was successful, except that Vidriani was replaced from Rome by Colonel Luca and could not totally follow totally the agreed plans. The only part of the deal that was carried out was the release from jail of Giuliano's family. Luca, the new commander, was determined to bring Giuliano to justice and squelch all the rumors of Giuliano's departure for America.

The demise of Giuliano finally came as the result of his trusted friend, confidant and lieutenant, Gaspanu Pisciotta's betrayal. In 1950, Giuliano was hiding in the De Maria house in Castelvetrano. On July 4th, a message from Vidriani warning Giuliano of the impending betrayal and of Pisciotta's plot to kill him was received by him. Giuliano confronted Pisciotta with this message. But Pisciotta convinced Giuliano to trust him and to disregard the message. In the middle of the night, while he was sleeping in his bed, Giuliano was killed by Pisciotta.

The official version of the story in police accounts is that Giuliano was killed by the *carabinieri* while trying to escape after being surrounded. Pisciotta claimed that he and not the police killed Giuliano at the Viterbo trail for the massacre at Portella della Ginestra. Pisciotta was found guilty of this massacre and sent to jail, but in 1954 he was mysteriously killed in his cell. After the claims of Pisciotta, the official version of Giuliano's death became questionable and the rumors about Mafia involvement in this matter were predominant. In 1960, when Benedetto Minasola, a Mafia intermediary between the police and the underworld, was found murdered, a lid was officially placed on the case, but several questions still remained unanswered.

Giuliano's short life, especially his campaigns for Sicilian independence and against the left, became the source of several admiring ballads and legends. His memory continued to live in the collective mind of Sicilians everywhere. He became a popular hero for many who barely had heard of him. His killing became the first step in the creation of a new Giuliano born to serve and to lead. To Sicilians, he became the voice of an idea which many outside the island did not understand. Dennis Mack Smith gives this assessment:

Giuliano's political allegiance, like Vizzini's, was at first
to the separatists, and in 1945 he was colonel in the Sicilian army of independence; but when separatism could no
longer guarantee him subsidies and high-level sponsor-
ship, it was noticed that the pattern of voting in his zone of
influence shifted significantly to the monarchists, and then,
again like Vizzini's, to the Christian Democrats. By 1947
his considerable powers of intimidation were engaged in
combating communism; and a few days after the elections
of April 1947 had favored the Left, he gave warning of his
intentions when the spectators at a defiant May Day meeting outside Palermo were mowed down by the automatic
rifles of his gang.[6]

These activities of Giuliano affected the Sicilian masses in a different way than the outsiders looking in. For Sicilians, Giuliano's exploits from
birth to death were shrouded with an aura of mystery and wonder. This gave
rise to a figure of Giuliano which bordered the mythological and the people
by meditating and reflecting on it reinforced the perception of Giuliano as
hero. This, at the same time, had the beneficial effect of strengthening for
everyone the popular culture of Sicily. This culture was rooted in millinery
customs and ideas which never changed, but continued to exist even under
different circumstances especially during foreign domination. Sicily for Sicilians is foremost a place of the heart and of the mind that only Sicilians can
understand at all times. By believing in Giuliano, the people allowed a sub-
stitutive gratification of their inner wishes and desires. By anointing him as
a new hero, who was young, strong and fearless and who fought and died for
the liberation of the motherland, a sacrament of atonement was established
for all. The dream of independence even after his death will live on and will
rise again from the ashes, like the phoenix, in another time.

Giuliano, in the silences of his personal despair, caused by the failure of achieving an independent Sicily, was able to reach the highest point
of a spiritual ascension toward his destiny. He became a conscience of his
people's supreme ordeal: the search for empowerment and greater affirma-

tion. The cultural world of Sicily beckoned to him to come and defend its reason for survival. Giuliano heard the call and joined the struggle, but the price was much greater than the one he had expected.

It is in this context of facts and identities of issues that Giuliano and his short life must be studied. In the confused interpretations of historical events, caused by different perspectives, the first film *Salvatore Giuliano* (1961) made by Francesco Rosi, must be analyzed. This film delves into the most intricate labyrinth of the history of the Mafia and post-war Sicily. The death of Giuliano is the starting point of the plot and must be taken as the necessary explanatory link between all his actions and historical events. The film proceeds with a quasi-documentary plot.

> Giuliano is a mythical figure, and as such he is powerful enough to make the investigation of the myth a thrilling dramatic experience. Rosi's interest focuses on a power struggle in which the "criminal hero" was hardly more than a pawn. Giuliano was first used by the Sicilian separatists, then by the Allies, the anti-communists, the Mafia, and by various sections of the state apparatus, even the judiciary. The evidence of this manipulation started coming together only at the trial of some of his accomplices, long after Giuliano had been murdered. But the truth remained obscure; Rosi does not pretend to have any answers to the questions surrounding the Giuliano myth. His camera, sometimes emotional, sometimes objective, reveals the drama of life and death as it had been performed in Sicily for centuries, with piles of corpses and no catharsis.[7]

The first shot of the film presents the bullet-ridden, lifeless body of Giuliano in a courtyard surrounded by police officers and photographers. The film then proceeds through flashbacks to the most important ideas that shaped Giuliano's life. History is interpreted by Rosi without any respect for chronology and the period between 1945-1960 is seen through a series of disorienting leaps back and forth linking one event with another with an "attempt to reach a satisfactory explanation of why these seemingly disconnected events occurred, but then Rosi is investigating the Byzantine interconnection between bandits, the Mafia, and Allied occupation forces, and politicians."[8]

The people of Sicily saw in Giuliano not only a man that stole from the rich and gave to the poor, but a hero, a liberator who could lead them forth from the bondage of years of servitude. Rosi's film indicates this when it points out that there is a far more important reality underneath all the facts and events narrated. When the journalist went to visit Giuliano, spoke to his men, the emphasis is about Sicily or being a Sicilian, because anyone who is not Sicilian cannot understand Sicily or anything Sicilian. The laws of honor and respect were the spiritual source of his power, a power nourished and strengthened by the unwritten practice of "omerta," through which he found protection and security.

Giuliano, to his countrymen, was greater than life itself. He was a fearless leader in the face of insurmountable difficulties. Even in death his figure loomed larger than life and anything comprehensible to the human eye. Rosi portrays this mythological aura surrounding Giuliano by showing his lifeless body in state at the cemetery before burial. The body is placed on a slab of marble to allow his mother to see him for the last time. Here Rosi presents a framed image of Giuliano from an angled perspective which recalls the painting of the *Dead Christ* by Mantegna. Rosi intended with this device to make the viewer meditate with the greatest possible intensity upon the personal meaning of Giuliano's death. The message is simple to understand: the sacrificial death of Christ is here the meter of comparison with Giuliano's death. This scene is one that will be repeated in Cimino's film *The Sicilian*. The profound psychological effect produced by this frame goes in a long way in reinforcing the director's perspective in presenting a man hailed as a liberator and leader who found premature death through the betrayal of his trusted acolyte.

In 1950, the great Giuliano, known as the King of the Mountain, had become just a name on the tombstone. But this is not the end, because Rosi in his tendency to blur the psychological outlines of his heroes converts them into emblems of factual inquiries.[9] The factual inquiring is overshadowed by the blurring of psychological study of the character, and this enhances Giuliano's meteoric rise to self-determination as it is understood by the view-

ers especially if his power-driven accomplishments are seen as a prelude for
the acknowledgments which followed his death. The investigation about his
death, as presented by Rosi, showed either the inefficiency or the culpability of the Italian State in finding the real culprits in the rise and fall of
Giuliano. These culprits together with the government are the Mafia, who
control through intimidation and silence the life of the poor and rich alike,
and the Church, which, by linking with the nobles and other unnamed forces,
oppresses the populace, and abandons its spiritual world and becomes alien
to itself by destroying the most noble elements of human life instead of protecting them.

In the end, Pisciotta betrayed Giuliano by going to the police and by
agreeing to do the killing for them. This must be taken either as an indication
that the Italian police were not able to deal with the problem at hand in an
efficient manner or that Giuliano was the beloved of the people. The police
by staging the killing of Giuliano in the courtyard emphasized their ability
to distort the truth through cover-up and other activities supposedly performed in defense of the people. In the trial of Viterbo, years later, Pisciotta
was found guilty for the peasants massacre at Portella della Ginestra and
condemned to a lengthy jail sentence but one day while serving his prison
term he was found poisoned to death. This from a viewer perspective will
forever muddle the truth about Giuliano's activities.

The creation of the three centers of powers: the Mafia, the Church
and the Nobles, is according to Cimino's *The Sicilian* (1986), the basis of
Giuliano's ascent to power and heroic status with the people. He glamorizes
the figure of this outlaw by presenting a character based on the romanticized
biographic novel of Mario Puzo, *The Sicilian*.[10] This work of Puzo is histori-
cally inaccurate and filled with revisionistic ideas. Emmanuele Macaluso in
an article published in *L'Unita`*, August 3, 1986, states:

> *I giornali ci hanno informato che Cimino ha come
> referimento il nuovo libro dell'autore del Padrino, Puzo,
> che ha scritto una storia romanzata, Il Siciliano, del
> bandito di Montelepre. Abbiamo letto il libro è
> francamente non vale niente. La ricostruzione segue un
> filo che e alcune 'varianti' volte a dare il ritratto di un*

*Giuliano forte e buono, coraggioso e generoso, amico dei
poveri e nemico dei ricchi che godeva della devozione
dell' intera popolazione dell'Isola. Balle. Il libro è
infarcito di luoghi comuni, di mediocri ovvita; i
personaggi sono colorati, caricaturali, improbabili. Puzo
non conosce la storia e la geografia della Sicilia, gli usi e
i costumi, il linguaggio e le abitudini dei siciliani. Il libro
e una paccotaglia per il grosso pubblico americano.*[11]

Throughout the film Cimino uses Puzo's historical revisionism in order to maintain the illusion that Giuliano was a Robin Hood of sorts, rather than the leader of a right wing death squad.[12]

A major difference between the Giuliano of history and Cimino's representation of myth created by the artistic powers of literature and cinema is the analysis of Giuliano's relationship with the left at the beginning of the Italian Republic. To understand this relationship is important because it ties in with much of the life of Giuliano especially in regard to the Massacre of Portella della Ginestra.

In Cimino's film, Giuliano was present during the massacre, but was disobeyed by one of his members who shot at the crowd. In Puzo's novel, Giuliano's whereabouts are unclear, however his orders are disobeyed and people are shot. Although the two fictional accounts are different, one thing stands out: the perception of Giuliano's concern for the people and their wish for emancipation and empowerment.

Generally speaking, he is presented as regretting the whole incident. Cimino goes a step further and presents Giuliano leading the leftists in their march toward a much brighter future. A more thorough reading of the historical Giuliano clearly points out a very different reality than the revisionist one advanced by Puzo and Cimino.

Giuliano had contempt for the Communist Party and this is supported by his letter to President Truman asking for military aid under the Marshall Plan and wanting to politically re-align Sicily with the United States. These facts make it hard to believe that he felt pity for any of the participating Communists who were killed on May 1, 1947. This is probably one of the only events which can be directly associated to Giuliano which did not seem to be for the "good of the Sicilian people" especially since many of the people killed were peasants whom Giuliano was supposedly protecting from the clutches of the Italian state. It is, however, understandable why this event has been altered by Puzo and by Cimino. Such a drastic event directly linked to the hero would seem to place more than just a small scratch on his character. If the revision had not taken place, the reader and the viewer would no longer put Giuliano on a pedestal to be idolized by rebuking the injustices which have been incurred upon him, but rather diminish him and place him in the category of political leaders whose ideas have gone awry.

With these factual truths about gentility it is easy to see how a character such as Giuliano could become glamorized, no one wants to believe that a man who is so mannered and gentle could commit so many vicious murders. The stereotypical villain is ugly, coarse and very publicly brutal. Giuliano was definitely not stereotypical, he was good looking, gentle and educated even though mostly through self-improvement. Another important aspect in the creating of the legend is Giuliano's premature death. His memory lives on and his death is seen by many as an unjust ending for such a great hero and thus he is made the martyr of a noble cause through his death.

Giuliano's life as bandit was a hard and complicated one: sneaking into and out of his house without being caught, staging attacks to police stations, and kidnapping rich landowners to finance his political and military campaigns. There is an element of reason and truth in all that he did but the difficulty factor was hardly evident until the last year of his life when all of his dreams were coming suddenly to an abrupt end. Although he had killed many *carabinieri* he was still able to freely give interviews with the press, visit his family and kidnap people in broad daylight with ease.

Another fictionalized aspect of Cimino's and Puzo's views about Giuliano is the interest he showed toward women. His gentleness with women was emphasized and this characteristic is exemplified in one of his first heists as a bandit when he steals a ring from the American born countess. He is never rough with her but simply asks her for the ring, although she pleads to keep it because of its sentimental value, Giuliano takes it anyway saying he will treasure it more so. According to other sources, he also asks to borrow a Steinbeck book which he does and actually returns it a week later as promised. The fictitious along with the factual accounts of his treatment of kidnapped prisoners are most honorable. One of his kidnapped guests even says, "he fed me well and treated me with respect."

The fictional element continues in Puzo and Cimino where wedding bells and a wife are added to the legend about the "King of the Mountain." This is a long stretch of the artistic imagination and includes a marriage of Giuliano to the sister of the leftist leader whom Giuliano joins in a battle against the noble landowners and during the rally at *Portella della Ginestra*. Giuliano's wife is expecting a child at the moment of his death and is ready to escape to America with the help of the same forces who decreed the death of her husband. In reality Giuliano did not have a great interest in women. However, one must realize that the fictitious Giuliano would have been a bit boring without at least a love affair, like the one with the American-born countess and an emotional and sentimental commitment to his wife.

Puzo and Cimino create a Giuliano who is the hero of the common people, a man who had a calling. It is also important to note that the endless list of good deeds which Puzo describes in the novel, and appear in Cimino's filmic rendition, were also intertwined with dishonorable behavior such as imposing his protection on anyone who could pay (a tactic which the mafia is famous for) and a number of merciless killings.

> Though the real Giuliano was more banal and quixotic than this fictional counterpart, Puzo has changed very few details or events in his life; instead, he has scrupulously pared away extravagances that made the real Giuliano ridiculous: the bandit's appeal for arms to President Truman, for instance, and his suggestion that Sicily become this country's 49th state. It works as well because Giuliano's virtue is set against the infinite corruption of nearly everyone around him.[13]

The mystery surrounding Salvatore Giuliano will probably never be fully solved for several reasons. It is also worth noting that the truth about him is not that important to Sicilians. Giuliano represents more than just a character in history, he is the embodiment of an idea and a belief about Sicily held by Sicilians all over the world. Cimino goes even a step further because he creates a character which combines the mythological and Christological characteristics of the hero based in the activities of the individual, his name, and his sacrificial death caused by a friend's betrayal. By passing through the crucible of death, Giuliano shows that he as a hero is not afraid of dying.

> Salvatore Giuliano succumbs to virtually all the temptations with which he is confronted. He is lustful, proud, and violent. He is a thief of ideas as well as of property. He has taken Silvio Ferra's message, that the people want land, and made it his own. But none of this matters because he will be, if not forgiven, certainly not forgotten. Like Christ, he dies voluntarily to insure that his myth, and perhaps his message, will be remembered both through his unborn child in America and through the boy who bids him farewell at the pier.[14]

Not knowing exactly what happened during Giuliano's reign of power enables writers and movie-makers to glorify something or someone which may not be possibly as great as they think. Like characters in the American past such as Billy the Kid or Bonnie and Clyde, who represent a symbol to the American people about the great western frontier, Giuliano is the symbol of Sicily because he represents the fight for a separate identity from Italy. He attempted to relieve the oppression imposed by foreigners and deeply felt by the peasants of Sicily, by making it possible for all Sicilians to have control over their own fate. Because of this he will always be a synonym with liberation and affirmation for Sicilians all over the world.

NOTES

1. Chandler, Billy Jones, *King of the Mountain: The Life and Death of Giuliano the Bandit* (Dekalb, IL: Northern Univ. Press, 1988), p. 23.
2. Turri, Mario, *Sicilia ai Siciliani*, 1943.

3. Chandler, p. 48.
4. Chandler, p. 105.
5. Chandler, p. 99.
6. Smith, Dennis Mack, *Modern Sicily*, After 1713 (Dorset Press, 1968), p. 530.
7. Liehm, Mira, *Passion and Defiance: Film in Italy from 1942 to the Present* (Berkeley: Univ. of California Press, 1984), p. 213.
8. Bondanella, Peter, *Italian Cinema* (New York: Continuum Books, 1991, p. 169.
9. Whitcombe, R. T., *The New Italian Cinema* (New York: Oxford Univ. Press, 1982), p. 175.
10. Puzo, Mario, *The Sicilian* (New York: Simon & Schuster, 1984).
11. Macaluso, Emanuele, "I ritorni di Giuliano," *L'Unita*, 3 (August, 1986):13.
12. Lawton, Ben, "America through Italian/American Eyes: Dream or Nightmare," in *From the Margin*, Anthony J. Tamburri, et al (eds.) (West Lafayette, IN: Purdue Univ. Press, 1990), p. 429.
13. Prescott, Peter S., "In the Name of the Godfather," *Newsweek* 11 (November, 1984): 108.
14. Lawton, pp. 419-420.

ADDITIONAL REFERENCES

Bliss, Michael, *Martin Scorsese and Michael Cimino* (Metuchen, N.J.: The Scarecrow Press, Inc., 1985).

Finkelstein, Monte S, "Sicilian Separatism, the Mafia and the Origins of Sicilian Autonomy, 1943-1946," in *Support and Struggle*, Joseph Tropea et al (eds.) (Staten Island, NY: AIHA, 1986), pp. 207-24.

Moorehead, Alan, "If You Value Your Life," *New Yorker* (February, 1950): 36-46.

13

ON THE POETICS OF JOSEPH TUSIANI'S *GENTE MIA*

FRANCO MULAS
UNIVERSITY OF SASSARI, ITALY

Joseph Tusiani is an Italian-American poet born in Italy, who writes highly original poetry without ever denying his *Italianità*. Born in San Marco in Lamis (Foggia), Dr. Tusiani, after receiving a degree in Foreign Languages and Literatures from the University of Naples, moved to the United States in 1946. He began his career as professor of Italian, scholar, translator and poet. Writing in English, Italian and Latin, he has authored several collections of poems which have brought him international recognition and honors. Of the long list of his publications, our interest here is centered on *Gente Mia and Other Poems*[1], a little volume of about 30 lyrics which, as Paolo Giordano has said, "is a poetical account that capture(s) the essence and pathos of what it means to be Italian in a foreign land that he must call home."[2] Fred Gardaphe has defined this book as "a collection of poems written in English, a language he had learned in Italy, through which he is able to give voice to the immigrants who came before him—the ones who did not, because they could not, write in the language of their new land."[3]

Tusiani's classical studies gave him a lyrical footing on which to base some of the main themes dear to Italian poets, such as Leopardi, Foscolo, and Carducci, whom he knew almost by heart. But this did not keep him from reaching for new poetic horizons. Of his lyrics, very few carry the

seasonal imagery or idyllic visions communicating a serene inner state; rather
they bring to us the hopes and cries of the Italian immigrants in America,
whose experience he lived in *prima persona.*

Primary in Tusiani's poetry are the feasts and celebrations of his
fellow immigrants in the New World. In these so brilliantly described commemorative moments, much of the pain and suffering of their struggle seems
to disappear. The emphasis instead is on the positive, the festive and often
intimate side of their presence in this foreign land:

> Last night your children were the chanting throngs
> behind your statue and the parish priest,
>> and now they once again
> are what they were—unknown, hard-working men.
>
> Yes, you are pleased remembering this new
> Procession in your honor, with a glare
>> of altar boys in red,
> a band, balloons slow-floating overhead,
>
> and from the sidewalks people throwing you
> signs-of-the-cross and kisses and a prayer:
>> three hours of paradise
> quite visible in all our mortal eyes.
>
> This morning everybody's back to work
> as if no holiday had ever been,
>> yet everybody's more
> resigned to life than ever, ever before.
>
>   ("The Day After the Feast")

In his poetic design Tusiani achieves both freedom and balance
which he seems to draw from his own inner depths. He never wanders cha-
otically as if conducted by conflicting memories. Even the clash of the first
impressions and feelings of his early childhood with those of the immediate
reality of life in the New World is never really in conflict, but rather is con-

trolled by his artistic maturity. He is at all times a scholar with a dreaming heart and soul, and a poet in whose veins runs pure Italian blood, who seems to have inherited, from some unknown, mysterious power, the gift to sing freely about everything his sensibility perceives of the joys and disenchantments of his fellow immigrants:

> Unhappy in his happy paradise,
> misunderstood in all this understanding
> gold of the Indian summer round his brow,
> unable to forget the Ocean now
> when he should but recall the joy of landing.
>
> ("Columbus Day in New York")

The lyric voice of this poet is unique and his genuine pathos recaptures perfectly the conflicting emotions which often result from deep pain and loss of affections, as on the occasion of the death of his uncle who used to bring him the figs from his own garden:

> "Figs from my backyard!"' you announced to me
> whenever, unannounced yet welcome most
> you wished to tell me of Italian skies
> here in the midst of this Atlantic fog.
>
> ("In Memoriam: Joe Pisano")

There is obviously no lack of drama in Tusiani's poems, for they are always both very personal and objective.

Gente Mia is made up of two parts, the first dealing with the life and manners of the common immigrant people, a recollection of a past agrarian society or a nostalgic remembrance of boyhood experience, and the second dealing with the poet's desperate need for new friendships and warm human contacts. These poems are not difficult to read and understand, yet Tusiani is always profound. He does not use symbols nor does he construct mythical worlds of his own that require exegesis. His language is always that of cultured speech and is used with extreme precision and clear, straightforward forms.

To listen to the voice of Joseph Tusiani, a voice of seemingly lim-

itless humanity, is to feel the anguish of those millions of immigrants from
Italy who had to make the final painful choice of leaving their birthplace.
How the author himself came to make that choice at the age of 23, soon after his graduation from the University of Naples, is addressed in one of his
poems "The Difficult Word." This poem, a deeply felt confession, recalls a
fatherless child growing up in a small village in Abruzzo:

> Christmas Day
> brought me, instead, the mystery of snow—
> an omnipresent coldness in the air
> with the heart-warming chirping, now and then,
> of a bird feeding fledglings in their nest.
>
> ("The Difficult Word")

The sadness which permeates this lyric constantly heightens the dramatic
representation of the intellectual and emotional experience of the poet, who
leads the reader into a prophetic world of final discovery. The process of
migration tears people from their loved ones, keeping them apart, and what
is even more tragic is that it keeps sons away from their fathers' love and
protection, making them strangers to one another forever:

> Oh, we have grown apart—you with no son,
> I with no father: Emigration's last
> and most uncharted tragedy is this—
> slowly it forces people to adjust
> to want to love, anticipating death.
> A reunited family means only
> reunion of faces, not of feelings.
>
> ("The Difficult Word")

His imaginative reconstruction of the language enables him to express his
concern about man's estrangement from the spiritual value of life as such,
until the difficult word becomes "a meaning in your soul."

While Tusiani never departs from the basic realism of modern poetry, he achieves transcendence in the use of aesthetic metaphors intellectually created from the raw material of his own life and of others he knows very

well. The word and the event in the hands of such a craftsman become a single experience charged with extraordinary feelings, and although original themes are not sought after in his poetry, they can easily be found, mainly because his poetic reflection reaches down to genuine humble people, his own people, and never gets left in the clouds.

His awareness of form and technique, his use of color, and his vivid, striking images owe something, no doubt, to his extensive background in literature. He makes spontaneous use of what he has learned and assimilated in his reading of all kinds of poetry. Unlike other modern poets, however, he avoids abstractions and philosophical conceits. His vision, nonetheless, is often complex, sometimes confused, causing certain perceptions to come forth bright in our minds as if breaking suddenly free of obscure situations. Most of the best qualities of Tusiani's poetry are exemplified in this collection of poems, particularly in "The Barrel-Organ," one of the most moving elegies ever written by an Italian American poet:

Music, music, only music is the language of the heart,
so new music I am playing in the heart of old
New York. Father says we have nobody but the
music and the stork: here is a song for everybody,
here's a song I know by heart.

Grandfather long ago
a piece of land had he

but God makes nothing grow
in southern Italy.

Grandfather was as strong
as any southern man
and knew that it was wrong
not to work and work again.

So in his piece of land
harder he worked that year,

sowing with his own hand,
praying with all his fear.

His land grew large and new
and rich as altar gold,
the sky more deep and blue,
the sun more bright and bold

In less than a half hour
a whole year's dream fell dead:

goodby, Grandmother's flour,
goodby, Grandfather's bread!

Grandfather did not curse,
though wholly bent and low,
but he was spared much worse,
dying before the snow.

Before he died, Grandfather
Had but one thing to say.
"This is no land," he said to Father;
"I curse you if you stay."

                              ("The Barrel-Organ)

In most of the poems in *Gente Mia*, Tusiani is directly concerned
with the life of the Italian immigrants in New York, where he has lived since
coming to the United States, feeling both the tension of their endeavor and
the pathos of their failures and successes. As an interpreter of their lives, he
portrays them as truthfully and objectively as he can, never giving an outward
show of his own emotions, although many of his poems have their origin in
deeply felt personal experiences. Tusiani knows that life and art are two different things and that there is no such thing as complete objectivity in art.
Therefore, in his poems, he does what an artist must do to give the illusion

of life: he tries to attain a realistic effect through specificity and richness of carefully selected details. He is not merely interested in the exterior realism of things, however, but in states of mind, the relationships of people, the consequences of actions.

Many of his lyrics contain a strong narrative element. Charged with pure lyric emotion they usually tell a story with a rich mixture of fantasy and real events. As a narrator, he shows both boldness and a sense of being at home with the world he knows well; he is a man who speaks rather than writes, treating the most disturbing situations with admirable calm. Whether he begins with a phrase like "Uncle I know now why this Spring began / so strangely cold," or with a question, "Why a museum now?" or an intriguing meditation, "It must be want of music makes me charge / this silence with a song I have not sung," he makes certain to develop the lead-in with a commanding accuracy. More like the Metaphysical poets than his modern contemporaries, he uses emotionally heightened states as occasions for clarity.

In general, his poetry embodies a passionate process of investigation which often implies a narrative, leading both speaker and reader through a sequence of rapidly changing images, even when all the action is interior. It is these investigations that structure his poetry, and the flexibility of his investigative movement could be the major reason why Tusiani generally seems to be content with common meter. Typically, his poems begin with a declaration or definition in the first two lines and proceed to a metaphorical breaking open of the original premise. One poem may question: "O new awareness of my ancient light / what's then so new about this earth of mine?" ("Ethnicity") Another may examine: "If per contraria we know all things / White from black, peace from war / Clear is the reason why these murmurings, so indistinct before, / are now the voice from some prenatal place / of human helplessness." ("The Italian Goat") Other poems, but fewer, begin with an observation which form the shell for the poem's argument: "I, Costantino Brumidi, declare / that Art and Liberty go hand in hand. / Pardon me, gentlemen, I did not know / that I had company." ("I, Costantino Brumidi")

In the middle of Tusiani's poems, we usually find a sequence of metaphors or metaphoric actions. Then the poems veer, often unexpectedly, into surmise, renewed rhetorical inquiry, or an open ending of the lyric, for many of the poems close with the clear indication that the debate does not finish with the poem:

> So here he is today, today at last,
> riding atop his bright Santa Maria,
> the navigator of the *Gente Mia*,
> light of my future, darkness of his past,
>
> the one who came to dig (for dig we must)
> for the high glory of the subway tracks,
> the immigrant who died and yet still lacks
> identity with this American dust.
>
> ("Columbus Day in New York")

Tusiani's poems are usually long poems and cover a great deal of subjects. However, they all have a common denominator, the life of the immigrant in the United States: his life, dreams, hopes, successes, failures and, above all, pain of separation from his native land. Who better than the poet himself to express the torments cf people forced to break away from their culture, language and history? Born a few months after his father's departure to America, Tusiani lived as he himself says in his biography "with a picture in my mind," until he finally met him in a strange land among strange sounds and strange people. For the poet the calvary he must bear is not over upon the reuniting of the family:

> a reunited family means only
> reunion of faces, not of feelings.
>
> ("The Difficult Word")

In this foreign land, Tusiani finds difficulty understanding not only the world around him, but ever more so his *paesani* and, above all, his own father. The Italians he meets in the Bronx where his family settles are different from the Italians he has left back in Italy; they are neither Italians nor Americans. They have lost their identity and although they try very hard to hold on to the language (mostly their dialects) and to the celebrations of their hometowns, a great deal of the old life has been irremediably lost. Tusiani is aware of what the tragic experience (of migration) has done to his *paesani*, and since it seems to be sort of natural law, he himself feels the same loneliness as the other immigrants. Most lyrics of the second group of *Gente Mia* deal with this existential problem of the poet, and we can hear distinctly, between the lines, his cry for hope and human understanding, which we believe will be heard forever.

NOTES

1. Tusiani, Joseph, *Gente Mia and Other Poems* (Italian Cultural Center, Stone Park, IL, 1978.
2. Giordano, Paulo, "Tusiani Explores Lives of Italian Immigrants," in *FRA NOI* (Chicago, November 1987), p. 25.
3. Gardaphe, Fred, "Fact in Fiction: Oral Tradition and the Italian American Writer," in J. Krase and W. Egelman (eds.), *The Melting Pot and Beyond: Italian Americans and the Year 2000* (Staten Island, NY: American Italian Historical Association, 1987), pp. 165-74.

14

IL CAFFE`

MARY RUSSO DEMETRICK

The pastry's warm
here in this shop
they talk about me
I recognize the words

the *tazza d' espresso*'s hot
the *sfogliatelle* has citron
and a center soft and creamy
carta di Sicilia covers
tiled walls
curved wrought iron
chair presses into my spine
reminding

lemon rind on the saucer
crumbs on the plate
notebook open
my pen moves across the page
the Italian soccer game
on *la televisione*

Each customer saunters
in after church
the language forms a backdrop
words that define
illuminate, roll from the tongue
envelop, invite in
they form the formless

here in the shop
my *caffè* becomes cold
the pastry sticks to my fingers
Sicilia looks more frayed
than I first noticed
the brick is fake
the tiles cheap

maybe I am not olive skinned enough
to appear that I fit
perhaps our grandparents
rode horses together
in Messina
noi cugini lived
in stone huts
on the same rocky shore
but for today I intrude
for the promise of *il caffè*
ushered out with cruel words
they don't know I understand

IL CAFFE`

MARY RUSSO DEMETRICK

Sweet juice runs
through my fingers
as I bite
the purple skin

Seeds push against
my tongue
as it prods
the milky cavity

How do I explain
the joy of a fresh-
from-the-tree fig
to a non-believer

It's like trying
to experience grapes
when you have only tasted
raisins

I recall
my grandfather
how he buried the tree
each fall, digging
a trench before the frost

moving the promise
of ripe fruit underground

Now, at the market
I imagine their taste
their color beckons
seems just right
Yet thick juice
resides around
hard seeds and mealy pulp
No sweetness yields
from my tongue's pressure

Memory just suffice
aroma helps
perhaps in a warmer climate
I can marry the memory
with the dream

Like those Sicilian
saplings wrapped in cloths
carried with hope
planted in New Jersey
connecting
with all that is sweet
in Messina

PART VI
STUDIES IN ASSIMILATION

15

ADJUSTMENT AND INTEGRATION: THE ITALIAN EXPERIENCE IN COLORADO

JANET E. WORRALL
NORTHERN COLORADO UNIVERSITY

Colorado in the nineteenth century is often characterized as a frontier society. Recent scholarship portrays it more accurately as an area of rapid change where mining towns were "industrial islands" dominated by large corporations.[1] Cities like Denver reflected this industrialization brought on by the mining economy. By 1887, Denver had four smelters, several manufacturing companies producing mining equipment, three large railroad shops, stockyards, and several textile factories. Immigrants, attracted to these industries, flocked to Denver after the Civil War. British (including Welsh and Scottish), Irish, Germans, and Scandinavians (especially Swedes) dominated the labor scene bringing their churches, newspapers, ethnic celebrations, and immigrant societies. Gradually Italians began to trickle in, showing a dramatic increase between 1900 and 1920 (along with the German-Russians). Denver as well as mining towns experienced the growing pains of industrialization — low wages, crowded living conditions, poverty, and exploitation of an immigrant working class. The traditional, Protestant based population of Denver was challenged and alarmed by the growing number of Catholics, first Irish and Germans, and then Italians. Their fears were reflected in the rapid growth of the American Protective Association (APA) in the 1890s and domination of Colorado's government by the KKK by 1926.[2]

The Italian immigrant population in Colorado grew steadily from 3,882 in 1890 to 12,580 in 1920. Mines provided work for many of the Italians with the inevitable result that they became involved in labor struggles of that time. While some immigrants found jobs in the precious metal mines of Central City, Georgetown, Empire, Leadville, Creede, and Cripple Creek, the majority worked in the coal mines in southeastern Colorado. Prior to 1890, northern Europeans, Mexicans, and Americans provided labor in the southern Colorado coalfields; after 1890, Italians and Slavic immigrants entered the mines in growing numbers. In 1900 (when the first statistics are available for individual counties), 44 percent of Colorado's Italians (2986 of 6818) lived in the four southeastern counties where coal mining dominated the economy (Las Animas, Pueblo, Huerfano, and Fremont). That number grew in 1910 to 69 percent of Colorado's Italian population, then dropped to 46 percent in 1920. Not surprisingly, Italians participated in numerous labor strikes as the miners tried to organize the Rockefeller controlled coalfields of the Colorado Fuel and Iron Company (CF&I). (CF&I used the coal to provide coke for its steel mills — coal mining was secondary to the company's steel mills.) Among the most memorable strikes were those of 1903-04 and that of 1913 ending in the Ludlow Massacre of 1914.[3]

The United Mine Workers of America (UMW) led the struggle to organize workers in the southern Colorado coal fields. Miners sought to achieve recognition of an eight hour day; a 10 percent increase in wages; an end to the use of scrip; improved health and safety regulations; and better company housing. In 1903, when company representatives refused to meet with UMW representatives, 90% of the coal miners in Las Animas and Huerfano walked out. When company officials responded by evicting workers from company housing at Hastings where many workers lived, violence followed. Governor James H. Peabody called out the national guard and as many as 98 workers (including many Italians) were escorted across the border into New Mexico. As Philip Notarianni points out in his perceptive study of this strike, Governor Peabody's actions reflected his hatred of unions as well as Italians.[4]

Numerous other labor conflicts in the coalfields culminated in the tragic Ludlow Massacre several years later. For years the UMW had been trying to organize workers in the northern and southern coalfields. In September 1913, southern miners voted to strike demanding higher wages, an 8 hour day, and recognition of their union, but the Colorado Fuel and Iron Company was intransigent. Miners at the Ludlow coal camp, 15 miles north of Trinidad, joined the general strike. In the following months, struggles broke out between miners and strikebreakers, including Mexicans and Japanese brought in by the mine owners. Miners and their families had moved to tent colonies near the mines and were supported by union funds. The inevitable confrontation broke out with firing between the militia and miners at 10:00 a.m., April 20, 1914. No one knows who fired the first shot; gunfire continued throughout the day and claimed the lives of ten men and one child. Even worse, when the temporary tent colony housing 900 men, women and children caught fire, two Italian women and eleven children, who had dug under a tent to escape the gunfire, died of suffocation. In all, 24 lives were lost. Armed miners invaded the coalfields and town of Trinidad—gunfire continued and mine buildings were set on fire. Only when Federal troops were called in was order restored by the end of the month.[5]

Northern Europeans also dominated coal fields in northern Colorado until the 1890s when increasing numbers of Italians, Slovenians, and Poles entered. The 1903-04 strike had little impact in the northern part of the state. No strikebreakers were called in and the UMW negotiated an agreement with the northern mine operators. Because of greater labor peace in the northern fields there was less worker turnover and racial lines seemed clearly drawn. Supervisory jobs went to native born and Northern Europeans while miners and general laborers were Southern Europeans.

Discrimination by employers as well as the workers was shown toward Chinese, Japanese, and Blacks. In short they were never offered jobs in the northern fields. Greeks were marginally acceptable, in times of labor scarcity which rarely occurred in the northern fields.[6]

While the majority of Italians outside Denver worked in some aspect of the mining industry, many others found employment with railroad companies which recruited them and often paid their passage to Colorado. In

1881, Adolfo Rossi was one of 70 Italians brought by the Denver, South Park and Pacific Railroad (later the Union Pacific). Believing that they would be employed as timekeepers, cooks, and carpenters, Italian immigrants instead were sent to a railroad camp at 11,000 feet where they cleared a forested area to make way for new track. The work was far harder than anticipated for a paltry salary of $2.50 per day with room and board. They made the best of their situation spending leisure time with their musical instruments which they had fortuitously brought along, much to the amusement of their Irish working partners.[7]

Not so fortunate was another Italian railroad worker near Gunnison. In a confrontation with a contractor named Hoblitzell, the Italian shot and killed him. The Italian escaped, but was later caught and confined in the courthouse in Gunnison. Through a ruse, the prisoner was abducted and hanged. Gunnison residents feared retaliation by the Italian community, but nothing came of the incident which probably reflected a mining town mentality more than anti-Italian sentiment.[8]

The railroad companies and the padrone system both exploited Italian workers. The Union Pacific left several hundred jobless in 1884 and when Denver residents raised money to help them, natives objected to charity which they feared would encourage joblessness.

Through their work in mines and on railroads, Italians contributed much to the growth of Colorado. Unfortunately, due to the nature of those industries, workers became embroiled in labor strife and violence which often reflected negatively on them and in the worst cases led to loss of life. We have presented merely an overview of Italians in mining and railroad camps. Much research remains to be done on the local level to fully understand the role of Italians in these industries as well as their interaction with other immigrants.

Many immigrants eventually settled in the growing southern towns of Trinidad and Pueblo where they found work in steel mills. Newspapers testify to their numbers. In Trinidad, *Corriere de Trinidad* served the Italian colony with articles in both English and Italian. Starting around 1900 and continuing into the 1940s, the paper carried mainly international news. In Pueblo the best known and longest published Italian paper was *L'Unione*, starting in 1907. Vincent Massari, a leader of Pueblo's Italian community, was its editor and publisher from 1921 until publication ceased in 1947. Massari, born in Italy in 1898, came to the U.S. in 1915 joining his parents in Pueblo. His father was a coal miner and union organizer who served as Secretary/Treasurer of the Pueblo Smeltermen's Union and helped reorganize the miners after the Ludlow Massacre. Vincent Massari became a U.S. citizen in 1923. He was a leader of Pueblo's Italian community and an active member of the city's mutual aid society. A vocal Democrat, Massari served in both the Colorado House of Representatives and Senate for over twenty years.[9]

According to census reports, the Italian population in Denver nearly tripled between 1900 and 1920, increasing from 1,000 to 2,872. These figures are probably on the low side as many Italian workers who had migrated to Denver due to poor working conditions and a decline in jobs in railroad and mining camps were missed by census takers. The actual size of the Italian-American population is difficult to determine. In 1907, an Italian newspaper in Denver claimed that there were 15,000 Italians in Denver and 60,000 in the state.[10]

The Zarlengo family is an example of a migrating family which eventually settled in Denver. Charles or Gaetano aged 13, came to Colorado with his father, Francesco, in June 1890. His five brothers migrated later from their rocky, family farm in Campobasso. Charles worked as a waterboy for a railroad section gang. Francesco disliked subjecting his son to the dangers of blasting and earth moving, and they moved to the mining area of Silver Plume, Colorado where a second brother, George 14 years, joined them in 1895. There the family contracted to supply wood as fuel for the silver and gold mines and eventually hauled ore from the mines to the railroad. During snowbound winters, they learned English from another Italian immigrant who had picked up the rudiments over the years.

In 1910, when the mines declined the family moved to Denver. Having the language and some knowledge of business operations, they took advantage of the numerous opportunities offered by the growing city and started the Zarlengo Brothers Contracting Company. Their firm expanded from unloading coal and ore at the smelters to operating their own coal and lumber enterprise. In turn they hired hundreds of newly arriving Italian immigrants, in many cases paying for their passage over.

George married Elizabeth Fabrizio while his brother, Charles, returned to Italy in 1905 to bring his childhood sweetheart back to Denver. Each couple had nine children who attended Catholic schools in Denver and eventually entered the professions of law, teaching, and medicine.[11]

Many Italians in Denver followed their agricultural inclinations by settling along the South Platte River. Railroads owned the land, but tracks occupied only part of it. Most of the immigrants came from southern Italy, especially Potenza and Naples, but a few were from Genoa and Milan in the North. Denver was a place of mixed blessings for immigrants. Land was cheap, but the hazards of poor sanitation, the smell of garbage treatment plant, and the refuse carrying diphtheria and typhoid fever made it a less than desirable place to live. Homes were often one room cottages or tents.

Poverty conditions of the inhabitants evoked little sympathy from Denverites. Children gathered watercress along the banks and sold it uptown where they picked up cigar butts to sell back in the Bottoms. As one local said, "The majority of the children belong to these dagoes, who would probably follow the same thing if they had thousands of dollars."[12] Young boys often landed in jail for stealing pieces of wood or coal from railroad cars as a desperate effort to keep the family from freezing in the cold winter months.

Yet immigrants quickly turned the fertile land into vegetable and flower gardens giving Italians a monopoly on supplying Denver's growing population with fresh fruits and vegetables. Farmers took their produce to the City Market (Colfax and Speer) by 4:00 a.m. in horse-drawn wagons often accompanied by women and children. Mothers put hot bricks in the wagon to keep the children's feet warm. For many this was a social event. Sometimes women did the selling as Sam Santangelo recalls, "... husbands came to town all dressed up and went to the bars." Retailers, often Italian peddlers, sold produce door-to-door throughout Denver or out of their wagon on street corners. So good was the reputation of Italian growers that grocers came up from Colorado Springs twice a week for fresh produce.[13]

John Figliolino, a native of Italy, was one of the peddlers who regularly bought his produce at City Market. His son, Tom, followed the trade, and had peddled fruits and vegetables in Denver for 55 years until 1978, when he finally cut back on his schedule. He rose at 4:00 a.m. and drove his 1950 green Chevrolet pickup truck, with a cornucopia painted on the side, to the Denargo Market. There he loaded his truck and was home by 5:30 a.m. to have breakfast with his wife and daughter. Then he traversed the neighborhoods where his customers waited. Some he had served for three generations. Those who could not be home would leave their orders. Knowing where keys were placed, Tom would fill the order, place it inside, and lock the house again. Many remembered Tom from Depression days when he would give fruit to children. He was so well regarded that some of his customers remembered him in their wills.[14]

The Garramone family came from central Italy in 1901, settling on a farm on the outskirts of Denver. Sons Mike and Tony subsequently bought 30 acres in the river bottoms, then known as Frog Hollow, in 1916 for the rather high price of $2,000 an acre. Their specialty was bedding plants, petunias, snapdragons, and a few vegetable items, mainly lettuce. They sold their products to grocery stores, first the Piggly Wiggley chain and then Safeway. Mike's wife, Elvira, from Denver's Italian colony, worked side by side with him in the field in addition to raising a family and keeping an immaculate house. As an Italian co-worker said, "Women did a tremendous amount of work ... up at 3:00 o'clock in the morning to make coffee for the men to go out into the fields. Then shortly afterward, they'd be out there themselves. You don't find this breed of people anymore."[15]

The rise of Italian newspapers reflected the growing Italian community in Denver. Angelo Noce, born in Genoa and having emigrated to American in 1850, published the first one in 1885, *La Stella*, an Italian weekly. However, this was somewhat premature, given the limited Italian population in the city, and the paper ceased publication in 1889.[16]

Probably the most influential and best patronized Italian weekly at the beginning of the century was *Il Grido del Popolo*, published by Frank Mancini. It encouraged Italians to become U.S. citizens and even carried the questions and answers for a citizenship test in a 1907 issue. In a push to Americanize Italians, the paper stated that it would begin publishing articles in English, "so that the American people may read them and when they see that the Italian people want to become not only a part of the Great American Republic, but a necessary part, they cannot but help respecting them for the interest and service and they render to the Land of their Adoption. {sic}"[17]

In an effort to increase readership the paper lowered its price from $1.50 to $1.00 per year. Touting the virtues of Italians, *Il Grido* stated that an American dealer in the Italian district said that, "... he had never yet lost a bill owed by an Italian creditor; and this speaks well for the Italians." [18]

Several other Italian newspapers were published in Denver in the first decades of the twentieth century, some continuing into the 1940s. These included *Il Risveglio*, directed by Frank Mancini for a time, *La Capitale, La Frusta*, and *La Roma*, the last published by one of Denver's leading businessmen, Peter Albi.

Catholic churches and schools were vital to Denver's Italian community. The first permanent Catholic Italian priests were two Jesuits, who came in 1879 and started the Sacred Heart Church at 28th and Larimer streets. They laid the cornerstone within two months of their arrival. The following year a school opened and in 1888 Regis College was started, then known as Sacred Heart.[19]

In the 1890s, the Italian community gradually moved from the bottomlands to nearby north Denver forming the city's "Little Italy." There in 1893, newly appointed Jesuit Father Mariano Lepore initiated construction of Our Lady of Mount Carmel, the Italian national church at Navajo and West 36th streets. LePore, a handsome, dynamic young man, lived in the Italian community and quickly won the support and affection of his flock. But LePore soon reflected and exacerbated the growing dissension in the Italian community. Some members objected to Lepore's involvement in secular activities. He published his own newspaper *La Nazione* and encouraged his congregation to join the Democratic Party. Others questioned his morality around the opposite sex and some men prohibited their wives, sisters, and daughters from speaking to him. So strong was antagonism to Father LePore, that leaders of the Italian community tried to have him dismissed from the parish.[20]

Matters worsened in 1898 when Mount Carmel caught fire and burned by what firemen suggested was a deliberately set fire. Father Lepore had left the church unlocked after mass, as was the custom. He heard about the fire when he was downtown; he rushed back to find the wooden building completely destroyed. The anti-LePore faction, led by Frank Damascio, then built a chapel nearby on the corner of Osage and West 36th streets. The bishop, however, refused to appoint a priest and the building became the Mount Carmel Grade School. Meanwhile, Mt. Carmel Church was rebuilt and dedicated on December 18, 1904.[21]

The end of the dissension came tragically with the murder of Father Lepore in 1903. The assassin, a laborer, Giuseppe Sorice, also died in the confrontation, leaving motives and details unanswered.[22]

Without doubt the most famous of the Catholic leaders in Colorado was Mother Cabrini. In 1902, she led the first group of the Sisters of the Sacred Heart to Denver where they established the Mt. Carmel School on Navajo and West 34th streets. Three years later, Mother Cabrini opened the Queen of Heaven Orphanage nearby. Apparently two Sisters of the Sacred Heart Order happened upon two weeping little girls, who had no place to go as their mother was dead and their father worked. They were afraid to stay home alone. At the time of its founding, the orphanage was the largest in Denver.[23]

Italians loved processions, feast days, and societies. One of the most important for the Denver colony was the feast of San Rocco, named after one of the most beloved saints, patron of the sick and plague-stricken. Denver had its first San Rocco celebration on August 16, 1892 in the chapel of what now is Regis University. Two years later, a special San Rocco chapel was completed there which added to the festiveness of the occasion.[24]

With the opening of Mt. Carmel Church and the friction in the Italian community, each parish had its own San Rocco celebration. The two parishes tried to outdo each other and attract the most followers with raffles, fireworks, flowers, and music. Once the factionalism subsided, the religious nature of the day dominated again. Italian societies bid for the honor of carrying San Rocco in the procession ending in the San Rocco Chapel—all joined in the celebration.[26]

The major festival for Mt. Carmel Church was the celebration of La Madonna del Carmine (Our Lady of Mt. Carmel), first held July 16, 1896.

People came from all over the state to participate in the daylong activities of processions, mass, and the final carnival-like celebration with fireworks, brass bands, and flower covered booths.[27]

Columbus Day generated nearly as much excitement in the Italian colony as religious holidays. In 1892 a committee of Denver's leading Italians planned a celebration for the 4th centenary of Columbus' landing. Later they tried to take credit from the printer, Angelo Noce, who led the campaign for constructing a statue to Columbus and for recognizing October 12 as a legal holiday. Noce persuaded Governor Jesse McDonald to designate the date as Columbus Day and wrote the bill which was introduced in the Colorado House and Senate in 1905. It failed, but was reintroduced and passed two years later. Colorado became the first state to recognize Columbus Day, October 12, as a legal holiday. As tribute to Noce for his efforts, he led the parade as grand marshal on October 12, 1907.[28] To many first generation Italians, Columbus symbolized hope and pride, and the parade unified the Italian community.

The incidents surrounding Father LePore and Angelo Noce raise the issue of factionalism and perhaps regionalism. Leaders of the Italian community were wealthy businessmen including Agostino Roncaglia, banker and businessman; Frank Mazza, a wealthy merchant; Frank Damascio, designer and donor of San Rocco Chapel and one of the richest Italians in Denver; Luigi Mosconi, restaurant owner; and A. Abiati, an artist. These were the leaders in Denver's first Italian organizations. They were uncomfortable with Father LePore and resented his outside activities, especially promotion of the Democratic Party among his congregation. Later they shunned Noce and took the credit for promoting Columbus Day. Noce lived in east Denver rather than the Little Italy of northwest Denver where Damascio resided. No doubt other issues also caused hostility between Noce and the Italian leaders. There was obviously a wealthy, educated group who came in the 1880s and seem to have provided leadership well into the twentieth century. Still to be determined, however, is whether regionalism, status, politics, or other factors accounted for a person gaining status in the Italian community. However important in their own colony, Italians had not earned acceptance in Denver "society" as had wealthy Germans and English. For example, no Italians could join the prestigious Denver Club or the exclusive Denver Athletic Club.[29]

Colorado was the center of nativism in the West in the late 19th and early 20th centuries. Denver was white, Protestant, and conservative with a reputation for intolerance. Indicative was the increase in membership of the American Protective Association which rose from 3,000 in 1893 to 10,000 in 1894 as older residents became alarmed at the increasing number of Catholic immigrants. The 35,000 first and second generation Catholics in Denver in 1920 frightened nativists more than the usual nativist causes of white supremacy and anti-Semitism, and led to the Klan's dominance of government in Colorado by 1924. While historians have yet to assess how nativism directly affected the Italian community, the incident surrounding the lynching of Daniel Arata in Denver in 1893 has manifestations of nativism.[30]

On Tuesday night, July 25, B. C. Lightfoot, a 63 year old Civil War veteran, went to Daniel Arata's saloon, the Hotel Italia, for a beer. After finishing it, Arata asked Lightfoot if he wanted another, he replied, yes. Upon finishing the second Lightfoot began to leave, Arata asked him for payment for the second. As Lightfoot had no money and thought the second drink was free, he refused to pay. Arata, in a drunken state, attacked Lightfoot first with his fist and then struck him on the head repeatedly with a heavy chair. As Lightfoot seemed ready to fall off the chair, Arata shot him in the chest, then dragged him out of the saloon into a narrow courtyard. A crowd gathered, the police came and arrested Arata who was described in the newspaper as a native of Italy, 28 years old, and with a very bad reputation having been engaged in several shooting episodes.[31]

Wednesday night, July 26, a mob of 10,000 broke into the Denver jail and dragged out Arata. The mob action appeared to start when a half dozen Grand Army of the Republic (GAR) men, led by a Colonel C. F. Brennan, urged a group of just dispersed men who had gathered to discuss the hard times, to "Follow me." (Brennan maintained that he was of the Forty-eighth Pennsylvania regiment during the war and wore a GAR medal prominently on his breast.) A mob temperament quickly took over and they let out a yell to "Hang the Dago! Hang Arata!" Their number grew as they approached the jail.[32]

The sheriff and police were helpless in their efforts to halt the mob of 10,000 who eventually found Arata and dragged him out to a nearby cottonwood tree. There they lynched him and filled his body with bullets. His body was cut down and dragged through the streets—then strung up on a telephone pole—a grisly sight.[33]

While there was no question over Arata's guilt, the lynching was a mob reaction tinged with nativism was reflected in the frequent cries of "Hang the Dago" and in the reverence shown to the GAR. On July 28, the *Rocky Mountain News* carried a story on the event labeling lynchings as outrageous and unacceptable in a civilized country. The article explained the action as resulting from an atrocious act by a "member of an organization so venerated by the country and in which sentiment plays so strong a part, the criminal, being of a nativity against which a deep and exaggerated prejudice exist. . ."[34]

In the following days, attention was focused on culpability—did it lie with the sheriff's office or police? Both took considerable criticism. Stories in the *Rocky Mountain News* indicated that citizens of Denver should be shocked and ashamed that such barbarous actions could take place in their city.

Some feared that the Italian colony would retaliate and there were rumors that, ". . . the Italians were concocting dreadful schemes in the bottoms as a revenge for the bloody execution of their fellow countryman."[35] Further research will show whether this was an isolated event or had the overtones of nativism reflected in the growth of the APA and KKK in Denver. Careful examination must be made of incidents which on the surface appear to be racist, but may be the result of mob reaction. As the *Colorado Catholic* editorialized, "No one will contend that Arata would have met the same fate had he been of a nationality other than Italian."[36]

This paper has been a preliminary study of Italians in Colorado. While the Italian population was never very large in Colorado or Denver, if compared to that of eastern states in 1920, Italians were the second largest immigrant group in the state, after the Germans from Russia. Now it is time for more probing, detailed studies on nativism, residential patterns, associational life, regionalism, newspapers, voting patterns, community leadership, and generational changes. Ultimately, this will allow for comparative studies of the Italian experience in the less urbanized West and the more industrialized, urbanized East.

NOTES

1. David Thomas Brundage, "The Making of Working-Class Radicalism in the Mountain West: Denver, Colorado, 1880-1903," PhD dissertation., University of California, Los Angeles, 1982, p. 4; see Lyle W. Dorsett, *The Queen City: A History of Denver* (Boulder: Pruett Publishing Company, 1977) for overview of Denver.

2. Brundage, Chap. 1.

3. U.S. Census Office, *Twelfth Census, 1900*, vol. 1, pt. 1, Table 34, pp. 739-41; *Thirteenth Census, 1910 Supplement for Colorado*, Table 1, pp. 594-606; *Fourteenth Census, 1920 State Compendium for Colorado*, Table 12, pp. 39-40; U.S. Congress, Senate, *Reports of the Immigration Commission*, S. Doc. 633, 61st Cong., 2nd sess., pt. 25, 1911, p. 259; H. M. Gitelman, *Legacy of the Ludlow Massacre A Chapter in American Industrial Relations* (Philadelphia: Univ. of Pennsylvania Press, 1988), p. 4.

4. Philip F. Notarianni, "Italian Involvement in the 1903-04 Coal Miners' Strike in Southern Colorado and Utah," in George E. Pozzetta (ed), *Pane E Lavoro: The Italian American Working Class, Proceedings of the Eleventh Annual Conference of the American Italian Historical Association* (Toronto: The Multicultural History Society of Ontario, 1980); Luciano J. Iorizzo and Salvatore Mondello (eds), *The Italian Americans* (Boston: Twayne Publishers), pp. 93-4.

5. Gitelman, pp. 17-20; see Manfred F. Boemke, "The Wilson Administration, Organized Labor, and the Colorado Strike, 1913-1914," PhD dissertation, Princeton Univ., 1983, for full account of Ludlow Massacre; Reports of the Immigration Commission, pt. 25, p. 260.

6. Reports of the Immigration Commission, pt. 25, pp. 241-56.

7. Andrew F. Rolle, *The Immigrant Upraised Italian Adventurers and Colonists in an Expanding America* (Norman: Univ. of Oklahoma Press, 1968), p. 171.

8. George A. Root, "Gunnison in the Early `Eighties'," *Colorado Magazine* 9 (6, November 1932): 201-13.

9. Vincent Massari Collection, Univ. of Minnesota Immigration History Research Center, see description for file.

10. *Il Guido del Popolo*, Denver, Colorado, October 2, 1907.

11. Massari file, unidentified newspaper clipping.

12. Stephen J. Leonard, "Denver's Foreign Born Immigrants 1859-1900," PhD dissertation, Claremont, 1971, p. 189.

13. *Denver Post, Empire Magazine*, December 17, 1978.

14. Ibid.

15. *Denver Post*, Section C, May 9, 1976.

16. Giovanni Perilli, *Colorado and the Italians in Colorado* (Denver, n.p., 1922), p. 14.

17. *Il Guido del Popolo*, October 2, 1907.

18. Ibid.

19. Perilli, p. 31.

20. Leonard, p. 194; Christine A. Derose, "Inside `Little Italy': Italian Immigrants in Denver,"

Colorado Magazine 54 (3, Summer 1977): 284-6; Ruth Eloise Wiberg, *Rediscovering North-west Denver Its History, Its People, Its Landmarks* (Denver: Bradford Printing Co., 1976), p. 40.
21. Ibid.
22. Leonard, p. 195.
23. Pirelli, p. 32.
24. "Colorado Festivals—Pt. II," *Colorado Magazine* 29 (3, July 1952): 189.
25. Ibid., pp. 188-9.
26. Ibid.
27. Ibid.
28. Perilli, p. 14; DeRose, pp. 280-81.
29. Leonard, pp. 192-195; Derose, pp. 278, 286.
30. Kenneth T. Jackson, *The Ku Klux Klan in the City 1915-1930* (New York: Oxford Univ. Press, 1967), pp. 215, 219.
31. *Rocky Mountain News*, July 26, 1893
32. Ibid., July 27, 1893.
33. Ibid.
34. Ibid., July 28, 1893.
35. Ibid.
36. Leonard, p. 209.

16

MORAL FAMILISM: ITALIAN-AMERICANS AND *SOCIETÀ*

FRANK A. SALAMONE
IONA COLLEGE

> . . .inability to concert action beyond the immediate family arises from an ethos—that of "amoral familism."[1]

The controversy surrounding Banfield's thesis of "amoral familism" has raged for over thirty years and reveals no sign of abatement. Much heat and even a little light has been shed on the issue. Banfield's original statement of the thesis limited it to a situation in which three factors were present, namely, "a high death rate, certain land tenure conditions, and the absence of the extended family." However, both Banfield and his opponents have tended to disregard the very limited case in which "amoral familism" is supposed to exist. In any case, very careful studies have indicated that even in the presumed type-case, that of "Montegrano," the hypothesized characteristic features of "amoral familism" do not conform to the reality.[2]

This paper examines the very real moral and social nature of Italian gregariousness—the adhesion to groups that extend beyond the family and set up networks which are useful in coping with the often hostile surrounding cultural and social environment. It examines southern Italians who migrated to Rochester, New York, from the second half of the nineteenth century to their descendants' preparation to merge more fully into Rochester society at the brink of World War II. These southern Italians, mostly Sicilians, were perfect candidates for Banfield's "amoral familists" when they left their Sicilian villages. They already had the skills to form and join organizations well-equipped to negotiate with hostile forces and further their own interests. They did not suddenly develop these skills when freed from the *padrone*'s clutches. To believe such requires more faith than sense. It is much easier to see their organizational skills as continuations of abilities and experiences already present in their environments and eminently pre-adapted to successful manipulation of the difficult social situation present in Rochester, New York.

THE ROCHESTER SETTING

The population of Italians in Rochester, including Sicilians, was negligible until the turn of the century. The following table gives an idea of the growth of the community.

TABLE 1 – Growth of Italian Popluation in Rochester, New York*		
Date	Number of Italians	Total Population
1865	9	50,940
1870	16	62,000
1875	30	81,722
1890	516	133,896
1910	14,816	218,149
1940	56,329	330,000

* Table based on figures in Ray and Keen.[40]

As early as 1910 Italians formed over 10% of Rochester's white population of foreign birth or of those who had at least one parent born outside the United States. By that definition, there were 142,680 foreign born people in a total population of 218,000. 14,816 of those people were from Italy. Most Italians were from the South, the vast majority of whom came from Sicily.[3]

Zissler[4] indicates that Domenico Sturla was the first Italian in Rochester. He lived in an area named "Sleepy Hollow," north of Andrews Street between St.Paul Street and the Genesee River. Sturla came to Rochester some time in the 1860s and applied for citizenship in 1868. Evidently, Sturla failed to receive citizenship for "the first Italian to be granted citizenship was ... Paul Rigali" in 1876.[5] Between 1920 and 1960, approximately half of all people naturalized as citizens in Rochester from 1890 to 1929 came from Italy.[6]

"Sleepy Hollow," the first center of Italian settlement in the 1880s, was the same area in which the Genoese immigrant Domenico Sturla settled. The next major settlement area, still near the river, was on Front and Mill Streets. Problems that marked later settlement were present in these early ones. For example, there was a language problem and *padroni* served as labor recruiters and go-betweens, with all the evils inherent in the system. When Italian immigrants sought to learn English in night school, they were frequently turned away because they did not know the language. The irony of the situation led a group of prominent Rochester women to found "a mission to teach English, arithmetic, and 'Americanness'" to Italian men.[7]

This mission appealed to the public who donated "First and Second Readers to educate Italians."[8] The Italian Mission had acquired a room which it used as a school room. Its location at 61 State Street placed it near the river in the heart of the Italian community of the time. The mission, following the age-old tradition of Christian charity, solicited help from children. It was their old books they asked for - and received. The mission continued in existence until other agencies, Catholic and secular, encroached on its territory. Certainly, it had a healthy life into the 1890s.[9]

Meanwhile, in spite of the efforts of voluntary agencies such as the Italian Mission, landlords and employers joined forces to oppose housing reforms, a long-lived alliance that certainly has echoes beyond the Italian experience. Employers benefitted from high rents since it made workers desperate for employment of any kind. Certainly, the short term benefits of slum conditions to landlords are obvious. The costs to the immigrants, however, were enormous.

To lessen those costs, Italian quickly began to participate in cultural activities of the general community. Characteristically, they formed various types of societies which included the Good Time Club (Buontempone), the Cristoforo Colombo Society, and a host of mutual aid societies. These societies were further proof that immigrants sought to reproduce as much as they could of their traditional society in Rochester as a means of protecting their way of life. At the same time, they used these associations to secure a niche within Rochester's urban life.

As early as 1909, immigrants organized a Columbus Day Parade in which 20,000 people participated. Its grand finale took place at Seneca Park. Since there were less than 15,000 Italians in Rochester at the time, it is clear that other members of the Rochester community worked along with Italians.

It is true that organ grinders formed a significant number of the first Italian immigrants to the United States.[10] Rochester appears to have had its share of these musicians and their offspring. However, in a relatively short time they appear to have turned their talents to more conventional instruments and found employment with local musical groups. Thus, two Italian bands competed for the top prize at Exposition Park in 1913.[11]

In sum, Rochester's Italian immigrants, in common with their compatriots in other areas, turned to mutual aid, cultural and, later, professional associations to advance their interests. These associations formed bridges between individuals, their families and the wider society outside their tightly-knit family and friendship groups. Within them immigrants could enjoy the coziness of primary groups while reaping the benefits of instrumental groups advancing specific causes. It is no accident that these groups first became prominent in Italy at the time of unification and were an integral part of the immigrants mental baggage.

SOCIETA` IN ROCHESTER SOCIETY

The first Italians in Rochester faced problems common to immigrants elsewhere. Basically, they were outsiders, but, contrary to the myth that Italians were welcomed in America before the large immigration of the later nineteenth century, were made to feel that hostility from earlier settlers.[12] Since it was impossible to advance their common interests individually, they chose to do so through various societies, using these societies to specific categories of interest: financial (mutual-aid), cultural (upgrading the image of Italians), and professional and business (easing individuals into the mainstream of Rochester's financial life). Although the objectives often overlapped, with mutual-aid societies advancing business and cultural goals, or cultural societies aiding professionals promoting financial needs, in general these categories mark clear-cut boundaries among the types of associations found in their customary pursuits.

It is interesting that the first Italian group mentioned in the local history is an Opera Company. In 1864, a promoter made "a proposition to citizens of Rochester that if they guarantee him 150 subscribers at $5.00 each, he would bring the troupe here for 3 nights."[13] Granted that the company was not a Rochester association and that in 1864 there were at most only nine Italians in Rochester, hardly enough to support an opera company, cultural societies were just the sort of activity that could unite Italians from various regions and political persuasions.

The need for such pursuits is brutally obvious in the following summary of an 1883 *Union & Advertiser* newspaper article:

> Some of the traits linked to the Italian include:
> • Early marriage, because Italian marriages are somewhat experimental and their marital vows are not undertaken with the view of 'permanence.'
> • Getting satisfaction on 'less than an average American wastes regularly.'
> • The woman does not clean the house, and the man 'is satisfied with the filthy manner she keeps it (the residence).'
> • Italian men are addicted to gambling, to the point of leaving their families on the 'verge of starvation.'[14]

At the time of the article, there were less than five-hundred Italians in Rochester, five of whom were citizens.[15]

Accordingly, it was obvious that political and cultural activities had to proceed rapidly in a complementary fashion if Italians were to merge into Rochester society. Alongside "purely" cultural societies Italian political clubs soon sprang up. As early as 1897 the Sixteenth Ward Italian Political Club elected officers.[16] The previous year's newspaper reported that an Italian-

American Political Club elected two officers.[17] It is not clear from the article whether this club is the same or different from the Sixteenth Ward Political Club. In any case, it is clear that Italians soon began to feel the need to become citizens and to exercise their rights if they were to survive and thrive in Rochester.

The first recorded mention of discrimination against Italians in Rochester occurred in an 1897 article. A workman, John Ronzone "declared that contractors at the canal work refuse to employ Italian labor.[18] "Ronzone's affirmation of discrimination was but the first in a long series of complaints. These acts of discrimination led to other Italian societies. As another newspaper account has it, in 1925 even in the midst of immense prosperity "various ethnic groups ... faced a lot of discrimination in the United States. So Angelo Maggio and 11 other Rochester men who found themselves outside the mainstream got together one October night and formed the Italian American Business Men's Association."[19]

When The Chamber of Commerce did not recognize them, they formed their own organization. According to Maggio, the organization was composed of insurance agents, doctors, lawyers, judges, and other professionals who were refused admittance into mainline professional associations. Once again the motivation for the group's organization was to achieve group aims that also aided the individual. The association was *not* organized to combat the wider society but to aid members in functioning within that society, and to demonstrate to that society that it was wrong in rejecting people who adhered to its values.

The theme of Americanization, therefore, is important in understanding the manner in which these groups operated. Their strong patriotism is remarkable only when one neglects to take into account the needs of their members and the social and cultural environments in which they operated. Italian immigrant organizations that did not stress Americanism, such as the radical organizations of bolsheviks and anarchists were not known for their successes in aiding the average immigrant nor for promoting security in the American context.

The need for security is patent. Table Two clearly indicates the proletarian nature of Italian immigration to Rochester.

TABLE 2–Occupations of Italian Male Passport Holders (per 100 emigrants)[41]					
	Agrarian	Construction	Excavation	Artisan & Manufacturing	Professional	Other
Sicily	41.74	8.72	28.22	12.40	0.21	8.67
Total	36.18	11.63	35.12	10.26	0.37	6.46

Italian societies reflected the security needs of working people, living in the worst slums of Rochester. The need for a Bersaglieri Lamarmora or similar mutual aid societies is evident when one understands the conditions which early immigrants found. As early as April 8, 1892, the Bersaglieri was well-established and elections of their officers made the local paper.[20] A brief description of living conditions underscores the need for mutual aid societies and others which promoted the interests of Italian immigrants.

In all of Rochester in 1914, there were 19 people per acre. In the Italian seventh ward, there were 55 people per acre. In the Lewis Street section of the basically Sicilian sixteenth ward, the area bordered by North, Scio, and Woodward Streets, there were 74 people per acre, a population of 2,357.[21] The effects of overcrowding took their toll as overcrowding correlated with a general lack of concern for the lot of the immigrants in Rochester.

Garbage collections were irregular. Garbage was piled under the outside staircases of homes, presenting a fire hazard. Spontaneous combustion could and did occur frequently. Even schools in the area suffered under the erratic regime of refuse collection. Food spoiled quickly in homes without refrigeration. Milk in the area was often the cause of tuberculosis. In schools common cups were the rule for drinks. Canned milk replaced breast milk for babies in many families.

Ray[22] cites a survey undertaken in 1911. Fifty-four of two-hundred families had both parents working all day. More than 25% of mothers of young children found it necessary to work in an attempt to balance the budget. And that in a community in which, presumably, "a woman's place was in the home." Many other women worked in cottage industries within the home. How many it is impossible to state precisely since no records were kept. Many of the children fed canned milk were, not surprisingly, children of working mothers. These children were at greatest risk for infant mortality and tuberculosis.[23] Although there were agencies that did social welfare work among the immigrants and were accepted by them, most notably The Practical Housekeeping Center, later known as Lewis Street Center, and the Practical Nursing Association, the Italian immigrants became noted for their desire to solve their own problems and to buy their own bills. The instrument that enabled them to do so was the society or voluntary association.

Interestingly, although many of these associations were based on *campagna* or *regione*, such as the Caltanisetta or Vulgarnara Societies, very quickly they served to present a united Italian ethnic identity. Even the use of regions united villages which otherwise were distinct in "the Old Country." It is an irony not often appreciated that Calabrians, Sicilians, and others had to come to America to become Italians. A significant part of that transformation occurred in clubs as a necessary response to prejudice and discrimination in the Rochester environment.

The local Gannett paper's attitude toward Italians has been noted above. It continued to treat Italians as either quaint or dangerous depending on the circulation needs of the moment. An interesting example is its illustrated article on the description of immigrants in Rochester.[24]

The house depicted as a typical "Arcadian" dwelling is, in reality, a summer house used by people to do some farming in a section they termed "le lotte" (the lots) and to get some fresh air. The purpose of the article was to stress the alien and inscrutable nature of Italians, a nature so different it would bar them from participating equally in Rochester's society.

Therefore, it is understandable that the immigrants pushed to emphasize their willingness to become Americans. At the same time they began to underscore Italian contributions to western civilization from which American values ultimately sprang. As I noted earlier, this meant using communication media to get the message across. As early as 1895 there are notices of the Italian Society's holding a ball in Germania Hall[25], an interesting comment on cultural pluralism in itself, the celebration of Victor Emmanuel day[26], and other events that help define Italian ethnicity.

And security was the overriding need for immigrants. Pre-1900 accounts note the election of officers to mutual-aid societies. In 1892, for example, the Bersaglieri Lamarmora Italian Society elected its officers. The Rochester Union and Advertiser duly noted the election and listed its officers.[27] The Bersaglieri was but one of many mutual-aid societies that ensured its members that medical and burial costs would be met.

It was also important that the immigrants combat negative stereotypes through stressing their ordinary activities, for example, their ability to have a wholesome good time. Therefore, they publicized the event when the Italian Society of Rochester Held a ball at Germania Hall.[28] Similarly, the Italian celebration of Victor Emmanuel Day was highlighted.[29] These public celebrations, unfortunately, could backfire.

Clement Lanni, a prominent politician and publisher of a Rochester Italian language newspaper, notes that he attended a parade in which his father participated. The Italian band was dressed in their elaborate and colorful uniforms and Lanni was elbowing his way to the front of the line when he heard an observer comment, "Here come those dagos!"[30] He slinked back into the bosom of the crowd made to feel shame at his Italian identity.

In general, however, the various societies stuck to their campaign of stressing Americanization and combating ethnic stereotypes through emphasizing positive aspects of Italian culture. Two groups, *Il Solco* and *Il Circolo Italiano* illustrate the manner in which ethnic stereotyping was combatted through emphasizing positive aspects of Italian culture.

Il Solco was an outstanding Rochester cultural organization Organized in 1943, it attempted to unite Italians and non-Italians who enjoyed Italian culture. A typical program consisted of a Sunday afternoon social hour after a musical presentation in one of the Eastman School of Music's buildings. *Il Solco* promoted the study of the Italian language through awarding scholarships to Middlebury College's summer school of language.[31]

Joe LoCurto, who was active in both the Italian Cultural Society and *Il Solco*, describes the work of the Italian Cultural Society in this passage from an interview:

> There was a lecture every time we met, and we . . . involved the community into something new for them, to encourage the new generation and the old generations to do

something altruistically and something for their own children at the same time, so that this is our Italian Cultural Society, starting way back in 1939, primarily made up of the organizers who were teachers. Di Francesco, Flora Rizzo, DaManda, myself, Henry Fino, Benny Pestiani, and others . . . We met primarily at the University of Rochester. We met once a month on Sunday afternoons. Very nice affairs—as I said, some lecture or a little musical program; we socialized, had coffee and whatever . . . I was president three times . . . but unfortunately, as the older generation passed away, they couldn't convince or inveigle the younger generation to keep it up . . . But through that organization some efforts were made to embrace the study of Italian in the high schools. And I myself and others started to approach the various schools and to ask why wasn't Italian being taught and the same old answer was given: there's no demand. Well if you don't offer the course, you're not gonna get a demand. And advisors advise the kids to study French or Spanish, so how are they gonna get Italian? If there isn't a teacher here who is going to try to gather some students together to form a class, how are they gonna have Italian in the schools? Well you know, the attitude was not very pleasant—so we went to work , and we gathered some 600 signatures and presented them to the Board of Education. They were signatures by students and their parents who wanted Italian. Well the Board of Ed. had some objections to it—they had no teachers. So we went out and found teachers. So we gradually, slowly, started to get Italian in the public schools—and at the same time we made efforts in the Catholic high schools, very successful there. And we had a few schools teaching Italian. It moved slowly but we did succeed . . . .[32]

The Italian Cultural Society in common with *Il Solco* promoted cultural studies. Its meetings differed from *Il Solco* in combining a lecture-discussion with music and a social hour. The Rochester Democrat and Chronicle of October

31, 1958 lists a typical meeting in this manner.

> Thomas A. Fabiano, a social studies teacher at Monroe
> High, will be the speaker at the Italian Cultural Society at
> 3:30 p.m. Sunday at Cutler-Union. The topic will be
> "Mazzei's Contribution to American Political Thinking."
> A musical program will be presented by Benny Prestianni.
> Mrs. Anne Nolfi will be the hostess.

It also differed in that it sponsored dinners, parties, and larger-scale events
to supplement its Sunday intellectual meetings. Moreover, as LoCurto makes
clear, the Italian Cultural Club was comprised essentially of Italians and Italian-Americans who sought to preserve whole areas of Italian culture, as they
defined it, and to gain respect for Italians and their descendants in the process. They were pleased to enlist non-Italians in their cause, such participation added validity to their arguments, but the records of the society demonstrate that much more than *Il Solco*, the Italian Cultural Club was Italian organized and run.

"Anne T. Cummins teacher of French and Italian at Eastman School
of Music of the University of Rochester," for example, founded *Il Solco*. It
is interesting that when the society disbanded it did so "because there is no
longer need for such a group-sponsored scholarship." Members stated that
"other funds are available to persons seeking higher education." *Il Solco* had
"also awarded prizes to high school winners of Italian language essay-writ-
ing contests." Interestingly, when it disbanded the group donated its book collection to Rochester's main public library along with its treasury funds so that
the library would purchase books on Italian subjects.[33]

Although Rochester had no Order of the Sons of Italy in America
to unite its various mutual aid, regional, and cultural clubs, Italians there did
recognize the need for an umbrella organization of their own devising. Certainly, they were in general accord with the Sons of Italy's overall aims:

> 1) to unite in a single organization persons of Italian ori-
> gin who are living in the United States; 2) to increase the
> prestige of the Italian people by spreading Italian culture
> and making known the many contributions of Italians to

the progress of America; 3) to promote the advancement
of its members and to help charitable associations; and 4)
to promote Americanism based upon absolute loyalty to
the Constitution.[34]

Rochesterians in general, however, are quite suspicious of organizations that originate outside of Western New York. Therefore, it generated its own umbrella organization, The Italian Civic League. At its fiftieth anniversary in 1985, the Italian Civic League attracted four hundred people to its dinner.[35] In addition to roast beef stories of the founding of the league were featured at the dinner.

Louis Valenza, one of League's founders. who was 84 in 1985, for example, recalled that more than forty organizations existed in Rochester in 1935. At that time more than 20,000 Rochesterians were born in Italy. The League espoused the rights of Italian Americans through opposing discrimination wherever it was found: in jobs, housing, or education. In 1985, the League had representatives of nine civic and social groups, a drop from the fourteen of just ten years before.[36]

At their annual Columbus Day meetings, the League generally recruited a prominent Rochester Italian-American to speak. In 1975, for example, New York State Supreme Court Justice Clarence Brisco praised Italians for their "great contributions" to the growth of the city of Rochester. He compared Rochester's Italian population to Columbus. Both travelled uncharted waters and possessed a sense of adventure. In common with Columbus, other Italians in America have contributed greatly to the welfare of the country to which they came as strangers.

Judge Brisco's talk was in conformity with others over the years.[37] Basically, these talks extolled the virtues of Italians and their descendants while focusing on one or two specific instances. They did focus on general issues that united members of the constituent organizations, functioning to bolster the nascent Italian-American ethnic identity which, at least situationally, replaced more regional identities.

Thus, it remained neutral in the controversy surrounding a potentially rival umbrella group, the Italian American Civil Rights League. The League grew up in the period of various "power" movements of the late

1960s and early 1970s. Given Rochesterians' antipathy to "New York" organizations, however, the Italian Civic League did not really have much to fear from the Civil Rights League. Wisely, it decided to take a neutral stance publicly on the Civil Rights League.

The Italian American Civil Rights League eventually admitted early links with the Mafia, but Frank Cimino, its President, stated that those links were broken in 1973 with the jailing of Frank Valenti. Charges, however, continued to plague the Civil Rights League and payoffs to mob members on its grounds were cited as continued mob connections. Older organizations, generally, ignored the brash new group. The "inadvertently" forgot to invite it to the 1973 Columbus Day Dinner, for example. Eventually, it faded away in Rochester while the more established organizations continued to represent their remaining members.

Salvatore Mondello identified the situation correctly when he noted that the formation of groups such as the Italian American Civil Rights League were a reaction to the black revolution. Other people who faced discrimination and overcame its effects tended to become impatient with the black power movement. Their grievances are often summarized as "Where are Italian-American studies?"[38]

In common with many groups asserting both their own ethnic identity and their right to be called American, Italian-Americans have turned to community involvement. For example, the Paisano Club in Fairport consists of a "dozen or so men and wives and children" who make spaghetti for about two hundred senior citizens. The club has been making spaghetti for more than twenty years. Membership is limited to fifteen men so that each member must be active.

The club follows a familiar Italian-American pattern in using church facilities for its work. In this case, it uses the dining hall of a local church to serve its meals.

Albert "Hawk" DiRisio, owner of a local restaurant, is a co-founder and key historian. In 1958 DiRisio and Herman Stolt were lamenting that as members of the VFW they had not been using the local VFW hall enough. They decided to get a group together to play bocce and spend money. The men began a Paisano Day at VFW and that led to the formation of the Paisano

Club. There were other Italian events; for example, a Paisano Ball with a pig roast. They use the proceeds to pay for the Seniors' spaghetti. In addition, they run a teen center. Unfortunately, DiRisio laments that there is no longer a bocce tournament. The neighborhood has changed. There are, however, new members in the Paisano Club, some of whom are not Italian.[39]

DISCUSSION AND CONCLUSION

Italian-American clubs served to meet immediate needs of their members, needs that individuals could not meet for themselves. These needs included burial and social service needs, certainly. Even in the earliest days, however, they were not limited to these requirements alone. There were social-psychological requisites as well. These necessities included respect, an end to prejudice and discrimination, and movement into the American mainstream.

In order to achieve these goals clubs had to establish that Italian were like other people within Rochester, that Italian culture had helped form the basis of Western culture, and that modern Italians were heirs to that culture. Clubs had to seize every opportunity to hammer home these points, often to the point of redundancy and ethnic cheerleading. In addition, each successful Italian became a symbol of what other Italians could do if given the opportunity.

Society officials exerted diligence to separate the "majority" of Italians from criminal elements while protesting against discrimination resulting from media glorification of criminals. Societies walked a difficult line in asserting Italian-American civil liberties, protesting discrimination, and asserting the compatibility of a dual identity. While club members may have been free to admire Mussolini or consort with reputed criminals, the clubs themselves had to remain neutral on issues that divided their members, always asserting and demonstrating allegiance to American customs and the Constitution of the United States.

As times changed, so did the role of the societies. Increasingly, they became more social, cultural, and political. Mutual aid aspects declined and the number of societies did also. Politicians of both parties and from Rochester's numerous ethnic groups found it beneficial to attend picnics sponsored by the Vulguernera society as well as the Columbus Day Dinners of the Italian Civic League.

For second and third generation Italian-Americans the more regional societies became a mild embarrassment during the 1950s and early 1960s. The emphasis was on the American part of the hyphenated identity. As Jerre Mangione has it in the opening of *Mount Allegro*, "When I grow up I want to be an American!" Italian-American college graduates wanted to move to the suburbs, climb the corporate ladder, drink Scotch instead of red wine and fit into the American dream.

Those societies that endured did so as a means for helping people achieving that dream. Many societies focused more strongly on identifying and eliminating bias from job opportunities and in protesting against stereotypes in the mass media. They still handed out scholarships to young Italian-American scholars and celebrated Columbus Day. Over time, however, the more "cultural" societies began to decline and cease to exist.

In the 1960s many Italian-Americans who paid little attention to their heritage other than to attend an occasional opera, eat pasta, and visit their parents regularly began to discover that they were not truly accepted into the wider society. There were exceptions for the extraordinarily gifted, but even those individuals faced the no longer so funny ethnic humor. The phoney Italian accents of their fellow-workers began to irritate rather than amuse. In sum, they found that although the prejudice and discrimination were more subtle, they still existed and closed top positions to them.

At that time, the middle and late 1960s various power movements began to emerge. No serious scholar can doubt the validity of the grievances that compelled the emergence of Black, Red, Feminist, Gray, Gay, and sundry other movements." Older ethnics," however, found themselves forgotten in the various non-quota quota systems that burst on the scene. Suddenly, second, third, and even fourth generation Italian-Americans who had given little thought to their "ethnicity" began to ponder the meaning of that heritage.

Societies took on a new life to counter other "power" groups. That is the real meaning of the rise of the Italian-American Civil Rights League in Rochester. That it was outmaneuvered by Rochester's older societies speaks to something important about Rochester's unique Italian heritage. It does not mean that Rochester's Italians were insensitive to discrimination. The record speaks against that interpretation. It reflects the general suspicion of New York City held in Western New York.

Currently, younger people are once again identifying themselves as Italian-Americans. Young Xerox business executives flock to Italian-American comedians, vocalists, playwrights. They seek out and read Italian novelists. Italian history courses fill quickly, surprising many who take them with their content. Many travel to Italy and are astonished with its differences from what their grandparents or great-grandparents prepared them to see.

Societies, very different from those founded in the late 1800s and early 1900s, still seek to serve community interests. The nature of voluntary associations is to bridge the gap between primary and secondary groups. The *societa`* have performed that task and continue to do so. In so doing, they have been a powerful social force in the fostering and promotion of a new ethnic identity, that of Italian-American.

NOTES

1. Banfield, Edward, *Moral Basis of a Backward Society* (New York: Free Press, 1958), p. 10.
2. Colombis, Alessio, "Amoral Familism and Social Organization in Montenegro: A Critique of Banfield's Thesis," *Peuples Mediterraneens* 25 (1983): 20-23, trans.
3. See Ruth M. Keene, "Acculturation of the First and Second Generation Italians in Rochester, NY," M.A. Thesis, Univ. of Rochester, 1946, for a detailed study.
4. Zissler, Alice, "Rochester's claim to Italian heritage," *Times Union* (July 21, 1977).
5. Corvai, Patrizia, *The Children of Columbus in Rochester* (Rochester, NY: Columbus, 1991), p. 6.
6. *La Stampa Unita*, October 24, 1929, cited in Corvai, 1991; Zissler, 1977.
7. Ray, Charles P., "American and Italian Women: A Decade of Progressive Reform at the Practical Housekeeping Center of Rochester, NY, 1906-1917," Senior Thesis, Univ. of Rochester, January, 1976, p. 8.
8. "Italian Mission: First and Second Readers Wanted," *Union & Advertiser*, Mar. 21, 1889:3-1.
9. "Speech by Ariel Bellondi on Behalf of the Italian Race," *Union & Advertiser*, Mar. 13, 1896:8-1.

10. Zucchi, John, "Italian Child Street Musicians in New York in the 1870s," *Italian Americana* (10, 1991): 7-29.

11. Zissler, 1977.

12. See Alexander DeConde, "Endearment or Antipathy? Nineteenth Century American Attitudes toward Italians," *Ethnic Groups* (4, 1982):131-48, on the myth of America's love of earlier Italian immigrants.

13. "Italian Opera Company," *Union & Advertiser*, Jan. 5, 1864:2-1.

14. Corvai, 1991, p. 7.

15. See Clement G. Lanni, "The History of the Italians of Rochester from 1876-1926," Rochester Historical Society Papers First Series (6, 1927), pp. 188-91, for a discussion of Italians in early Rochester history.

16. "Italian Political Club Elects Officers," *Union & Advertiser*, Dec. 17, 1897:12-2.

17. "Italian-American Political Club: Meeting Officers Elected," *Union & Advertiser*, May 6, 1896 :10-5.

18. "Discrimination against Italians Charged," *Union & Advertiser*, Dec. 27, 1897:7-7.

19. "Italian American group's founder honored. Area man helped form business club in 1925," *Democrat & Chronicle*, Oct. 24, 1988.

20. "Bersaglieri Lamarmora Italian Society Officers Elected and Listed," *Union & Advertiser*, Apr. 8, 1892:6-2.

21. Ray, 1976, p. 11.

22. Ray, 1976, p. 14.

23. Storey, Marjory, Strong Museum, Rochester, NY, July 2, 1991.

24. "Rochester's Arcadians," *Union & Advertiser*, Jan. 31, 1889:3-2.

25. "Italian Society Holds Ball at Germania Hall," *Union & Advertiser*, Apr. 19, 1895:8-2.

26. "Italians Celebrate Victor Emmanuel Day," *Union & Advertiser*, Sep. 20, 1895:6-1.

27. "Bersaglieri Lamarmora Italian Society Officers Elected and Listed," *Union & Advertiser*, Apr. 8, 1892:6-2.

28. "Italian Society Holds Ball at Germania Hall," *Union & Advertiser*, Apr. 19, 1895:8-2.

29. "Italians Celebrate Victor Emmanuel Day," *Union & Advertiser*, Sep. 20, 1895:6-1.

30. Lanni, 1927.

31. "Il Solco Disbands," *Times Union*, Apr. 5, 1969; Lo Curto, Joseph, Il Solco Meets in Dormitory, *Democrat & Chronicle*, Feb. 26, 1951.

32. Lo Curto, 1992.

33. "Il Solco Disbands," *Times Union*, Apr. 5, 1969.

34. Biaggi, Ernest L., *The Purple Aster: A History of the Sons of Italy in America* (New York: Veritas Press, 1961), p. 26.

35. Myers, Jim, "Italian Civic League draws 400 for roast beef and tales of old times. Group celebrates 50th anniversary," *Democrat & Chronicle*, Oct. 15, 1985.

36. "Justice Brisco Praises Italians," *Times Union*, Oct. 13, 1975.

37. See, for example, "Italian League Fetes Columbus," *Times Union*, Oct. 12, 1962.

38. See "League To Install Schiolino," *Times Union*, Dec. 9, 1975; *Times Union*, Oct. 13, 1973; Akeman, Thomas, "Mafia Link Gone Now, Says Rights Unit Aide," *Democrat & Chronicle*, May 20, 1976; "Civil Rights Reaction Split - `We're Americans', say Letters to the Editor," *Democrat & Chronicle*, Apr. 25, 1971; O'Brien, "Why Rochester's Italian-Americans Are Up in Arms," *Democrat & Chronicle*, Apr. 18

39. Barbara Gerber, "In Fairport, a Taste for Camaraderiem," *Times Union*, Apr. 19, 1990.

40. Ray, 1976, pp. 4, 11; Keene, 1946, p. 36.

41. Adapted from John Walker Briggs, *An Italian Passage: Immigrants to Three American Cities, 1870-1930* (New Haven: Yale Univ. Press, 1978).

ADDITIONAL REFERENCES

Democrat & Chronicle

1985	July 7. "A tale of two Sicilys. From Caltanissetta, Grotte, Valguarnera and other towns, they brought their dreams to a new world in Rochester." By Jim Myers.
1970	February 21. "'Social Club' Search Just Routine Say Police."
1965	September 4. "Societadi Gerace Will Have Dance."
1958	October 31. "Cultural Group Lists Speaker."
1958	July 14. "Hot Pizza, Politics Mix at Valguarnera Fete."
1992	January 3. Interview. Wunder's Restaurant, Rochester, NY. By Jerre Mangione.

Times Union

1973	October 9. "Columbus Day Lunch Goes Undiscovered."
1973	September 8. "Parrinello, Sparacino Honored."
1973	June 7. "Italian Dinner `Will Be a Bash'." By Charlie Wagner.
1970	November 20. "Scholarship Dance Slated."
1969	December 26. "Defends the Vulguernerians." By Larry Farsace.
1969	December 22. "No Way to Promote Americanism."
1969	December 30. "Community Action Hits Gamblers."
1959	November 9. "Valguarnera Society Lists Carlino Talk."

Union & Advertiser

1993	July 22. "Italians Have More than Doubled in the Past Five Years."
1890	February 24. "Italian Mission Celebrates Its First Anniversary."
1883	December 14. "Italian Population."
1875	March 18. "Antonio Pasche."

Mount Allegro. (New York: Columbia Univ. Press, 1981 [1942]).

17

THE ITALIAN AMERICANS: CULTURAL TRAITS AND SOCIO-ECONOMIC ACHIEVEMENTS

LOUIS J. GESUALDI
ST. VINCENT'S COLLEGE OF ST. JOHN'S UNIVERSITY

In an attempt to understand and explain various characteristics of Italian-Americans many researchers from the 1950s to 1990 have provided an explanation which states that aspects of the present day behavior of Italian-Americans (and other ethnics in the United States) are principally the outcomes of enduring norms, values and attitudes brought over to America from their country of origin.[1] This explanation will be referred to as the cultural trait approach. Cultural traits will be defined as norms, values and attitudes which were developed in the ethnic group's country or area of origin and maintained by the group in the United States. This paper critiques the cultural trait approach by reviewing and discussing some of the research on the educational and occupational achievements of Italian-Americans. It examines the cultural traits of the family and the social and economic situations in explaining this group's achievements.

Works by Rosen, Strodtbeck, Glazer and Moynihan, Covello, Gottlieb and Sibbison, Thernstrom, Kessner, Yans-McLaughlin, Egelman and Milione use the cultural trait approach to explain Italian-American behavior.[2] Italian-Americans, according to these writers, had fewer success stories because their inherited attitudes toward education, work savings and career planning did not lead them to the highest paying jobs. They have argued that the cultural traits of the Italian-American family which include a mistrust of educators and educational institutions outside the family circle are the cause of the claimed underachievement in the United States. There exist other works, however, that provide different interpretations and conclusions from the ones presented by these researchers. Joseph Lopreato, for example, pointed out that the "apparent low achievement" of Italian-Americans is misleading, and indicated that the American school and teachers were hostile to the Italian family. He argued that early Southern Italian immigrants did not value the education of the American high school because in school Italian children were advised to train for working class occupations and many educators judged that these children lacked the mental capabilities necessary for high status jobs. Moreover, Lopreato commented that Italian families, seeing this, felt that the trades could be learned on the job while at the same time their children would be financially rewarded.[3]

John W. Briggs' account of Italian communities in Utica and Rochester, New York and in Kansas City, Missouri during the migration period of 1880 to 1920 in America, indicated that the Italian immigrants' ideas concerning self-help, group organization, social mobility and the economic value of education, which were developed in Southern Italy, had become very useful in America. Briggs stated that once Italians had decided to stay in America, rather than return to Italy after having accumulated some money, they began achieving social and economic success in the United States while maintaining their cultural traditions. He also argued that the Southern Italians did value educational attainment as a way of access to personal and family betterment.[4]

Albert Grande stated that the high percentages of Southern Italian-Americans in the learned professions was proof that the Italian immigrant family did not have a negative attitude toward education. The Buffalo area, according to Grande, provided an excellent example. Grande noted that there were large numbers of Italian-American physicians, lawyers, dentists and engineers, mostly from Buffalo's Sicilian West Side, and large numbers of Italian-Americans in highly responsible professional positions. He indicated that these accomplishments could not have been attained by persons rooted in family values that mistrusted intellectual and educational attainment.[5]

Lopreato also presented a study by Leonard Broom and his associates, which ranked different racial and ethnic groups on the basis of education, income and occupations, using the native whites as a standard. Their findings indicated that the Russians, Greeks and Italians (in that order) had shown the highest degree of achievement while old immigrants (Anglo-Canadians, Germans, French-Canadians and Irish) ranked in achievement either below the native white norm or slightly above it. This study also showed that second generation Italian-Americans were at the norm in educational attainment, slightly higher in occupation and much higher in income.[6]

Richard Gambino stated that in a 1969 survey of Americans, by the U.S. Bureau of the Census, the figure for Italian-Americans between 25 and 34 completing high school was 50.4 percent and that this was the second highest percentage of all Americans in that age group.[7] Gambino, in 1978, reported that Italian-Americans were attending college at a rate much higher than the population average and that in New York they made up large percentages of the student body at SUNY, CUNY and the state's Catholic colleges.[8] Similarly, as stated by Gambino in 1974, 34,000 out of the 169,000 students (or approximately 20%) at CUNY were Italian-Americans. In the 1970s, Italian-Americans accounted for 50 percent of Fordham University's student body.[9]

Richard Alba, in disagreement with the researchers who have utilized the cultural trait approach, pointed out that Italian-Americans (and for that matter, other white ethnic groups) are becoming similar to majority Americans in the important matters of social standing as well as those of culture. Although ethnic norms, values and attitudes (traits) pertaining to Italian-Americans had not altogether disappeared, his data indicated that these factors did not constitute a barrier to the high level of occupational and educational achievement of the Italian-Americans of the 1980s, and were not serious impediments to social relations such as intermarriage. Alba listed, however, the significant changes which occurred among Italian-Americans over the past century. These changes included the loss of the Italian language by the third generation, the shrinkage of Italian immigrant communities, a considerable economic and occupational mobility of this group over the past decades, the erosion of past cultural attitudes, and the Italian-Americans' increasing rates of intermarriage with other ethnic and religious groups. Thus, Alba demonstrated that ethnic norms, values and attitudes associated with Italian-Americans were disappearing and concluded that this disappearance is an outcome of socio-economic conditions which exist in the United States.[10]

The authors cited above (Lopreato, Briggs, Grande, Broom and his associates, Gambino and Alba), argued on the whole that Italian-Americans are above the general population average in education and income. These studies indicated that Italian-Americans were not underachievers and that cultural traits therefore, did not hinder them. These studies, in contrast to other literature, suggested that the behavior of Italian-Americans involving education and income was not associated with a so-called enduring Italian trait concerning a mistrust of education from outside the family circle.

What of the other studies, then, which demonstrated the low achievement of Italian-Americans? As a possible explanation for some of these authors' allegations concerning the Italian-Americans' lack of income and educational achievements, Lopreato stated that there has been a tendency among social scientists to do their research concerning Italian-Americans in working class or poor areas where they are sure to find many idle people who do not mind being interviewed (unlike middle class areas where career and activities monopolize one's time). Under these circumstances, what observers have found may be relevant to Italian-Americans of the lower and working classes; however, this may say little about Italian-Americans in general.[12]

Lopreato also points out that, over the years, there has been a tendency by scholars to compare Italian-Americans to more successful ethnic groups (i.e., Jewish-Americans and Irish-Americans) and then suggest that Italians are low and poor achievers.[12] Grande has argued, however, that there was little basis for the comparative study of occupational achievement in the United States between Southern Italians and Jews. Grande pointed out that Southern Italian immigrants had the highest rate of illiteracy among the European immigrant groups. In contrast, most Eastern European Jewish immigrants could read and write Yiddish and knew enough Hebrew to read prayers. In other words, the advantage that Jews had upon their arrival in

America in terms of urban skills (education) was great in comparison to the Italians. The upward mobility of the Jews had been more rapid, because Jewish immigrants came from different levels of European society including the commercial, professional and educated classes—while the Italian mass immigration was made up predominantly of poorly educated people from the lowest economic level.[13]

Stephen Steinberg, in a similar discussion, indicated that in spite of their poverty Jewish immigrants (that is, from 1899 to 1910) were concentrated in economically advanced parts of their countries of origin, and they had experiences and occupational skills that would serve them quite well in the expanding industrial economy of the United States. In contrast, he stated that the vast majority of Italians who came to America during the same period were farmers or farmhands. Steinberg noted that for Jewish immigrants, 67 percent of the adult labor force were skilled laborers, while only 15 percent of the adult labor force of the Southern Italian immigrants were skilled. The upward economic mobility of Jewish-Americans had been more rapid than the Italian-Americans because they entered the United States at a higher rung of the occupational ladder.[14] It is important to note that Italians and Jews are frequently compared (possibly because they emigrated to the United States at about the same time and were two of the largest groups of immigrants), and these comparisons have been reached mistaken conclusions about the Italians.

Finally, differences in socio-economic achievement between the Italian and Irish-Americans can at least partly be explained by the differences in migration patterns and time of migration. Over 60 percent of the Irish immigrants came to the United States between the years of 1820 and 1900,[15] while 60 percent of the Italian immigrants arrived in this country between 1900 and 1914.[16] The Irish, in general, came to America one, two and even three generations before the Italians and thus had a significant head start in socio-economic advancement over the Italians. Furthermore, when the Irish emigrated to the United States, they came with their families and intended to stay in America. In contrast, between 1900 and 1914, most Italian immigrants were men traveling without their families, many of whom returned to Italy.[17] Rodney Stark pointed out that a great many Italians with family who stayed in America because of the outbreak of World War I and the bad conditions that existed in Italy after the war decided to wait for a later time to return to their country of origin. However, Stark also noted that many Italians never did go back and he argued as long as the Italians thought they would return, they were likely to maintain Italian cultural values. This would include a mistrust of educators and educational institutions outside the family. As time passed, the maintenance of Italian cultural values and norms by the immigrants began to disappear and the Italians began to participate more fully in American society.[18]

It has been common for many American researchers and writers to argue that the lack of educational and occupational achievements by Italian-Americans in comparison to other ethnic groups is mainly a result of an enduring cultural trait against education outside the family. This cultural trait approach, however, does not provide an adequate explanation of the behavior of Italian-Americans. In agreement with Steinberg, Lopreato and Alba, socio-economic conditions need to be investigated in order to understand the social realities for an ethnic group. These conditions include: 1) the historical migration patterns of the group (that is, the time period of the ethnic group's migration, the area of the United States where the group settled and the permanency of the migration); 2) the material resources that each ethnic group brought with them when they came to a particular section of the United States (that is, the educational and occupational background of the group before their migration to the United States or to a particular area of the United States); and 3) the economic opportunities that were available to the different ethnic groups within the different areas of the United States and during the different time periods of American history.[19] While investigating socio-economic conditions, one can determine how some cultural traits develop and/or remain with certain ethnic groups while other traits disappear or seem to disappear. Cultural traits are created and maintained due to environmental circumstances (that is, cultural traits cannot exist on their own).

It should be noted that the social scientists who use the cultural trait approach tend to view cultural traits as constants. They do not investigate socio-economic conditions that exist in the United States, and do not examine cultural traits as adaptive strategies. Furthermore, some social scientists' discussion on cultural traits of the different ethnic groups are based on their own impressions and speculations and not based on substantial data and evidence. Based on the evidence, it can be stated that the cultural traits of an ethnic group are often adaptive strategies to socio-economic predicaments and furthermore can change due to socio-economic conditions. In studying Italian-Americans or any other ethnic group, researchers need to examine not only the cultural traits but also the factors that exist outside a group's realm which affect these traits. More studies need to acknowledge that cultural traits common to an ethnic group are non-stagnant and to investigate how cultural traits are developed and/or maintained by certain groups as an outcome of environmental predicaments.

NOTES

1. Thomas Sowell, *Ethnic America: A History* (New York: Basic Books, 1981).
2. Bernard C. Rosen, "Race, Ethnicity and the Achievement Syndrome," *American Sociological Review* 4 (1959): 27-60; Fred L. Strodtbeck, "Family Interaction, Values and Achievement" in Marshall Sklare (ed), *The Jews: Social Patterns of an American Group* (New York: Free Press, 1958), p. 150; Nathan Glazer and Daniel P. Moynihan, *Beyond the Melting Pot* (Cambridge: The M.I.T. Press, 1971), p. 198; Leonard Covello, *The Sociological Background of the Italo-American School Child* (Leiden: E.J. Brill, 1967), p. 403; Dave Gottlieb and Virginia Sibbison, "Ethnicity and Religiosity: Some Selective Exploration Among College Seniors," *International Migration Review* 8 (1974): 43-58; Stephen Themstrom, *The Other Bostonians: Poverty and Progress in the American Metropolis, 1880-1970* (Cambridge: Harvard Univ. Press, 1973), pp. 99-125; Thomas Kessner, *The Golden Door* (New York: Oxford Univ. Press, 1977), p. 173; Virginia Yans-McLaughlin, *Family and Community: Italian Immigrants in Buffalo, 1880-1930* (Ithaca: Cornell Univ. Press, 1977), p. 251; William S. Egelman, "Italian and Irish Americans in Education: A Sociohistoric Analysis" in Francis X. Femminella (ed), *Italians and Irish in America* (Staten Island: American Italian Historical Association, 1988), pp. 163-76; Vincenzo Milione, "Occupational and Educational Attainment of Italian-American Professionals in New York City" in Joseph V. Scelsa, Salvatore J. LaGumina and Lydio Tomasi (eds), *Italian Americans in Transition* (Staten Island: American Italian Historical Association, 1990), pp. 153-63.
3. Joseph Lopreato, *Italian Americans* (New York: Random House, 1970), pp. 150-60.
4. John Walker Briggs, *An Italian Passage: Immigrants to Three American Cities, 1870-1930* (New Haven: Yale Univ. Press, 1978).
5. Albert Grande, "The Intellectual Image of Italian-Americans," *Unico Magazine* 35 (5, 1980): 127.
6. Lopreato, *Italian Americans*, pp. 162-65.
7. Richard Gambino, *Blood of My Blood* (Garden City: Doubleday and Company, 1974), p. 246.

8. Richard Gambino, "This Italian-American Voter: Is This His Year? *Empire State Report* 1 (3, 1978): 24-27.

9. Gambino, *Blood of My Blood*, p. 266.

10. Richard Alba, *Italian Americans into the Twilight of Ethnicity* (New Jersey: Prentice Hall, 1985).

11. Lopreato, *Italian Americans*, p. 161.

12. Ibid., pp. 164-65.

13. Albert Grande, "The Cultural and Intellectual Experience of Italian-Americans: Some Observations" in Humbert Nelli (ed), *The United States and Italy: The First Two Hundred Years* (Staten Island: American Italian Historical Association, 1977), pp. 217-21.

14. Stephen Steinberg, *The Ethnic Myth* (Boston: Beacon Press, 1981), pp. 97-8.

15. Frank A. Stone, *The Irish of Connecticut* (Storrs: Ethnic Heritage Studies Series, The People of Connecticut, 1975), p. 22.

16. Alba, *Italian Americans into the Twilight of Ethnicity*, p. 45.

17. Steinberg, *The Ethnic Myth*, pp. 152-71.

18. Rodney Stark, *Sociology* (Belmont, CA: Wadsworth Publishing Co., 1985), p. 44.

19. Steinberg, *The Ethnic Myth*.

APPENDIX A

PROGRAM: AMERICAN ITALIAN HISTORICAL
ASSOCIATION 25TH ANNUAL CONFERENCE: NEW
EXPLORATIONS IN ITALIAN AMERICAN STUDIES

Dupont Plaza Hotel (Washington, D.C.)
November 12-14, 1992

Conference Chairperson
Richard N. Juliani

<u>Thursday, November 12</u>
Executive Council Meeting (2:00-5:00 pm)

<u>Friday, November 13</u>
Women's Network Breakfast Meeting (8:00-8:45 am)
Registration (8:30 am-4:00 pm)
Welcome (9:00-9:15 am)

9:15-10:45 am Concurrent Sessions

Session 1A
Social Mobility and Cultural Change
Chair: William V. D'Antonio,
Catholic University of America\George Washington University.
Anthony Rauche, University of Hartford
> "Economic Viability and Selective Ethnicity: Italian Musical
> Culture in Hartford, Connecticut"

Louis J. Gesualdi, St. John's University
"The Italian Americans: Cultural Traits and Economic
Achievements"
Angela Danzi, SUNY, Farmingdale
"Home is Better: Childbirth and Continuity, 1920-1940"

Session 1B
Others among Others: Lesbians and Gays in Italian American Culture
Chair: Lucia Chiavola Birnbaum, Stanford University
Rose Romano, Malafemmina Press
"The Italian American Lesbian in Lesbian Literature"
Wallace Silanpoa, University of Rhode Island
"The Community in Italian American Gay Fiction"
Ron Illardo, CUNY, Staten Island
"Themes in Italian American Gay and Lesbian Filmmakers"
Nanci Gaglio, New York University
"The Lesbian Artist: Restructuring Sacrifice and Respect –
L'Omertà"
Stephanie Romeo, CUNY, Hunter College
"Anger is an Energy: From Bensonhurst to Transcendence"

Session 1C
Italian Images in American Culture
Chair: Mario Aste, University of Massachusetts
John R. Mitrano, Boston College, and James G. Mitrano, Lehigh University
"That's Italian...Or Is It?: (Un)Popular Images of Italians in
American Mass Media"
Chris Newton, Tufts University
"From the Prince Macaroni Hour to Car Talk:
An Evolution of Italian American Radio"
Jerome Cangelosi Krase, Brooklyn College
"Traces of Home"

11:00 am-12:30 pm   Concurrent Sessions

Session 2A
Focus on Columbus
Chair: Vincent DiGirolamo, Princeton University
Salvatore J. LaGumina, Nassau Community College
"In Honor of Columbus: Places, Organizations and Celebrations"
Frank J. Cavaioli, SUNY, Farmingdale
"Columbus: A Slide Presentation"
Luciano Rusich, SUNY, Staten Island
"Religiosity and Mysticism in Christopher Columbus"

Session 2B
Representations of Italian Americans in the Arts
Chair: Carol Bonomo Albright, *Italian Americana*
Robert Casillo, University of Miami
"The Religion of Martin Scorsese"
Christopher Zinn, Reed College
"Don DeLillo's American Dream"
John Paul Russo, University of Miami
"The Italian American in Late 19th Century American Fiction"

Session 2C
Social Change and Ethnic Identity
Chair: Richard N. Juliani, Villanova University
Madeline Goodman, Carnegie Mellon University
"Ethnic Identity, Language and Generational Conflict in the
Interwar Period"
Joan Saverino, University of Pennsylvania
"Image Making though Historical Pageantry in the 1920's: The
Italians of Reading, Pennsylvania"
Joseph R. Gibino, Seminary of the Immaculate Conception
"Intensification and Resistence: Ritual and Gender in an
Italian American Community"

12:30-2:00 pm Lunch

2:00-3:30 pm   Concurrent Sessions

Session 3A
Immigrants and the Economy
Chair: Luciano J. Iorizzo, SUNYCO, Oswego
Michael LaSorte, SUNYCO, Brockport
    "Vengo per Fare l'America: The Sojourner Businessman"
Adele Maiello, University of Genoa
    "Italian American Merchants in California and Argentina"
Diane Vecchio, University of Wisconsin at Whitewater
    "Connecting Spheres: Women and Work in Milwaukee's Italian
    Third Ward"
Luciano J. Iorizzo, SUNYCO, Oswego
    "Dun and Bradstreet's Assessment of Merchants:
    A Neglect Source for Italian American Studies"

Session 3B
Le Avventure ed i Sogni – **Adventures and Dreams: Family History and
its Role in Creative Writing"** *prose and poetry readings*
Chair: Mary Russo Demetrick, Syracuse University
Participants: Mary Russo Demetrick, Syracuse University
Mary Bucci Bush, Memphis State University
Mary Fama, Philadelphia
Judy Zaccaria, SUNYCO, Oswego

Session 3C
Autobiography and Family History
Chair: Diane Francesconi Lyon, Silver Spring
Sadie Penzato, Highland Park, New York
    "Growing Up Sicilian and Female"
Robert Marchisotto, Princeton, New Jersey
    "Going Home: A Sicilian American's Odyssey"
Julia Volpelletto Nakamura, Nutley, New Jersey
    "Chronicle of an Unremarkable Family"

3:45-5:15 pm   Concurrent Sessions

Session 4A
Politics and War
Chair: Valentino Belfiglio, Texas Woman's University
Valentino Belfiglio, Texas Woman's University
   "The Roles of Italian Partisans in World War II"
Rose Scherini, Kensington, California
   "Effects of the Fascist/Anti-Fascist Struggle on San Francisco"
Rocco Caporale, St. John's University
   "Educational Opportunity and Social Mobility among Italian
   Americans"

Session 4B
Women's Studies: Values, Roles and Relations
Chair: Maria Elisa Ciavarelli, Rowan College of New Jersey
Davida Gavioli, Pennsylvania State University
   "In Search of the Mother's Lost Voice"
Edvige Giunta, Union College
   "Comic Women: Nancy Savoca and the Italian American
   Domestic Comedy"
Lucia Chiavola Birnbaum, Stanford University
   "Black Madonnas: Post-modernist Interdisciplinary History"

Session 4C
The Italian Experience: Settlers and Visitors
Chair: Letizia Argenteri, University of San Diego
Janet Worrall, Northern Colorado University
   "Adjustment and Integration: The Italian Experience in Colorado"
Anthony D. Cavaluzzi, Adirondack Community College
   "Un Viaggiatore nel America: Giuseppe Antonio Borgese's
   Atlante Americano"

7:00-9:00 **Annual Banquet, Casa Italiana Cultural and Social Center**
595 1/2 Third Street N.W., Washington, D.C.
Special Entertainment Provided by Marco Pezzano and Anthony Rauche

<u>Saturday, November 14</u>
Registration (8:30 am-3:00 pm)
Annual General Business Meeting (8:00-9:00 am)

9:15-10:45 am Concurrent Sessions

Session 5A
Research Perspectives in Italian American Studies:
A Roundtable Discussion
Chair: Joseph Velikonja, University of Washington
Participants: Donna Gabaccia, University of North Carolina
Ira A. Glazier, Temple University
Nancy Torrieri, U.S. Census Bureau

Session 5B
Goodfellas and Bad Girls
Chair: Paolo Giordano, Loyola University, Chicago
Mary Jo Bona, Gonzaga University
"The Voices We Carry Within: Contemporary Italian
American Women Writers"
Ben Lawton, Purdue University
"Good Fellas and Bad Girls: Images of Self and Other in Italian
American Cinema"
Anthony Julian Tamburri, Purdue University
"What's a Nice Girl Like You Doing in a Video Like This?:
The Madonna Complex"
Fred Gardaphe, Columbia College, Chicago
"Parody at the Border: Giose Rimanelli and Italian American
Postmodernism"

Session 5C
Community Organization and Public Action
Chair: Jerome Cangelosi Krase, Brooklyn College
Judith N. DeSena, St. John's University
  "The Influence of the Italian American Community on Social
  Activities in Greenpoint-Williamsburg, Brooklyn"
Frank Salamone, Iona College
  "Clubs: Cultural and Otherwise in Rochester, New York"

11:00 am-12:30 pm Concurrent Sessions

Session 6A
Sacco-Vanzetti: New Perspectives
Chair: Fred Milano, Appalachian State University
Paul Avrich, Queens College, CUNY
  "Sacco-Vanzetti: Dynamite and Consciousness of Guilt"
Nunzio Pernicone, Drexel University
  "Terrorism and Italian Anarchists"
Philip V. Cannistraro, Drexel University
  "Mussolini and Sacco-Vanzetti"

Session 6B
Italian American Authors
Chair: Emilise Aleandri, New York City
Joseph Fioravanti, Oneonta, New York
  Excerpts from a novel in progress
Blossom Kirschenbaum, Brown University
  "Mary Caponegro: Prize Winning American Italian Writer at the
  American Academy in Rome"
Jerre Mangione, University of Pennsylvania
  "The Problem of Being an Italian American Writer"
Louise Napolitano, SUNY, Farmingdale
  "*Christ in Concrete*: A Chronicle"

Session 6C
Poesia e Critica Oggi: Poetry and Literary Criticism Today"
Chair: Tonia Caterina Riviello, Santa Clara University
Dante Maffia, University of Salerno
   "Essere Poeti Oggi"
Luigi Reina, University of Salerno
   "Direzione della Poesia al Femminile"
Franco Mulas, University of Sassari
   "On the Poetics of Tusiani's *Gente Mia*"

12:30-1:45 pm Annual Membership Luncheon
Robert Viscusi, Brooklyn College
   "An Oration upon the Most Recent Death of Christopher
   Columbus

2:00-3:30 pm Concurrent Sessions

Session 7A
The United States and Italy in World War I
Chair: Monte Finkelstein, Tallahassee Community College
H. James Burgwyn, West Chester State University
   "Sonnino's Power Politics vs. Wilson's Idealism"
Charles L. Killinger, Valencia Community College
   "The Italian Democratic Left and Woodrow Wilson"
James E. Miller, U.S. Department of State
   "Wilson and Italy: A Comment"

Session 7B
Columbus and Other Visitors
Chair: Bruno Arcudi, SUNY, Buffalo
Frank J. Cavaioli, SUNY, Farmingdale
   "Columbus and the Rise of American Literature"
Harral E. Landry, Texas Woman's University
   "Christopher Columbus, What Have We Done to You? The
   Renaissance Paradigm"

Paolo Giordano, Loyola University, Chicago
"Images of America and Columbus in the Literature of Immigration

Session 7C
The Poetic Image: Readings from New Work
Chair: Carol Bonomo Albright, *Italian Americana*
Tonia Caterina Riviello, University of Santa Clara
Selections from *Foreign Soil*
Irene Lagorio, Carmel, California
Selected poems

3:45-5:15 pm Concurrent Sessions

Session 8A
The Celebration of Religious Life and Experience
Chair: Lydio Tomasi, The Center for Migration Studies
Mary Brown, Kutztown State University
"The Second Italian American Generation in a New York Italian
Parish, 1949-1960"
Denise Mangieri DiCarlo, New York City Board of Education
"Passion Plays at Our Lady of Pompeii Church"
Peter R. D'Agostino, University of Chicago
"Italian Ethnicity and Religious Priests in Chicago: A Case Study
of the Servants of Mary"

Session 8B
Politics and Community
Chair: Salvatore J. Lagumina, Nassau Community College
Stefano Luconi, University of Rome
"Italian Democratic Chieftains and the Making of a Democratic
Majority among Italians in Chicago"
Marco Rimanelli, U.S. Department of State
"The New Orleans Lynching of 1891: Consequences and
Implications"

Session 8C Images of Italy and Italians in Film
Chair: Franco Mulas, University of Sassari
Tonia Caterina Riviello, Santa Clara University
> "*Good Morning Babilonia*: Film Images by the Taviani Brothers"
Mario Aste, University of Massachusetts
> "Salvatore Giuliano: The Facts and the Myth from Literature to
> Cinema"

APPENDIX B

AMERICAN ITALIAN HISTORICAL ASSOCIATION PROCEEDINGS

Volume 1 ETHNICITY IN AMERICAN POLITICAL LIFE: THE ITALIAN AMERICAN CASE. Edited by Salvatore J. LaGumina (1968) pp. 36. Out of Print.

Volume 2 THE ITALIAN AMERICAN NOVEL. Edited by John M. Cammett (1969) pp. 35.

Volume 3 AN INQUIRY INTO ORGANIZED CRIME. Edited by Luciano J. Iorizzo (1970) pp. 87. Out of Print.

Volume 4 POWER AND CLASS: THE ITALIAN AMERICAN EXPERIENCE TODAY. Edited by Frances X. Femminella (1971) pp. 58.

Volume 5 ITALIAN AMERICAN RADICALISM: OLD WORLD ORIGINS AND NEW WORLD DEVELOPMENTS. Edited by Rudolph J. Vecoli (1972) pp. 80.

Volume 6 THE RELIGIOUS EXPERIENCE OF ITALIAN AMERICANS. Edited by Silvano Tomasi (1973) pp. 133.

Volume 7 THE INTERACTION OF ITALIANS AND JEWS IN AMERICA. Edited by Jean Scarpaci (1974) pp. 117.

Volume 8 THE URBAN EXPERIENCE OF ITALIAN AMERICANS. Edited by Pat Gallo (1975) pp. 177.

Volume 9 THE UNITED STATES AND ITALY: THE FIRST TWO HUNDRED YEARS. Edited by Humbert Nelli (1976) pp. 242. Out of Print.

Volume 10 THE ITALIAN IMMIGRANT WOMAN IN NORTH AMERICA. Edited by Betty Boyd Caroli, Robert F. Harney, and Lydio F. Tomasi (1977) pp. 386.

Volume 11   PANE E LAVORO: THE ITALIAN AMERICAN WORK-
ING CLASS. Edited by George E. Pozzetta (1978) pp. 176.
Volume 12   ITALIAN AMERICANS IN THE PROFESSIONS. Edited by
Remigio U. Pane, with an Introduction by Giovanni Schiavo (1983) pp. 290.
Volume 13   THE FAMILY AND COMMUNITY LIFE OF ITALIAN
AMERICANS. Edited by Richard N. Juliani (1983) pp. 191.
Volume 14   ITALIAN IMMIGRANTS IN RURAL AND SMALL TOWN
AMERICA. Edited by Rudolph J. Vecoli (1987) pp. 204.
Volume 15   THE ITALIAN AMERICANS THROUGH THE GENERA-
TIONS: THE FIRST ONE HUNDRED YEARS. Edited by Rocco Caporale
(1986) pp. 263.
Volume 16   THE INTERACTION OF ITALIANS AND IRISH IN THE
UNITED STATES. Edited by Francis X. Femminella, with an
Introduction by Geno Baroni (1985) pp. 308.
Volume 17   ITALIAN AMERICANS: STRUGGLE AND SUPPORT.
Edited by Joseph L. Tropea, James E. Miller, and Cheryl Beattie Repetti
(1986) pp. 312.
Volume 18   THE MELTING POT AND BEYOND: ITALIAN AMERI-
CANS IN THE YEAR 2000. Edited by Jerome Krase and William Egelman
(1987) pp. 318.
Volume 19   ITALIAN AMERICANS: THE SEARCH FOR A USABLE
PAST. Edited by Richard N. Juliani and Philip V. Cannistraro (1989) pp. 304.
Volume 20   ITALIAN ETHNICS: THEIR LANGUAGES, LITERA-
TURE AND LIFE. Edited by Dominic Candeloro, Fred Gardaphe, and Paolo
Giordano (1990) pp. 478.
Volume 21   ITALIAN AMERICANS IN TRANSITION. Edited by Joseph
Scelsa, Salvatore J. LaGumina and Lydio F. Tomasi (1990) pp. 283.
Volume 22   ITALIAN AMERICANS CELEBRATE LIFE. Edited by
Paola A. Sensi Isolani and Anthony J. Tamburri (1990) pp. 180.
Volume 23   A CENTURY OF ITALIAN IMMIGRATION, 1890-1990.
Edited by Harral Landry (1994) pp. 250.
Volume 24   ITALIAN AMERICANS AND THEIR PUBLIC AND PRI-
VATE LIFE. Edited by Frank J. Cavaioli, Angela Danzi, and Salvatore J.
LaGumina (1993) pp. 240.

Volume 25   NEW EXPLORATIONS IN ITALIAN AMERICAN STUD-
IES. Edited by Richard N. Juliani and Sandra P. Juliani (1994) pp. 246.
Volume 26   ITALIAN AMERICANS IN A MULTICULTURAL SOCI-
ETY. Edited by Jerome Krase and Judith N. DeSena (1994) pp. 302.

To order copies or for more information, write to:
AMERICAN ITALIAN HISTORICAL ASSOCIATION
209 Flagg Place
Staten Island, New York 10304

**PRESIDENTS
OF THE
AMERICAN ITALIAN HISTORICAL ASSOCIATION**

1. Rudolph J. Vecoli	1967-1970
2. Salvatore J. LaGumina	1971-1974
3. Luciano J. Iorizzo	1975-1978
4. George E. Pozzetta	1979-1980
5. Francis X. Femminella	1981-1982
6. Frank J. Cavaioli	1983-1984
7. Dominic Candeloro	1985-1988
8. Richard N. Juliani	1989-1992
9. Jerome Krase	1993-1994

THE AMERICAN ITALIAN HISTORICAL ASSOCIATION

Founded in 1966, the AIHA is an interdisciplinary organization that seeks to increase the understanding of the Italian experience in North America. With an international membership of historians, social scientists, language specialists, artists and writers, educators and others, the Association pursues the highest standards of academic scholarship in Italian American studies. The AIHA holds an annual conference and publishes its *Proceedings*. It also provides members with a quarterly newsletter that reports on current research and other information related to the field. A memorial fund supports a scholarship award to a student doing relevant research. The AIHA encourages the collection and preservation of historical records that can be used in research on the Italian American experience.

Membership is open to anyone interested in these objectives. Further information on joining the AIHA may be obtained by writing to the AIHA, 209 Flagg Place, Staten Island, New York 10304.